ⓈHORT**ORDER**

MACROMEDIA®

Dreamweaver® 4

STEVEN MONIZ

Short Order Macromedia Dreamweaver 4

Copyright © 2001 by Que

International Standard Book Number: 0-7897-2554-1

Library of Congress Catalog Card Number: 20-01086701

Printed in the United States of America

First Printing: April 2001

03   02   01   4   3   2   1

Trademarks

Warning and Disclaimer

EXECUTIVE EDITOR
Beth Millett

ACQUISITIONS EDITOR
Heather Banner Kane

DEVELOPMENT EDITOR
Laura Norman

MANAGING EDITOR
Thomas F. Hayes

PROJECT EDITOR
Heather McNeill

COPY EDITOR
Megan Wade

INDEXER
Erika Millen

PROOFREADER
Harvey Stanbrough

TECHNICAL EDITOR
Doug Scamahorn

TEAM COORDINATOR
Julie Otto

INTERIOR DESIGNER
Karen Ruggles

COVER DESIGNER
Aren Howell

CONTENTS AT A GLANCE

iv

CONTENTS

ABOUT THE AUTHOR

Steven Moniz is a consultant and trainer in the Boston area specializing in Web design, desktop publishing, and electronic prepress. He teaches regularly scheduled courses in everything from HTML Basics to Advanced Photoshop, Flash, Fireworks, and Dreamweaver. Steve often lectures on digital prepress and Internet topics and provides customized training for corporate clients on both Macintosh and Windows platforms. Steve is the author of *Photoshop 4 Studio Skills* and *Short Order Macromedia Dreamweaver 3*, coauthor of *Photoshop 4 Complete* and *Using Photoshop 5*, and technical editor of *Adobe Photoshop 5.0 Certification Guide* and *Teach Yourself GoLive 5*.

DEDICATION

This book is dedicated to Lisa and John. My sister and her husband, along with their four sons, are a constant reminder of what is truly important. They have come to my rescue more times than I can count, and devoted much of their precious time during the writing of this book to help me move, unpack, and settle into my new home. I could never do what I do without the love and support of my family.

ACKNOWLEDGMENTS

Thank you to everyone at Que who helped get this book on the shelves, especially Heather Banner Kane, Julie Otto, and Laura Norman. Laura really knows her stuff and, as always, patiently guided me in the writing of this book. Karen Whitehouse will always have a place in this section because of the writing opportunities I've had at Pearson Education due to her initial guidance. Thank you to Lisa, Billy, Adam, Andrew, Joshua, Mike, Charlie, Pauline, and Robbie for their photo contributions.

TELL US WHAT YOU THINK!

As the reader of this book, *you* are our most important critic and commentator. We value your opinion and want to know what we're doing right, what we could do better, what areas you'd like to see us publish in, and any other words of wisdom you're willing to pass our way.

As an executive editor for Que, I welcome your comments. You can fax, e-mail, or write me directly to let me know what you did or didn't like about this book—as well as what we can do to make our books stronger.

Please note that I cannot help you with technical problems related to the topic of this book, and that due to the high volume of mail I receive, I might not be able to reply to every message.

When you write, please be sure to include this book's title and author as well as your name and phone or fax number. I will carefully review your comments and share them with the author and editors who worked on the book.

Fax: 317-581-4666

Email: feedback@quepublishing.com

Mail: Beth Millett
         Que
         201 West 103rd Street
         Indianapolis, IN 46290 USA

INTRODUCTION

Short Order Macromedia Dreamweaver 4 was created for those interested in quick solutions to everyday problems and tasks. With step-by-step examples, plenty of illustrations, and valuable tips, you'll learn the intermediate-to-advanced tasks and commands—in short order.

Whether you are new to Dreamweaver or work with it on a daily basis, this book is a valuable reference. Short steps that cut through all the rhetoric found in larger tomes and manuals give you the solutions you need to be productive. You will find insights into tricks used by professional Web site developers and tips to help you avoid any pitfalls. Expand your Dreamweaver skills to include cutting-edge techniques and learn about all the great new features in Dreamweaver 4.

About Dreamweaver 4

Dreamweaver is one of the most user-friendly and intuitive WYSIWYG editors on the market for creating Web content. Aside from being a visual HTML tool, Dreamweaver incorporates all the state-of-the-art features that professional Web page developers need to produce effective and dynamic pages.

With Dreamweaver, you can visually create all the standard HTML elements, such as tables, frames, and forms, as well as the advanced elements, such as Dynamic HTML (DHTML), Cascading Style Sheets, and JavaScript. The built-in HTML editor enables you to view and edit your HTML code in three ways, and the timeline editor makes creating DHTML animations a snap. The powerful FTP client- and site-management features enable you to take full control of your Web site and easily manage changes and updates.

What You Can Do with Dreamweaver

Dreamweaver has the features you expect to find in an application designed to create Web pages. Formatting of Web pages is accomplished by using menu commands, panels (palettes), and inspectors—in particular, the Objects panel and Property inspector. Aside from the standard creation tools, Dreamweaver enables you to incorporate advanced features, such as JavaScript functions, Flash movies, Flash buttons, Flash text, and server-side includes. The round-trip Fireworks editing feature enables you to switch to Macromedia FIreworks to edit your content, and then switch back to Dreamweaver where the page is automatically updated. Dreamweaver's feature-rich interface enables you to create and manage your Web sites with familiar concepts and these productivity-enhancing tools:

- **Templates**—These enable you to keep the design separate from the content and produce and maintain a uniform style for your Web site.

- **Point-to-File Icon**—Use this method to link to files and images or drag content from the Site window right onto your pages.

- **Global Search-and-Replace Capabilities**—These enable you to make sweeping changes to every page on your Web site. Search for HTML codes or for complex patterns using regular expressions.

- **Layout Tables and Layout Cells**—Designers will love the control afforded by these features. Creating complex page designs and layouts that work in every browser has never been easier.

- **Web-Safe Color Palette**—Select colors from this palette or use your system color palette to specify any color in the RGB color space. You can even sample colors from anywhere on the screen, including images placed on your Web pages.

- **Plugins**—Play these elements, such as Flash and QuickTime movies, right in the Dreamweaver document window.

- **QuickTime, Flash, Shockwave, Java Applets, and ActiveX Controls**—Incorporate these elements on your pages and control all their properties without typing a line of code.

- **Assets Panel**—Use this new panel to track and manage all the assets, such as images, text, Flash, and Shockwave.

- **Reference Panel**—This enables you to search for information on HTML, JavaScript, and Cascading Style Sheets. It's like having three reference books at your fingertips.

- **Third-Party Extensions**—Customize and extend Dreamweaver with these extensions and extensions you write yourself. You can even add your own menu choices, commands, tools, and objects.

- **Synchronization**—Synchronize your remote site with your local site using a single command.

- **Check-In and Check-Out**—Use this, along with design notes, to create and manage a team development environment.

What's New in Version 4

The newest Dreamweaver version adds some powerful tools and features to an already impressive list. Integration with Fireworks and Flash, the addition of the Reference panel and Assets panel, and several other advanced features make it even easier to produce professional Web sites with a minimum investment of time. Some of the new features for version 4 include the following:

- The new Dreamweaver toolbar appears at the top of the Document window and enables you to view a page in Design view, Code view, or both. The toolbar also provides easy access to commonly used features, such as Preview in Browser and design notes.

- Edit non-HTML documents, such as JavaScript files, Active Server Pages, Cold Fusion Templates, and XML files, directly in Dreamweaver's Code view.

- The Reference panel provides a quick reference for HTML, JavaScript, and CSS. It provides specific information and syntax requirements for tags you are working with in the Code view or Code inspector.

- The Code Navigation pop-up menu enables you to select code for JavaScript functions described in an HTML document and insert the code in the Code view or Code inspector.

- The JavaScript Debugger helps you debug JavaScript while in Dreamweaver, enabling you to set breakpoints to control the sections of code you want to examine.

- Layout view enables you to quickly design Web pages, drawing boxes to create tables and table cells.

- Select from a predefined set of Flash buttons and Flash text from within Dreamweaver and incorporate your own templates for Flash buttons and text.

- Round-trip slicing enables you to switch between Dreamweaver and Fireworks 4 to make changes to sliced images.

- The Assets panel helps you to manage your site's assets. View all images, colors, external URLs, scripts, Flash, Shockwave, QuickTime, templates, and library items in the Assets panel. You also can print the list of items that appear in the Assets panel.

- View design notes in the Site window and attach e-mail addresses when using Check-In/ Check-Out.

- New Site reports test your HTML documents for common problems, such as missing <alt> tags. Write custom reports to suit your particular needs.

- The improved Package Manager (formerly Extension Manager) lets you install and manage extensions easily with a single click.

- Version 4 has integration and support for SourceSafe and WebDAV.

- Edit, add, and delete keyboard shortcuts to create sets of shortcuts you can alternate between.

How to Use This Book

I have made an effort to include tasks that are easy to follow with a minimum of steps while also incorporating advanced features throughout. The tasks are highlighted by a color bar at the top of each page, and tips and notes are included on nearly every page to enhance the information presented.

The tips should serve as memory joggers for the experienced user and as points to commit to memory for the novice-to-intermediate Web developer. The notes offer explanations to clarify task-specific details and provide commentary on some of Dreamweaver's more challenging aspects. Keep an eye out for links to Web sites in the tips and notes.

If a picture is worth a thousand words, then you'll find no shortage of visual verbiage here. Plenty of screenshots are provided to guide you through the tasks, along with callouts and captions that emphasize specific features of Dreamweaver's dialog boxes and inspectors.

This book includes directions for both Macintosh and Windows platforms. Although very few differences exist between the two platforms, screenshots for both platforms are included where the differences occur. Shortcut keys also are included for both platforms. You'll find Macintosh shortcuts in parentheses and Windows shortcuts in brackets, like this: (Command-Shift-P)[Ctrl+Shift+P].

What's in This Book

Treat *Short Order Macromedia Dreamweaver 4* as your briefcase-ready reference. This book is divided into chapters that contain collections of related tasks. I have worked to put everything you need in one place so you can quickly find the answer to your problem and get back to work. Although this book is not meant to be read sequentially from cover to cover, a general order does exist to the way the chapters have been organized so you can find what you need quickly.

Configuration and Setup

In Chapters 1, "Configuring Dreamweaver"; 2, "Setting Up Your Site in Dreamweaver"; and 3, "Editing HTML in Dreamweaver," you will find the information necessary to get started working with Dreamweaver.

Chapter 1 tells you about the interface and includes information on the panels, inspectors, and preferences you should be familiar with before creating Web pages. Chapter 2 tells you how to set up a site in Dreamweaver so you'll be able to start saving pages and creating your site hierarchy. Chapter 3 has everything you want to know about editing HTML in Dreamweaver and working with the Code view and Code inspector.

Text and Paragraph Formatting

Chapters 4, "Creating and Editing Text," and 5, "Working with Paragraph Elements and HTML Styles," deal specifically with the text on your Web pages. In Chapter 4, you will find all the information about creating and formatting text, as well as instructions on using the powerful search-and-replace features. Chapter 5 deals with paragraph features, such as heading levels, line breaks, lists, and special characters. You also will find information on using the HTML Styles panel and adding horizontal rules.

Images, Graphics, and Links

Chapters 6–9 cover the many ways you can incorporate images, graphics, links, and interactive imagery on your Web pages. In Chapter 6, "Working with GIF, JPEG, and PNG Images and Graphics," you will find tasks for inserting GIF, JPEG, and PNG images on your Web pages. Chapter 7, "Round-Trip Graphics Editing with Fireworks," deals specifically with editing images in Fireworks using the round-trip editing features of Dreamweaver. Chapter 8, "Creating Links," deals with the basics of creating links for text and images, and Chapter 9, "Inserting Interactive Images," tells you how to spice up your pages with interactive features, such as navigation bars and Flash buttons.

Tables, Frames, and Forms

Chapters 10–13 deal with overall Web page layout and the inclusion of forms to get information from users. In Chapter 10, "Building Tables," you will find everything you want to know about tables and table formatting. Chapter 11, "Designing Pages in Layout View," deals with Dreamweaver's new Layout view and the specifics of using layout cells and layout tables. Chapter 12, "Creating Frames," is about creating frame-based pages, whereas Chapter 13, "Creating and Customizing Forms," deals with creating forms for user input.

Cascading Style Sheets and Layers

Chapters 14 and 15 deal with two components of Dynamic HTML: Cascading Style Sheets and Layers. In Chapter 14, "Working with Cascading Style Sheets," explore the many attributes of Cascading Style Sheets for both CSS1 and CSS2, and create both internal and external styles. Chapter 15, "Creating Layers," deals with layers, a part of the CSS specification that enables you to build page content in floating layers that can be controlled with Dreamweaver's JavaScript™ behaviors. Learn how to convert layers to HTML tables and how to convert HTML tables to layers.

Advanced Features and Site Management

Chapters 16, "Using Behaviors"; 17, "Working with Timelines"; 18, "Managing and Inserting Assets with the Assets Panel"; 19, "Creating Templates and Libraries"; 20, "Adding Multimedia to Your Web Pages"; 21, "Managing, Synchronizing, and Cleaning Up Your Site"; and 22, "Customizing Dreamweaver," cover the advanced features of Dreamweaver, including Cascading Style Sheets (CSS), Dynamic HTML (DHTML), JavaScript behaviors, timelines, templates, libraries, and customizing Dreamweaver. Learn how to use the new Assets inspector in Chapter 18. In Chapter 21, you will find the procedures and tasks necessary to efficiently manage and clean up your Web site.

UltraDev, CourseBuilder, and Other Extensions

In Appendixes A, "Using Dreamweaver UltraDev"; B, "Using CourseBuilder for Dreamweaver"; and C, "Enhancing Dreamweaver with Extensions," you will

find information on some of the ways you can incorporate specific extensions, as well as information on
Dreamweaver UltraDev—Dreamweaver's database
interaction software.

Debugging JavaScript

Appendix D, "Debugging JavaScript with
Dreamweaver," gets you quickly up to speed on using
Dreamweaver's JavaScript Debugger to fix code prob-
lems and get your site up and running smoothly.

From basic Web pages to complex Web sites, *Short
Order Macromedia Dreamweaver 4* strives to break
through the complexities of Dreamweaver and deliver
what you really need, when you really need it.

CHAPTER 1

In this chapter, you will learn how to...

View Pages in the Document Window

View Dreamweaver's Panels and Inspectors

Modify the Launcher Panel

Modify Keyboard Shortcuts

Set Status Bar Preferences

Specify Page Properties

Select a Predefined Web-Safe Color Scheme

Specify Text and Background Color

Use the History Panel

Record Commands

Dreamweaver is a powerful tool for creating virtually every type of Web page—from very simple HTML markup to pages that include animation, sound, and interactivity. This chapter covers the configuration of features you will use for every Web page you create. Document setup options, such as setting the background color, setting the background image, and selecting color, are covered here.

CONFIGURING DREAMWEAVER

You also will increase your productivity by customizing the Launcher panel and modifying keyboard shortcuts. When using Dreamweaver, the Web-safe color palette is always available, and you can even choose from some preset color schemes to design your pages. Dreamweaver's versatile color palettes enable you to select color from a variety of palettes as well as any color you see on your desktop. You can sample colors from images—or anywhere else on your screen—easily with Dreamweaver's unique eyedropper color selection.

The History panel enables you to retrace every step you perform while creating your pages. You can build many of the steps found in the History panel into commands, and then perform these commands over and over again. With the live recording feature, you also can create commands while you're building your pages, saving time on repetitive tasks. For more information on customizing Dreamweaver, see Chapter 22, "Customizing Dreamweaver."

Viewing Pages in the Document Window

When working in Dreamweaver, you can build your pages in a variety of ways. The area where you put the content of Web pages is called the Document window. Within the Document window, you can build your page in a linear fashion using the Design view, as shown in (1.1). If you want more precise control over the positioning of objects and text on your Web pages, the Layout view enables you to create layout cells and position content within the cells. The layout cells can then be repositioned onscreen, as shown in (1.2). When you switch from Layout view to Design view, the content is depicted in table format—the most popular method for creating Web content at this writing (1.3).

1.1

Layout cells enable you to precisely position page content.

1.2

Layout cells are actually table cells as seen in Design view.

1.3

 O T E

See Chapter 11, "Designing Pages with Layout Cells," for more information on designing Web pages in table format. You also can design your pages using frames and layers; each is discussed in a separate chapter in this book. See Chapters 12, "Creating Frames," and 15, "Creating Layers."

a b c   d   e f g h j k

L   m n   o

1.4   The download time shown at the bottom of the
Document window is based on a connection
speed of 28.8 Kilobits per Second connection
by default. If you click on the page dimensions
at the bottom of the Document window and
choose Edit Sizes from the pop-up menu, you
can edit and add your own pages sizes as well
as change the Connection Speed.

Regardless of the view, the Document window always contains the Dreamweaver toolbar at the top of the window and a status bar at the bottom (1.4). The toolbar enables you to change the view of the current page and edit the page title. It also contains frequently used features, such as Preview/Debug in Browser, and File Management. The Status Bar shows the current status of your Web page and reports on page size, transfer speed, and the hierarchy of HTML code in the document. The Mini-Launcher is also included on the right side of the Status Bar.

(a) **Show Code View**

(b) **Show Code and Design Views**

(c) **Show Design View**

(d) **Web Page Title**

(e) **File Management**

(f) **Preview/Debug in Browser**

(g) **Refresh Design View**

(h) **Reference**

(j) **Code Navigation**

(k) **View Options**

(L) **HTML Code Hierarchy**

(m) **Window Size**

(n) **Download Time**

(o) **Mini-Launcher**

T I P

*Type (Option - Tab)[Alt + Tab] to toggle
between the Design view and the Code view.*

Viewing Dreamweaver's Panels and Inspectors

Dreamweaver has numerous panels and inspectors available under the Window menu in the menu bar. The Objects panel, Property inspector, and Launcher panel are the first three listed in the Window menu and the three that you'll use consistently while building Web pages (1.5). The Object panel displays the common objects by default. These are the objects you regularly use to add content to Web pages. The Objects panel contains a drop-down menu called the Objects Panel menu, which contains the other six Objects menu choices (1.6).

The Property inspector is a context-sensitive panel that displays the properties available for the object or text selected. Toggle between the reduced and expanded views of the Property inspector by clicking the white arrow in the lower-right corner of the inspector. The Launcher panel contains buttons for some commonly used features and can be displayed vertically or horizontally by clicking in the lower-right corner. The Launcher panel choices also appear in the Mini-Launcher at the bottom of the Document window.

 I P

If you find that the panels or inspectors are positioned off the screen and you can't seem to make them appear again, choose Window, Arrrange Panels to put them in their default positions onscreen.

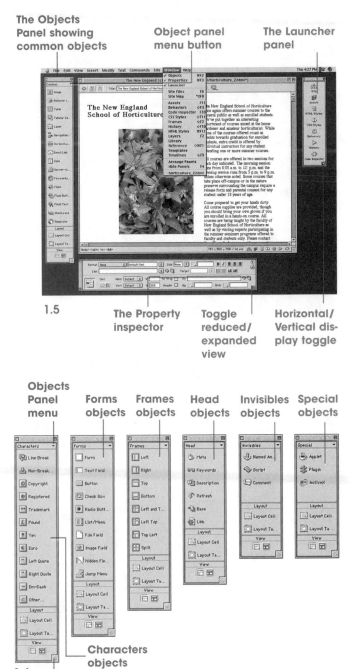

The Objects Panel showing common objects

Object panel menu button

The Launcher panel

1.5

The Property inspector

Toggle reduced/ expanded view

Horizontal/ Vertical display toggle

Objects Panel menu

Forms objects

Frames objects

Head objects

Invisibles objects

Special objects

Characters objects

1.6 **Resize Objects panel**

Modifying the Launcher Panel

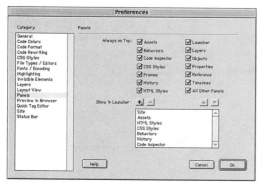

1.7

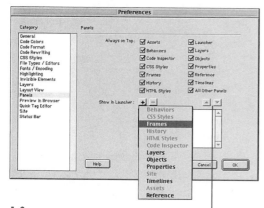

1.8

Click the up and down arrows to rearrange the order of the buttons in the Launcher panel.

The Launcher panel contains buttons for Site, Assets, HTML Styles, CSS Styles, Behaviors, History, and Code Inspector by default. Modify the Panels Preferences to add and remove buttons from the Launcher panel. For example, if you frequently use frames to design your Web pages, you can add the Frames button to the Launcher panel to quickly access the Frames panel. Changes you make to the Launcher panel are also reflected in the Mini-Launcher at the bottom of the Document window.

1. Choose Edit→Preferences to display the Preferences dialog box.

2. Choose Panels from the Category list on the left side of the Preferences dialog box to display the Panels Preferences (1.7).

3. To add another button the Launcher panel, click the plus (+) button and select a panel from the list (1.8).

4. To remove a button from the Launcher panel, select the panel name in the list at the bottom of the Panel Preferences dialog box and click the minus (-) button.

Modifying Keyboard Shortcuts

Use the keyboard shortcut editor to create shortcut keys, edit existing shortcuts, or use the shortcut sets included with Dreamweaver 4. The default sets are Dreamweaver 3, Bbedit, Homesite, and Macromedia Standard. The Dreamweaver 3 set uses the key commands you used in Dreamweaver 3 along with any new features in Dreamweaver 4. The Macromedia Standard is selected as the current set by default and contains the universal shortcuts for Dreamweaver, Flash, and Fireworks, as well as those specific to Dreamweaver 4.

1. Choose Edit→Keyboard Shortcuts to display the Keyboard Shortcuts dialog box (1.9).

2. Click the Current Set pop-up menu to display the list of predefined sets included with Dreamweaver 4, and any custom sets you've previously defined. Predefined sets are listed at the top of the menu.

3. Click the Duplicate button to duplicate the current set and assign a name to the set (1.10).

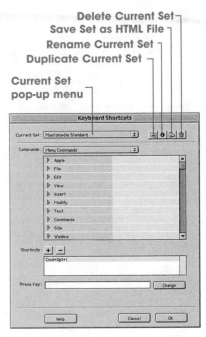

1.9

1.10

 I P

If you choose a keyboard shortcut that is already in use for another command, Dreamweaver displays a message to that effect at the bottom of the Keyboard Shortcuts dialog box.

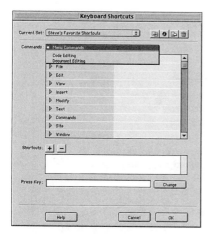

1.11

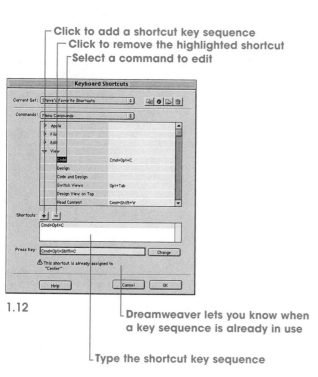

— Click to add a shortcut key sequence
— Click to remove the highlighted shortcut
— Select a command to edit

1.12

— Dreamweaver lets you know when
a key sequence is already in use

— Type the shortcut key sequence

4. Click the Commands pop-up menu and select which commands you want to display in the scrolling list box (1.11):

- **Menu Commands**— Modifies the commands in the menu bar

- **Code Editing**—Modifies the commands used for editing source code

- **Document Editing**— Modifies commands used to edit in the Document window

Windows users also have an additional choice for Site Menu Commands: the commands available under the Site Window's main menu bar.

5. Click the command you want to edit in the scrolling list, and then click the plus (+) button next the word Shortcuts. Type a new key sequence in the Press Key field and click the Change button to add the shortcut (1.12).

6. Click OK when you have finished editing the keyboard shortcuts.

 I   P

You can assign more than one keyboard shortcut for a command by separating the commands with a comma. For example, the shortcut for Undo is (Cmd - Z,Option - Delete)[Ctrl + Z,Alt + Backspace].

Setting Status Bar Preferences

A status bar at the bottom of the Document window (1.13) includes options for document size and transfer speed along with a mini-launcher that contains the same buttons as the Launcher panel. Preset page sizes are available, or you can create your own custom sizes to standardize your Web page design.

1. Choose Edit→Preferences to display the Preferences dialog box. Click Status Bar in the left column to display the options for the Status Bar (1.14).

2. To edit an existing window size, click the window size you want to edit and change the values. To create a new window size, click in the empty space under the Width column and enter the information for a new window size. The Description you enter here appears in the Status Bar pop-up menu at the bottom of the Document window.

3. Choose a Connection Speed from the pull-down menu or type a value into the field.

4. The Mini-Launcher is displayed at the bottom of the Document window by default (1.15). If you don't want to see the Mini-Launcher and would rather use the Launcher panel, uncheck the Launcher option. Click OK when you're done.

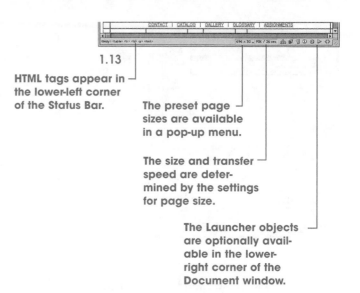

1.13

HTML tags appear in the lower-left corner of the Status Bar.

The preset page sizes are available in a pop-up menu.

The size and transfer speed are determined by the settings for page size.

The Launcher objects are optionally available in the lower-right corner of the Document window.

1.14

1.15

Specifying Page Properties

1.16

The title appears at the top of the browser window and is used as bookmark text.

1.17

The page properties in Dreamweaver determine the overall specifications for the Web page, such as title, background color, background image, and link colors. The first thing you do when creating a new Web page is set the page properties.

1. Choose Modify→Page Properties to display the Page Properties dialog box (1.16).

2. Enter a title for your Web page in the Title field. The title appears at the top of the Web page in the window's title bar (1.17). The title is also the text that is used when users bookmark your Web page, so keep this fact in mind when titling your Web pages.

(T) I P

If you want to set the default page properties for Dreamweaver, open the default.html file found in the Dreamweaver\ Configuration\Templates folder. Specify the page properties and save the file in the same place with the same name. Every new document you create will have the page properties specified for default.html.

(T) I P

Some search engines use the title of your page as the title for your site when users see the search results page, so it's a good idea to make it descriptive and not too generic.

Specifying Page Properties continued

3. To include a background image for your Web page, click the Choose button to select an image. If the background image is smaller than the browser window, the image is tiled to fill the space (1.18).

4. Click the color swatch to choose a background color or enter either the color name or hexadecimal value.

5. Indicate a color for the text in your document, as well as colors for links, visited links, and active links, by clicking their respective color swatches or entering the color value in the appropriate field (1.19).

6. The default left margin is 11 pixels from the left edge of the browser window, and the default top margin is 8 pixels from the top of the browser window. Specify the Left Margin and Top Margin values in pixels to change the left and top margins for Internet Explorer. Specify the Margin Width and Margin Height to change the left and top margins for Netscape browsers.

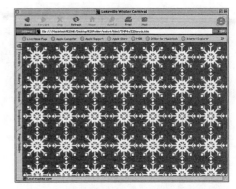

1.18 **The background image is tiled when it's smaller than the window dimensions. This background image is a GIF file that has a transparent background, so the background color shows through as well.**

Link Color   Visited Link Color

1.19
Active Link Color

I P

The active link color is the color the link changes to while you're clicking it—you have to watch closely to see this one.

The charset attribute of the \<meta\> tag indicates the font encoding specified in the Page Properties dialog box.

1.20

1.21

7. The character set to be used to display your Web page is indicated in the Document Encoding option. Select the Document Encoding method from the pop-up menu. The default Document Encoding is Western (Latin 1). Document encoding is specified using the \<meta\> tag in the \<head\> section of the HTML source code (1.20).

8. Click the Choose button next to the Tracing Image box to specify a tracing image. The tracing image is helpful when you have a preexisting layout from another program that you want to use as the basis for your Web page design (1.21). See Chapter 15, "Creating Layers," for instructions on how to use a tracing image.

 O T E

The Transparency option in the Page Properties dialog box pertains to the tracing image. You can change the opacity of the tracing image so it is faded in the background of the page, which makes positioning elements on top of it easier.

Selecting a Predefined Web-Safe Color Scheme

You can choose from a number of predefined Web-safe color schemes to specify the background color, text color, and link colors for your Web page rather than selecting them manually from the Page Properties dialog box.

1. Choose Commands→Set Color Scheme to display the Set Color Scheme Command dialog box (1.22).

2. Select a background color from the list of available colors.

3. Select a color combination for text and links from the color list that corresponds to the background color you select. Click OK when finished.

 **O T E**

To add your own color schemes to the Set Color Scheme Command dialog box, edit `Configuration/Commands/colorSchemes.js`, *located in the Dreamweaver application folder. Open this file in Dreamweaver's Code window. Edit the hexadecimal color values or copy and paste a color section to create your own scheme for background color, text, and links (1.21). Save a copy of the original* `colorShemes.js` *file before overwriting it. Edit the* `Set Color Scheme.htm` *file located in the same directory to modify the way the dialog box appears. Quit and restart Dreamweaver to see your changes reflected.*

1.22

```
10 function colorSchemes(){
11 var colorSchemes = new Array();
12 var i;
13
14 //TEAL SCHEMES
15 colorSchemes.Teal = new Array();
16 i=-1;
17
18 colorSchemes.Teal[++i] = new Array();
19 colorSchemes.Teal[i].name = "Black,Green";
20 colorSchemes.Teal[i].bgcolor = "#66CCCC";
21 colorSchemes.Teal[i].text = "#000000";
22 colorSchemes.Teal[i].link = "#009999";
23 colorSchemes.Teal[i].vlink = "#3399CC";
24 colorSchemes.Teal[i].alink = "#33CC66";
25
26
27 //BLACK SCHEMES
28 colorSchemes.Black = new Array();
29 i=-1;
30
31 colorSchemes.Black[++i] = new Array();
32 colorSchemes.Black[i].name = "Green,Grey";
33 colorSchemes.Black[i].bgcolor = "#000000";
34 colorSchemes.Black[i].text = "#339933";
35 colorSchemes.Black[i].link = "#33FF00";
36 colorSchemes.Black[i].vlink = "#666666";
37 colorSchemes.Black[i].alink = "#666600";
```

1.23

Specifying Text and Background Color

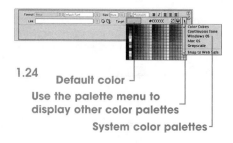

1.24 **Default color**

Use the palette menu to display other color palettes

System color palettes

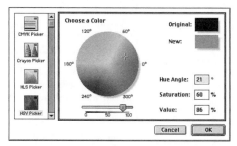

1.25 **The Macintosh color picker**

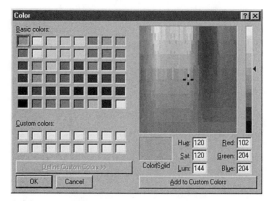

1.26 **The Windows color picker**

Whenever Dreamweaver gives you an option to specify color, you can click a color swatch to visually select a color from a color palette. The default color palette contains the Web-safe color palette. You can select one of these colors by clicking the swatch of the desired color, or you can use alternative methods of selecting color, such as your system's color palettes or even color from images and elements on your screen.

1. Click any color swatch once in Dreamweaver to display the palette of Web-safe colors (1.24).

2. Position the eyedropper cursor over the color swatch you want. The hexadecimal value for the color is displayed at the top of the color palette. Click the color to select it. You also can click anywhere on the screen to sample a color.

3. Click the Color Wheel icon to display the Macintosh color palettes (1.25) or the Windows color palette (1.26). Select a color and click OK.

 T I P

Visit http://graphicdesign.about.com for good information on the Web-safe colors as well as many other Web design topics.

Using the History Panel

The History panel records all the steps you've performed in the active document since opening it. Using the History panel, you can undo one or more steps, replay existing steps, and even save history steps as commands that appear in the Commands menu.

1. Choose Window→History to display the History panel (1.27).

2. Move the slider to a previous step to undo all the steps back to that point. When you perform another Dreamweaver function, all the grayed-out steps are deleted.

3. Click a step (not the slider) in the History panel, and then click the Replay button in the lower-left corner of the History panel to replay the selected step (1.28). Highlight steps to replay with the Replay button.

Move the slider to a previous step to undo subsequent steps.

Create a command from selected steps.

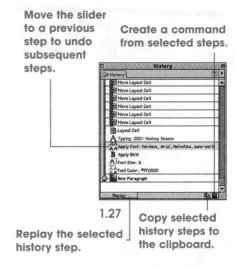

1.27

Replay the selected history step.

Copy selected history steps to the clipboard.

The History panel does not display steps you perform in the Site window, other documents, or other frames.

1.28

 I P

You can type (Command - Z)[Ctrl + Z] to undo the last step you performed, moving the slider in the History panel to the previous step. Then you can continue to type this command until you've exhausted all the steps in the History panel. Type (Command - Y)[Ctrl + Y] to redo the last undo.

The name you assign to the command appears under the Command Name menu.

1.29

After you clear the history, you can no longer undo the previous steps.

1.30

Enter a number between 2 and 99,999 in this field to set the maximum number of history steps.

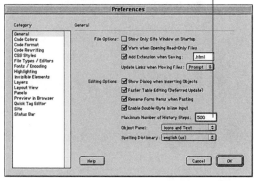

1.31

4. Select some steps in the History panel, and then click the disk icon in the lower-right corner of the History panel to create a new command in the Command Name menu (1.29). The divider lines in the History panel indicate breaks in the history that cannot be recorded, such as clicking or dragging in the document. Steps that show a red X in the icon cannot be replayed or made into commands.

5. Click the panel menu in the upper-right corner of the History panel and select Clear History to clear the existing History (1.30).

 I P

You can repeat the last step you performed by choosing the Edit, Repeat command or by typing (Command - Y){Ctrl + Y]. The Repeat command is not available immediately after an undo or a redo operation.

 O T E

Dreamweaver can record 2–99,999 steps in the History panel. Choose File, Preferences and click the General category to change the total number of steps saved in the History panel (1.31). The higher the number, the more memory the History panel requires.

Recording Commands

Dreamweaver enables you to temporarily record any number of steps
as a command. The steps you perform are recorded as you perform
them, so you don't have to select
multiple steps in the History panel.
Some events, such as clicking to
select something or dragging an element from one place to another, cannot be recorded and will be skipped
in the command.

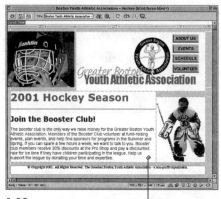

1.32

**The cursor changes to a cassette
icon when recording.**

1. Choose Commands, Start
   Recording; then perform the
   steps you want to record. The
   cursor changes to an audio cassette tape icon when recording
   (1.32).

2. When you're finished recording, choose Commands, Stop
   Recording.

1.33

3. Choose Commands, Play
   Recorded Command to play
   back the last recording. A step
   named Run Command appears
   on the History panel.

4. To save the recorded command
   in the Commands menu, select
   the Play Command step in the
   History panel and click the
   Save As Command button in
   the lower-right corner of the
   History panel.

5. Enter a name for the command
   and click OK. The command
   now appears in the Commands
   menu.

ⓝ O T E

*Dreamweaver does not record changes you
make when you switch to another document
while recording. The pointer changes to a
cassette tape icon when recording. If the
pointer does not display the record icon, the
changes are not being recorded.*

©HAPTER 2

In this chapter, you will learn how to...

Create a Local Site and Specify a Remote Site

Set Up a Local Staging Area

Set Up WebDAV and SourceSafe Access

Transfer Files to and from Remote Sites

Use Check In/Check Out

Manage and Link Your Files with the Site Map

Change Links Site-Wide

Specify the Site Map Layout

Set the Site Preferences

Include Design Notes for Your Site

Add Design Notes to Your Documents

Use File View Columns with Design Notes

Synchronize Remote and Local Files

The site management tools in Dreamweaver enable you to manage your entire site from Dreamweaver's Site window. You can display the content of your remote Web site in one pane while viewing the site content on your local hard drive in another. Whether you're the sole developer of a Web site or part of a group of developers, Dreamweaver has you covered. In the case of Web page development by more than one person, you can turn

SETTING UP YOUR SITE IN DREAMWEAVER

on Dreamweaver's Check In/Check Out feature so that only one person can make changes to a Web page at a time. You also can synchronize your remote site with the local site folder and manage and update multiple sites.

After you have created a site, you can use Dreamweaver's point-and-shoot icons to specify URLs and link to external assets, such as images, sound files, and video. The site map feature provides a graphical method of viewing the hierarchy of your Web site and presents the entire Web site as a flowchart of Web pages, URLs, and other assets. The site map is an ideal way to build a site from scratch, creating pertinent links and organizational structure before you begin creating the individual page content. The powerful Site window in Dreamweaver keeps track of where everything is on your Web site and informs you of any broken links or orphaned or missing files.

Creating a Local Site

The Site window in Dreamweaver provides a method of keeping your files organized for your Web site. The Site window is also an effective File Transfer Protocol (FTP) client that enables you to transfer your files to and from the Web server. Designate a local directory as the Site Root folder, and Dreamweaver does the rest, cataloging the files of the site to enable site-root–relative and document-relative links. After you upload the site files to the remote server, Dreamweaver keeps track of changes made to either the local or remote site to ensure that the Web content is always consistent and up to date.

1. Choose Window→Site Files or click the Site icon in the launcher to display the Site window (2.1).

2. Choose Site→New Site to display the Site Definition dialog box, and then select the Local Info category (2.2).

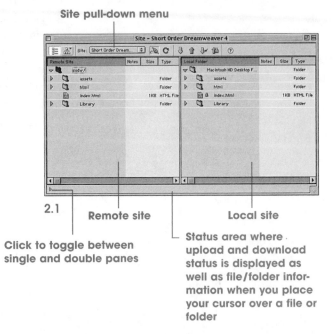

Site pull-down menu

2.1

Remote site

Local site

Click to toggle between single and double panes

Status area where upload and download status is displayed as well as file/folder information when you place your cursor over a file or folder

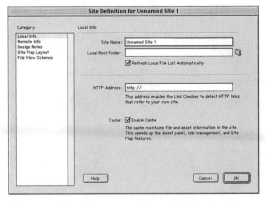

2.2

If you check the Enable Cache check box, a local cache is created to speed the link and site management tasks. If you do not check the Cache check box, Dreamweaver prompts you to create the cache prior to creating the site.

 I P

The Assets panel works only when the site cache is created. See Chapter 18, "Managing and Inserting Assets with the Assets Panel."

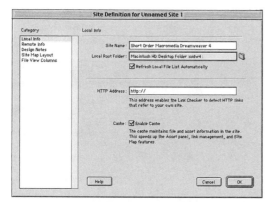

2.3

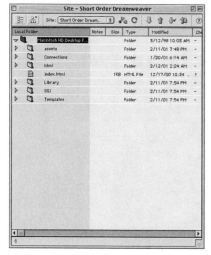

2.4

3. Enter a site name. The site name can be anything you want because it is used only by Dreamweaver and does not affect your remote Web site.

4. Enter the path of the local Root folder or click the Folder icon to select an existing folder that is the Site Root folder (2.3).

5. When you click OK, Dreamweaver evaluates the contents of the Site Root folder to create the site in the Site window (2.4).

 O T E

Type the address for your completed Web site in the HTTP Address field so that Dreamweaver can verify any absolute links used on your site. Dreamweaver uses this information to verify any links to pages on your site that are HTTP links. For example, if your site is called www.sneezing.com, you might reference a page on your sight with the URL http://www.sneezing.com/tissues.html, as opposed to using a site-root-relative or document-relative link.

Specifying a Remote Site

You must have the information (provided by your site administrator or ISP) to connect to your remote site via FTP. If you are using a local network connection and a staging server, you first must connect to the local server volume.

1. Choose Site→Define Sites and double-click the site you want to edit to display the Define Site dialog box.

2. Select Remote Info from the Category list and choose FTP from the Server Access pull-down menu (2.5).

3. Enter the FTP information and fill in the Login and Password fields.

4. Check the Use Passive FTP check box if your firewall requires the local software to set up the FTP connection. Check the Use Firewall check box if you are accessing the Internet from behind a firewall. Click OK.

5. Click Done to close the Define Sites dialog box.

6. In the Site window, click the Connect button.

 **O T E**

Choose Edit→Preferences to display the Preferences dialog box, and then select Site from the Category list to specify the settings for your FTP connection (2.6).

If you're not sure whether you must enter firewall information, ask your system administrator or firewall administrator for specific information.

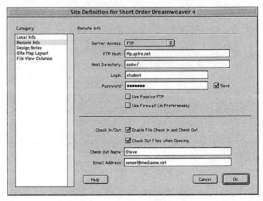

2.5

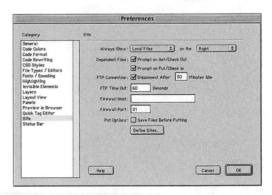

2.6

If you encounter problems with your FTP connection, choose (Site→FTP Log)(Window→Site FTP Log) to display the FTP log.

Setting Up a Local Staging Area

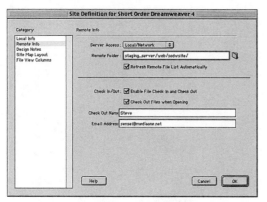

2.7   **Macintosh users should connect to the local server volume or hard drive so it appears on the desktop. Windows users can connect directly by browsing the network using Network Neighborhood in Windows 95/98 or My Network Places in Windows 2000. You can also can use a folder on your local hard drive as a staging area.**

The Local/Network option for server access in the Remote Info category of the Site Definition dialog box enables you to connect to a local or network drive instead of the FTP site. In most cases, a local hard drive or server volume is used as a staging area for Web sites, affording the system administrator more control over what is posted to the remote FTP site.

1. Choose Site→Define Sites, and then double-click the site you want to edit to display the Define Site dialog box. If the Site Definition dialog box is already onscreen, proceed to the next step.

2. Select Remote Info from the Category list and choose Local/Network from the Server Access pull-down menu (2.7).

3. Enter the path of the folder that corresponds to your Web site in the Remote Folder field, or click the folder icon to locate it.

4. Check Refresh Remote File List Automatically to refresh the file list in Dreamweaver's Site window whenever changes are made. Click OK.

Setting Up WebDAV and SourceSafe Access

Connect to any SourceSafe database readable from MetroWerks Visual SourceSafe client version 1.1.0 on the Macintosh or Microsoft Visual SourceSafe client version 6 on Windows. Similar to SourceSafe, WebDAV (Web Distributed Authoring and Versioning) is a Web standard that offers source and version control. You must have Visual SourceSafe installed on your system or have access to a WebDAV-supported system to take advantage of these features.

1. Choose Site→Define Sites, and double-click the site you want to edit to display the Define Site dialog box. If the Site Definition dialog box is already onscreen, proceed to the next step.

2. Select Remote Info from the Category list and choose SourceSafe or WebDAV from the Server Access pull-down menu (2.8).

3. Click the Settings button to display the connection settings (2.9).

4. Enter the URL, username, password, and your e-mail address. Click OK.

5. Click OK in the Site Definition dialog box, and click the Connect button in the Site window.

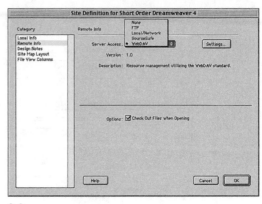

2.8

WebDAV settings dialog box

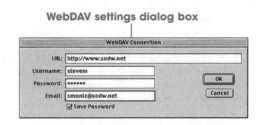

SourceSafe settings dialog box

2.9

Transferring Files to and from Remote Sites

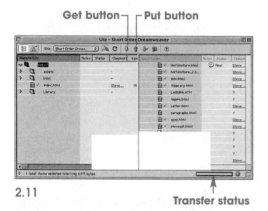

2.10

Get button ─┐ ┌─ Put button

2.11   **Transfer status**

You can click and drag files and folders from the local folder to the remote server and vice versa. (Cmd+click) (Right-click) files and folders in the Site window to display the context menu, and then select Put or Get.

The process of transferring files to and from your remote server is referred to as *putting and getting*. You can put and get single files, multiple files and folders, or the entire site.

1. Connect to the remote site and select the local file or folder you want to transfer to the remote location. Click the Put button at the top of the Site window. If the file(s) you are transferring has any dependent files, such as images or sounds, you will be prompted to include the dependent files in the transfer as well (2.10). The status of the transfer appears along the bottom of the Site window in the status area (2.11).

2. Select a file or folder on the remote server and click the Get button in the Site window to transfer the file or folder to the local folder.

ⓃOTE

If you're worried that the files you're transferring are replacing newer versions of the files, you can select all newer files on either the local site or the remote site before putting or getting them. On the Macintosh, choose either Select Newer Local or Select Newer Remote from the Site→Site Files View menu. Windows users choose Select Newer Local or Select Newer Remote from the Edit menu.

Using Check In/Check Out

If multiple developers are working on your Web site, you can use Dreamweaver's Check In/Check Out feature to prevent more than one developer from editing the same file at the same time. When another Dreamweaver developer checks out a file on the remote server, a check mark appears next to the filename, and the username of the person working on the file appears in the Checked Out By column in the Site window. Add Dreamweaver's Design Notes to communicate with members of your team and click the name of the person who has a file checked out to send e-mail.

1. Choose Site→Define Sites, and then double-click the site you want to edit to display the Site Definition dialog box (2.12).

2. Choose Remote Info from the Category list on the left, and check the Enable File Check In and Check Out check box.

3. Select Check Out Files When Opening to automatically check files out when you open them locally or from the remote server (2.13).

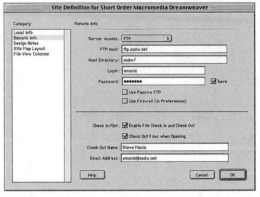

2.12

When you activate the Check In/Check Out feature of Dreamweaver in the Site Definition dialog box, the Check Out and Check In buttons are added to the Site window.

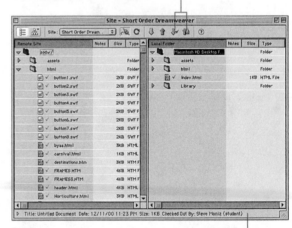

2.13

Hover the cursor over a file with a check mark next to it. The date it was checked out and who it was checked out by will appear in the status line.

 **O T E**

All developers working on a Web site with the Check In/Check Out function activated must select this option from the Define Site dialog box and enter their names in the Check Out Name field.

Check In/Out is not available when Web Server Access is set to None in the Remote Info category of the Site Definition dialog box.

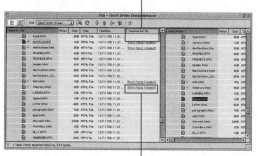

2.14

Click the name in the Checked Out By column to launch your e-mail program with a message addressed to that person.

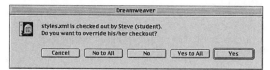

2.15

2.16

4. Enter your name and e-mail address in the Check Out Name field and Email Address field, respectively.

5. Select a file or files in the Site window and click the Check Out button in the upper-right corner. You can select the file from the remote server or the local folder. A green check mark appears next to a checked-out file on both the remote server and local folder, and the username appears in the Checked Out By column **(2.14)**. If you select a file on the remote server, the file is copied to the local folder, and you are prompted to overwrite the existing file if one exists that is older or newer than the one being copied **(2.15)**. If you attempt to check out a file that is already checked out by another user, you are prompted to override the checkout **(2.16)**.

(N)OTE

If the files you are copying contain dependent files, such as GIFs, JPEGs, and Flash movies, a dialog box appears asking whether you want to include the dependent files. If you click Yes, the dependent files are copied and placed in the same relative location on the site to which you're copying. Folders are created when necessary to match the hierarchy of the site from which you're copying.

Managing Your Files with the Site Map

The site map provides a flowchart-type picture of your site and can depict the links, e-mail addresses, and images contained in each file. In addition to displaying a pictorial view of your site hierarchy, the site map enables you to create links between files by simply clicking and dragging. If you have a good idea of the files your site will contain and the overall hierarchy of the files on your site, you can create an empty site with all the files in place. Use the Site window to create the empty folders and files, and then use the site map to drag links, with the Point-to-File icon, from one page to another. The links appear at the bottom of the pages when you edit them, and all you have to do is assign the links to the text or object you want.

1. Click the Site button in the launcher to display the Site window if it isn't already onscreen.

2. Click the Site Map icon in the upper-left corner of the Site window to display the site map (2.17).

3. Click the plus sign to the left of the file to display the links for that file. The icons to the right of the file's Thumbnail icon indicate that file's status, as seen in Table 2.1.

Click the minus signs to contract the dependent files and links.

Position your cursor over the arrowheads pointing to the files in the site map; then click and drag to increase or reduce the space between items.

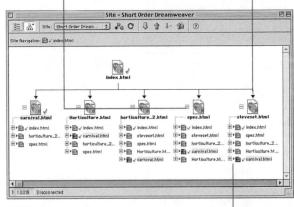

2.17

Click the plus signs to show the dependent files and links.

Table 2.1   File Status Icons

Icon	Description
	Green check marks indicate files you have checked out; red check marks indicate files checked out by others.
	The Padlock icon indicates that the file is locked or read-only. Padlocks appear on local files when the files are checked out.
	A link to a file that does not exist on the site.
	Text displayed in blue and marked with a globe indicates a file on another site or a special link, such as e-mail or scripts.
	Plugin, Java, and text files are depicted with the standard Page icon.
	A Cascading Style Sheets file that is linked.
	The Shockwave icon appears for both Shockwave and Flash.
	An image file, such as a GIF or JPEG.

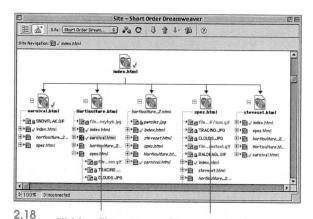

2.18

Hidden files are indicated with italics.

Dependent files include JPEG, PNG, and GIF files.

Click the original root file to resume viewing the site map from the root file after you've selected another file to view as root.

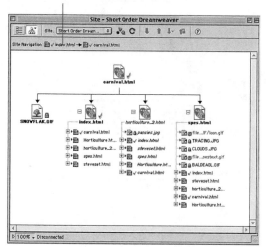

2.19

Hover your cursor over any file-name in Site Map view to see the path of the file. This feature is disabled when you have the Show Page Titles feature enabled.

4. Macintosh users can hold down the Ctrl key and click a file to display the context menu, and then choose Show/Hide Link to hide linked files. Choose Site→Site Map View→Show Files Marked as Hidden to show hidden files in italics. Windows users click a file with the right mouse button and choose Show/Hide Link to hide files. Choose View→Show Files Marked as Hidden in the Site window to display the hidden files in italics. Choose (Site→Site Map View→Show Dependent Files)[View→Show Dependent File] to display dependent files, such as JPEGs and GIFs **(2.18)**.

 I P

*Click a file to select it; then choose (Site→Site Map View→View as Root) [View→View as Root] to treat the selected file as if it were the root file **(2.19)**. You can click the original root file in the Site Navigation bar above the site map to return to the full site map.*

 I P

Choose (Site→Site Map View→Show Page Titles) [View→Show Page Titles] to show page titles instead of page names in the Map view. The `<title>` tag in the `<head>` section of HTML documents indicates the page title.

Linking with the Site Map

You can decrease the time-consuming linking process either by creating links from one file to another in the Site Map pane of the Site window or by linking to files in the Local folder. Linking with the site map is an effective way to build your Web site visually, using empty HTML files to begin.

1. Click a file in the Site Map pane of the Site window to display the Point-to-File icon.

2. Click and drag the Point-to-File icon and release on a file you want to link to the selected file (2.20).

N O T E

Click to select a file, and then choose Site→Site Map View→Remove Link to remove a link in Site Map view.

N O T E

When you use the Point-to-File icon to link files in the Site Map view, a text link is placed at the bottom of the selected page. Reassign the links in the file when you edit it, or simply change and reposition the text if the link is to remain a text link (2.21).

You can point to a file in the Site Map pane or the Local Folder pane of the Site window when creating a link.

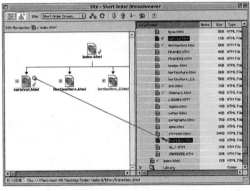

2.20

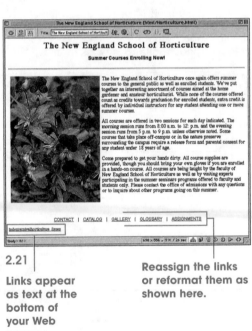

2.21

Links appear as text at the bottom of your Web pages.

Reassign the links or reformat them as shown here.

Changing Links Site-Wide

If you select a file in the Site window before choosing Site→Change Link Sitewide, the file path is automatically inserted in the Change All Links To field.

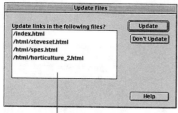

2.22

2.23

When the Update Files dialog box appears, it seems that you can selectively update the files in the list, but all the files in the list will be updated regardless of which ones you select.

Changing a link site-wide relinks all pages on your site to a new file you specify. This procedure is helpful if your site has links that change periodically—for example, if you have a client who designs a single page on her site every month, she can name the files `junesale.html`, `aprilsale.html`, and so forth. In the Site window, specify which files to swap, and all links to the sale page on the site are updated without eliminating previous sale pages.

1. Choose Site→Change Link Sitewide to display the corresponding dialog box (2.22).

2. Enter the link you want to change in the Change All Links To field. Enter the replacement link in the Into Links To field and click OK.

3. When the Update Files dialog box appears, click the Update button to update all the files in the list (2.23).

(N) O T E

After a link is changed site-wide, the selected file becomes an orphan because no files on your local site point to it. You can safely delete it without breaking any local links. Manually delete the corresponding file on the remote site and put a check in any files in which links were changed. Synchronizing your site can accomplish this in a single step, although you will still have to delete the orphaned file.

Specifying the Site Map Layout

The Site Map Layout is in the Define
Site dialog box and enables you to
specify the appearance of the site
map. You can specify how to display
the files in the Site Map view to fit
the type of data you need to manage
your site.

1. Choose (Site→Site Map
View→Layout) [View→Layout]
to display the Site Definition
dialog box with the Site Map
Layout category selected (2.24).

2. Indicate the home page for
your site in the Home Page
field. The home page is typically named index.html,
default.html, or home.html,
depending on the server.

3. Enter the maximum number of
columns, as well as the maximum column width. If you set
the Number of Columns to a
low number, such as 2, you can
view the Site window in a
more columnar format (2.25).

4. Choose the Icon Labels and
Display Options, and then
click OK.

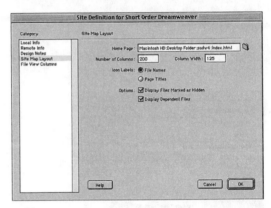

2.24

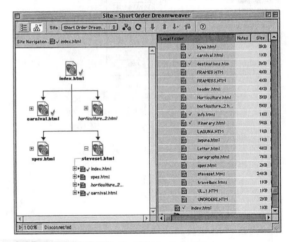

2.25

 **O T E**

*If you don't specify a home page in the Site
Map Layout category of the Site Definition
dialog box, Dreamweaver prompts you to
identify the home page when you choose the
Site Map Layout. If you have a file named
index.html or index.htm on your site,
Dreamweaver uses that file.*

Setting the Site Preferences

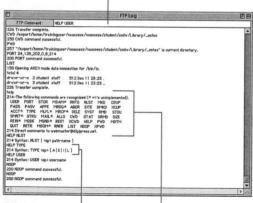

2.26

2.27

Type FTP commands in the FTP Command line and press (return)(Enter).

2.28

Type help followed by a command to get more information on the command.

Type help in the FTP Command line to list the available FTP commands.

The Site category in the Preferences dialog box is where you can specify how Dreamweaver interacts with files on the remote server. You can jump directly to the Define Sites dialog box from the Preferences dialog box after you specify the parameters for remote connections.

1. Choose Edit→Preferences to display the Preferences dialog box, and select Site from the Category list on the left (2.26).

2. Choose the way you want to work when connected to a remote site. If your remote server is behind a firewall, you must enter the firewall host and firewall port (usually 21) in the appropriate fields.

3. Click OK or click the Define Sites button to jump directly to the Define Sites dialog box.

(N)OTE

If you experience problems while transferring files using FTP, display the FTP log as a troubleshooting aid. Choose (Site→FTP Log)[Window→Site FTP Log] to display the FTP log (2.27). Type help *in the FTP Command line to list the available FTP commands for your site (2.28). You can enter these commands in the FTP Command line. Type* help *followed by an FTP command to get help on the command and to see the correct syntax for the command.*

Including Design Notes for Your Site

Use the Design Notes command to keep track of extra information associated with your documents, such as image filenames and comments about the file status. Design Notes are ideal for saving information that is private and that you don't want available in your source code. It's also a good way to keep track of which changes have been made to a document when working in a multiple-developer environment in which more than one person can work on the same file. You can see which files have Design Notes attached in the Site window. You also can create a Design Notes file for each document or template on your site. Additionally, you can create Design Notes for images, Flash movies, Shockwave objects, applets, and ActiveX controls.

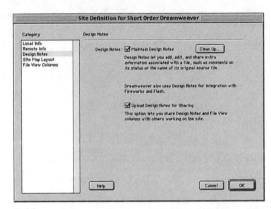

2.29

1. Choose Site→Define Sites, select a site, and click Edit to display the Site Definition dialog box. Select Design Notes from the Category list (2.29).

2. Check the Maintain Design Notes check box to enable Design Notes for your site. When Maintain Design Notes is selected, you can create Design Notes for all the files and templates in your site. Whenever a file is copied, moved, renamed, or deleted, the associated Design Notes file is also copied, moved, renamed, or deleted as well.

2.30

3. If you want to share your Design Notes with other developers working on your site, check the Upload Design Notes for Sharing check box. Deselect this option to save space on the server if you are the sole developer of your site.

4. If you click the Clean Up button, Dreamweaver deletes all Design Notes not associated with a file on your site (2.30). Click Yes in the warning dialog box to proceed.

5. Click OK.

 O T E

When defining your site, you can specify that Dreamweaver save file information in Design Notes for each file and template on your site.

 I P

If you add Design Notes to a template, any documents based on the template will not inherit the Design Notes of the template.

Adding Design Notes to Your Documents

To add Design Notes to your files, the files must be open in Dreamweaver's Document window. With Design Notes, you specify the status of the file to indicate in which development stage the document is. Include date-stamped notes as well as your own customized fields with values, such as an Author field with the author's name as the value.

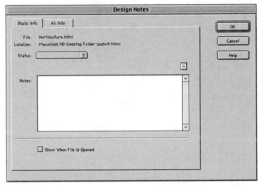

2.31

1. Make sure a document is opened in the Document window; then choose File→Design Notes to display the Design Notes dialog box **(2.31)**.

2. Indicate the status of the file on the Basic Info tab by selecting from the Status pull-down menu **(2.32)**.

2.32

3. Type any notes you want to make about the file or messages to other developers in the Notes field. Click the Date button above the Notes field to insert the current date **(2.33)**.

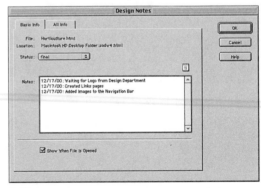

2.33

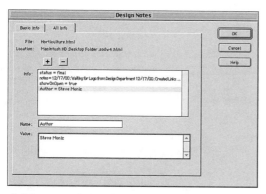

2.34

2.35   **Double-click to read Design Notes.**

4. On the All Info tab of the Design Notes dialog box, click the plus sign to add more key fields; then type a name and value. The Info field is automatically updated (2.34).

5. Click OK to save the notes.

Select a file in the Site window and select File→Design Notes to add Design Notes. You must either check out files on the remote server or get the file (copy it to the local drive) to add Design Notes.

 O T E

Design Notes are saved in a subfolder called __notes, in the same location as the current file. The filename is the document's filename, plus the extension .mno. For example, if the filename is training.html, the Design Notes file is named training.html.mno. The Notes folder is not visible in the Site window within Dreamweaver, but you can click the Design Notes icon in the Notes column of the Site window to read the Design Notes (2.35).

 O T E

To add Design Notes to individual objects on your Web page, such as images or Flash movies, (Ctrl-click)[Right+click] the object to display the context menu and choose Design Notes.

Using File View Columns with Design Notes

You can customize the columns that appear in the local and remote file list of the Site window. Reorder columns, add new columns, delete columns, hide columns, associate Design Notes with columns, and share columns with users connected to the site. The default columns are Name, Notes, Size, Type, Modified, and Checked Out By.

1. Choose (Site→Site Files View→File View Columns)[View→File View Columns] to display the File View Columns category of the Site Definition dialog box **(2.36)**.

2. Click the plus (+) button to add a column and assign a name in the Column Name field. Use a name that corresponds with one of the Design Note fields, such as Status or Priority.

3. Click the pull-down menu to the right of the Associate with Design Note field to indicate which Design Note information you want displayed in this column **(2.37)**.

Add a column¬   ┌Delete a column   Rearrange the column order

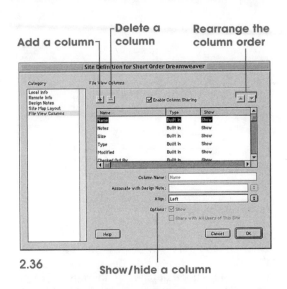

2.36   Show/hide a column

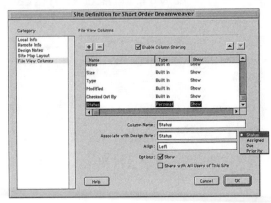

2.37

N O T E

You cannot delete, rename, or associate a Design Note with any of the default built-in columns. However, all columns can be hidden, with the exception of the Name column.

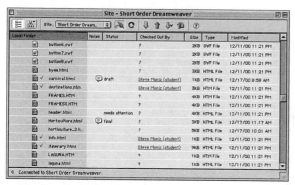

2.38

4. Choose an alignment option from the pull-down menu to the right of the Align field.

5. Check the Show check box to display the column in the Site window and check Share with All Users of This Site to make the column available to others viewing the remote site.

6. Use the up and down arrows in the upper-right corner to move the new column; then click OK. Display the Site window in Files view to see your new column (2.38).

 O T E

When you position the cursor between the column heads, the cursor icon changes to a line with arrows pointing left and right. Click between the column headers and drag to resize the columns.

 **O T E**

You can generate a workflow report detailing the Design Notes on your site. Refer to the section titled "Generating and Using Workflow Reports" in Chapter 21, "Managing, Synchronizing, and Cleaning Up Your Site."

Synchronizing Remote and Local Files

Use the Synchronize command to synchronize the files between your remote site and your local site. Dreamweaver will generate a list of files that need to be put or retrieved for the local and remote sites. You also can synchronize specific files and folders by first selecting them in the Local or Remote Site window.

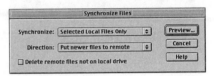

2.39

1. Choose Site, Synchronize to display the Synchronize Files dialog box (2.39).

2. To synchronize only selected files, choose Selected Local Files Only from the Synchronize pull-down menu. Choose the Entire Web Site option to synchronize the entire site.

3. From the Direction pull-down menu, choose the direction in which you want to synchronize the files (Table 2.2).

4. Check the Delete Remote Files Not on Local Drive check box if you want to remove any files that exist on the remote site but do not exist on the local site.

Table 2.2   Direction Options for Synchronizing Files

Option	Description
Put Newer Files to Remote	Uploads all the local files that have more recent modification dates than their counterparts on the remote server.
Get Newer Files from Remote	Downloads all remote files that have more recent modification dates than the local files.
Get and Put Newer Files	Places the most recent versions of the files on both the local and the remote sites.

 O T E

If you choose Get Newer Files from Remote in the Synchronize Files dialog box, and also check the Delete Remote Files check box, Dreamweaver deletes any files in your local site for which no corresponding remote files exist.

2.40

2.41

2.42

5. Click Preview and Dreamweaver evaluates and compares the files on your local and remote sites.

6. In the Synchronize dialog box that appears when Dreamweaver has finished checking your site, place a check mark in the Action column for all the files you want to update. Uncheck files you don't want to update **(2.40)**. Click OK.

7. Dreamweaver reports the status of the synchronization in the Status column of the Synchronize dialog box **(2.41)**. Click the Save Log button to save the status log to a text file **(2.42)**.

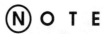

To see which files are newer on the local site or which files are newer on the remote site—without synchronizing—choose (Site→Site Files View→Select Newer Local)[Edit→Select Newer Local] or (Site→Site Files View→Select Newer Remote)[Edit→Select Newer Remote].

CHAPTER 3

The ability to edit the HTML source code of your Web pages within Dreamweaver provides the ultimate control over your Web pages and Web site. Even though you can design most of your Web content visually using the tools and features of Dreamweaver, sometimes it is helpful to edit the raw HTML code.

EDITING HTML IN DREAMWEAVER

Dreamweaver enables you to edit the HTML code through the Code view, the Code inspector, or the Quick Tag Editor. If you want to learn HTML, you can create page content in the Document window and simultaneously see the HTML code being written in the Code view or Code inspector. Use the Dreamweaver Reference panel to look up HTML codes to gain an understanding of individual codes.

Dreamweaver also enables you to open HTML files written outside Dreamweaver. Using the round-trip HTML feature, you can use your favorite text editor to modify the HTML code and then pop right back into Dreamweaver with your changes in place. In addition, you can use commands in Dreamweaver to clean up the HTML code, removing redundant tags, resolving nesting problems, and stripping out special codes, such as those used in Microsoft Word HTML files.

Using the Dreamweaver Reference Panel

The Dreamweaver Reference panel contains reference information for HTML tags, JavaScript objects, and CSS styles. If you are not familiar with HTML codes, the Dreamweaver Reference panel contains extensive explanations of each code as well as the correct syntax and usage. Experienced developers can benefit from the Dreamweaver Reference panel by tracking down problems and researching browser compatibility issues.

1. Select something on your page, such as formatted text, a table, or an image. You can select anything in the Design view or Code view window.

2. Choose View→Toolbar to display the toolbar if it isn't already onscreen.

3. Click the Reference button in the toolbar (3.1) or choose Window→Reference to display the Reference panel (3.2).

Display Reference panel.

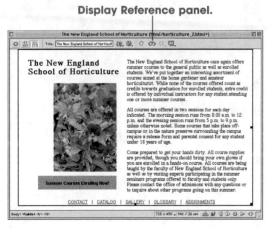

3.1

Select a tag, object, or CSS style.   Choose from available attributes.   Choose reference book.

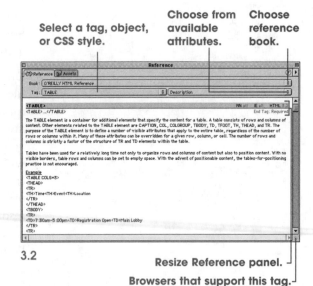

3.2

Resize Reference panel.
Browsers that support this tag.

Ⓝ O T E

HTML tags and scripts are color-coded in the Code view and Code inspector. You can specify your own colors in the Code Colors preferences. See the section titled "Changing the Code Colors" later in this chapter for information on changing the colors for the Code view and Code inspector.

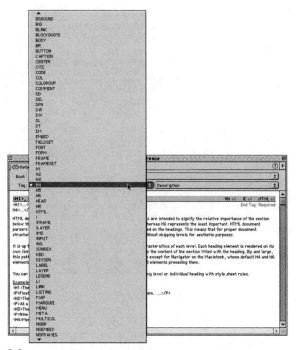

3.3

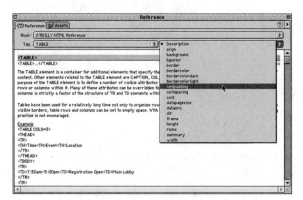

3.4

4. To look up other HTML tags, choose O'REILLY HTML Reference from the Book pop-up menu and select a tag from the Tag pop-up menu in the Reference panel **(3.3)**.

5. Choose a specific attribute for the tag in the pop-up menu to the right of the Tag pop-up menu **(3.4)**.

 I P

You will occasionally run into an HTML tag that Dreamweaver does not recognize, and some tag attributes are available only when typing directly into HTML code. For example, the bgsound attributes of the <body> tag and the <blink> tag are not available in Dreamweaver, but you can type them in the Code view or Code inspector. Dreamweaver also uses the <center> tag or the <div align=center> tag to center text in a table cell. If you want to add the align=center attribute to the <td> tag, edit the HTML code and all the cell contents will be centered and displayed that way in Dreamweaver's Document window.

 I P

To indent or outdent sections of code in the Code view or Code inspector, choose Edit→Indent Code or Edit→Outdent Code. You can check that your tags are balanced and have the appropriate opening and closing tags by choosing Edit→Select Parent Tag, which highlights enclosing tags.

Using the Code View and Code Inspector

The Code view displays the HTML code for the current document in the Document window and enables you to make changes to the HTML source code. You have the option of working entirely in the Code view or splitting the Document window to display both the Code view and the Design view.

1. Choose View→Code or click the Show Code View button in the upper-left corner of the Document window to display the HTML source code (3.5).

2. Edit the HTML source code or insert additional code, and then click the Show Design View button in the upper-left corner of the Document window to see the result.

3. Click the Show Code and Design Views button in the upper-left corner of the Document window to split the Document window (3.6).

4. Click the Refresh button in the Property inspector or press the F5 key to update the Design view with your changes. You also can click inside the Design view pane to see your changes.

5. Choose Window→Code Inspector or click the Code Inspector button in the Launcher panel to display the Code inspector (3.7).

Show Code view
Show Code and Design views
Show Design view

3.5

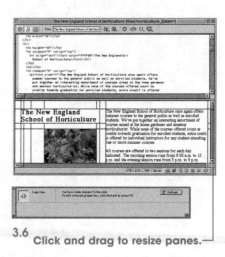

3.6   Click and drag to resize panes.

The Code inspector enables you to edit the source code in a separate panel and behaves just like the Code view.

3.7

Setting Code View and Code Inspector Options

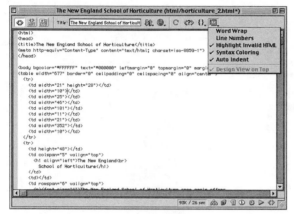

3.8

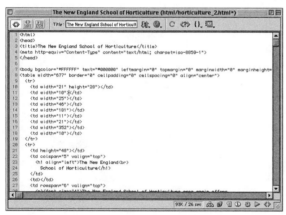

3.9

You can control how the source code is displayed in the Code view or Code inspector by selecting the settings in the View options pop-up menu. To access the Options menu, you must have the Code view or Code inspector onscreen.

1. Choose View→Toolbar if the toolbar is not visible at the top of the Code view window.

2. Click the Show Code View button in the upper-left corner of the toolbar to display the Code view in the Document window.

3. Click the View Options pop-up menu in the toolbar and select from the following options (3.8):

   - **Word Wrap**—Wraps the code to fit the width of the window.

   - **Line Numbers**—Adds line numbers along the left side of the code (3.9).

   - **Highlight Invalid HTML**—Turns on Dreamweaver's error highlighting. HTML that is not supported by Dreamweaver is highlighted in yellow.

   - **Syntax Coloring**—Turns on and off the color-coding specified in the Code Colors preferences.

   - **Auto Indent**—Turns on and off the code indenting specified in the Code Format preferences.

Using the Quick Tag Editor

The Quick Tag Editor is available in the Property inspector, through the context menu, or by simply pressing (Command-T)[Ctrl+T]. When you use the Quick Tag Editor button in the Property inspector, the Quick Tag editor pops up. If you use the context menu choices or type (Command-T)[Ctrl+T], the Quick Tag Editor appears at the insertion point in the Design view.

1. Click in the Design view where you want to insert an HTML tag.

2. Type (Command-T)[Ctrl+T] to display the Quick Tag Editor (3.10).

3. Type in the HTML code or double-click a code in the Hints pop-up list; then press (Return)[Enter].

4. Click and drag to select some text; then press (Command-T)[Ctrl+T] to display the Wrap Tag option of the Quick Tag Editor (3.11).

5. Type in an HTML tag or double-click a tag in the Hints pop-up menu; then press (Return)[Enter].

6. To edit an existing tag with the Quick Tag Editor, select an object (such as an image) or click a tag in the lower-left corner of the Document window; then press (Command-T) [Ctrl+T] (3.12).

Pause for a few seconds and the Hints menu appears, displaying HTML tags and attributes you can select using the up and down arrow keys or by double-clicking.

3.10

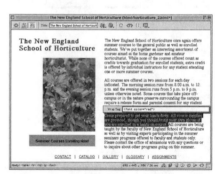

3.11

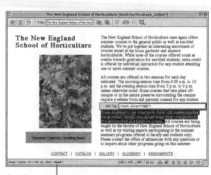

3.12   **Click an HTML tag to use the Edit Tag option of the Quick Tag Editor.**

Changing the Code Colors

Click the color swatches to indicate the colors for the HTML Source.

Select specific tags and indicate a unique color.

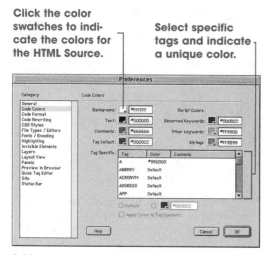

3.13

Color-coded HTML tags make locating specific source code in the Code view and Code inspector much easier.

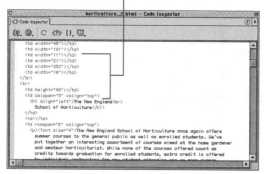

3.14

The Code view and Code inspector display sections of code in different colors to enable you to easily locate the code in the document. You can choose any colors you want to denote particular tags by editing the Code Colors preferences.

1. Choose Edit→Preferences to display the Preferences dialog box, and then select Code Colors from the Category list on the left (3.13).

2. Click the color swatches or enter a color specification in the color field adjacent to Background, Text, Comments, and Tag Default to set the colors for the display of these elements (3.14). To specify colors for specific tags, select the tag in the scrolling list and enter the color information in the field below the list. You can enter color names or hexadecimal values to specify color.

3. Check the Apply Color to Tag Comments check box if you want the color you specify to apply to both the HTML tag and the contents of that HTML tag.

 **O T E**

The Script Colors are used to denote any scripting keywords and strings in the Code view and Code inspector.

Setting Code Format Preferences for the Code View and Code Inspector

Edit the Code Format preferences to affect the way the Code view and Code inspector behave when you are entering and editing HTML code. Select from the Code Format preferences to specify indents, tab size, text wrap, and type case for tags and attributes.

1. Choose Edit→Preferences to display the Preferences dialog box, and then select Code Format from the Category list on the left (3.15).

2. Check the Indent check box if you want your HTML code to be automatically indented. Specify how you want the indents to be handled by selecting either Spaces or Tabs from the pull-down menu.

3. By default, Dreamweaver applies additional spacing to table rows and columns, as well as to frames and frame-sets. This setting makes sense because tables and frames often involve nested HTML code (3.16).

4. Specify an indent size if you are using spaces or a tab size if you are using tabs for indents. Specify values by entering them into their respective fields.

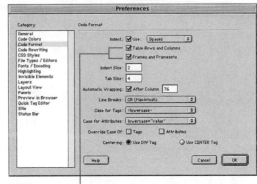

3.15

If you do not want to apply additional indent levels to tables and frames, uncheck their respective check boxes in the HTML Format preferences.

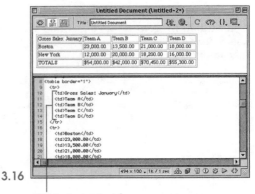

3.16

Table indented two spaces.

 I P

Changes you make to the Code Format preferences apply only to code that is subsequently added. To apply the source formatting to the existing code, choose Commands→Apply Source Formatting.

When you open an HTML file formatted
with the Macintosh line breaks (cr) in
Notepad for Windows, the line breaks
are ignored because Windows requires
the carriage return and linefeed (cr/lf)
in the source.

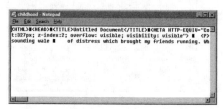

3.17

When you open an HTML file formatted for
Windows (cr/lf) in SimpleText for the
Macintosh, boxes represent the linefeed (lf)
character because the Mac uses only the
carriage return (cr).

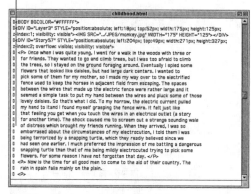

3.18

5. To automatically wrap the
HTML code in the Code view
and Code inspector, check the
Automatic Wrapping check
box. You can indicate the point
at which the text will wrap by
specifying it in the After
Column value.

6. You can specify the type of line
breaks used at the end of the
each line of HTML code. Each
of the three most popular operating systems uses a different
line break code to designate
the end of a line.

*Choosing the correct line break method for
your HTML code enables the hosting system
to display the HTML code correctly. Keep in
mind that, if the operating system you use is
different from the one you specify for line
breaks, the HTML code might be displayed
incorrectly when using simple text editors,
such as Notepad (3.17) or SimpleText
(3.18). The Dreamweaver HTML Inspector
displays the code correctly regardless of
which line break option you choose.*

*If you check the Wrap option at the top of
the HTML Inspector, the HTML code wraps
to fit the size of the HTML Inspector window and overrides the AutoWrap setting in
the Preferences dialog box.*

Setting Code Format Preferences for the Code View and Code Inspector continued

7. Specify how you want the HTML code to be displayed by choosing the Case for Tags and Case for Attributes options from their respective pull-down menus (3.19).

8. To center objects or text on your Web page, select Use Div Tag or Use Center Tag (3.20).

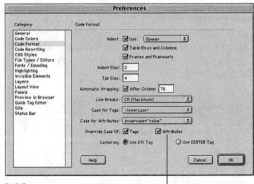

3.19

Choose Override Case of either Tags or Attributes, or both, if you want your specifications for case to be applied to HTML documents when you open them in Dreamweaver. Choose Commands→Apply Source Formatting to override the case of the HTML code in an open document.

 **O T E**

When the World Wide Web Consortium (W3C) released version 3.2 of HTML, the <center> tag was deprecated in favor of the <div align="center"> method of centering objects and text. Some Web page designers still prefer to use the <center> tag—hence the reason for these choices. Dreamweaver defaults to the more current <div align="center"> method.

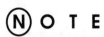 **O T E**

The center alignment options apply only to the elements of the Web page that do not have an attribute for centering, such as images.

3.20

Specifying Code Rewriting Preferences

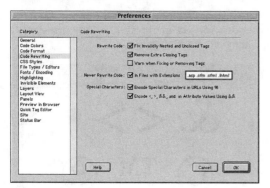

3.21

The line number and column number are indicated to make locating the corrected HTML code easier.

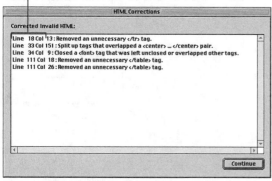

3.22

You can tell Dreamweaver to fix HTML tags that are incorrectly nested or that have too many closing tags, and to leave code intact for Active Server Pages, Cold Fusion, PHP, and others.

1. Choose Edit→Preferences to display the Preferences dialog box, and then select Code Rewriting from the Category list on the left (3.21).

2. Select the check box for Fix Invalidly Nested and Unclosed Tags if you want Dreamweaver to automatically fix nesting problems and close any unclosed tags when opening a document.

3. Check the box for Remove Extra Closing Tags to remove any redundant closing tags.

4. Check the Warn When Fixing or Removing Tags box to display the HTML Corrections dialog box before Dreamweaver makes any changes to your HTML code (3.22).

 I P

The code rewriting preferences apply only to code that is imported into Dreamweaver from an outside source and not when the text is edited in Code view or with the Code inspector.

Specifying Code Rewriting Preferences continued

5. Check the Never Rewrite Code check box to prevent Dreamweaver from writing HTML into files with the specified file extensions.

6. Leave the two Special Characters check boxes checked to ensure that Dreamweaver correctly interprets and codes special characters. Only uncheck these when you're opening a file that includes the specified characters as codes (3.23).

By default, Dreamweaver automatically codes special characters so they appear correctly on Web pages.

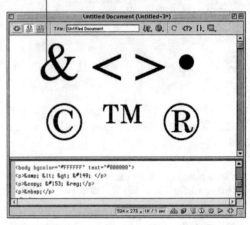

3.23

 **O T E**

If you turn off the HTML rewriting preferences, invalid code is displayed in the Document window and highlighted in both Design view and Code view (3.24).

3.24

 **O T E**

Server-side processing technologies, such as ASP, ColdFusion, JSP, and PHP, use special codes along with HTML codes. For example, in ASP and JSP, blocks of code appear between the <% and %> characters. If you do not check the Never Rewrite Code check box in the Code Rewriting preferences, Dreamweaver converts the codes to entity references and the file will no longer work with ASP or JSP.

Cleaning Up Microsoft Word HTML

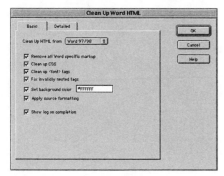

3.25

You can open documents saved as HTML files by Microsoft Word. The Clean Up Word HTML command removes any formatting specific to Microsoft Word and enables you to set some basic attributes. Be sure to save a copy of the HTML file if you want to open it again using Microsoft Word because once you clean up the code, Word will not properly interpret the page.

1. In Microsoft Word, save a document as an HTML file.

2. Choose File→Import→Import Word HTML; then select a file to open.

3. Dreamweaver automatically opens the Clean Up Word HTML dialog box (3.25).

4. The Basic tab of the Clean Up Word HTML dialog box offers the options shown in Table 3.1. Select the options you want to apply to the Word HTML file.

Table 3.1   Clean Up Microsoft Word HTML Basic Options

Option	Description
Remove all Word specific markup	Removes all Word-specific HTML, including XML, custom meta data and link tags in the `<head>` section, conditional tags and contents, and empty paragraphs and margins from Word styles.
Clean up CSS	Removes all Word-specific CSS styles, style attributes beginning with mso, and non-CSS styles.
Clean up `<font>` tags	Removes HTML tags and sets all body text to HTML size 2.
Fix invalidly nested tags	Removes the font markup tags inserted by Word outside the paragraph and heading tags.
Set background color	Word documents have a gray background by default. Enter a hexadecimal color or color name.
Apply source formatting	Applies the source formatting indicated in the HTML Format preferences.
Show log on completion	Displays an alert box detailing the changes made to the document when cleanup is completed.

 I P

The options you set in the Clean Up Word HTML dialog box are automatically saved as the default for this dialog box.

Cleaning Up Microsoft Word HTML continued

5. Click the Detailed tab to specifically indicate how the Remove Word Specific Markup and Clean Up <font> Tags options behave **(3.26).**

6. Click OK. If you checked the Show Log on Completion check box, an alert dialog box appears indicating the changes that were made **(3.27).**

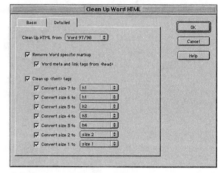

3.26

3.27

T I P

If you already have an HTML file created with Microsoft Word open in Dreamweaver, choose Commands→Clean Up Word HTML.

N O T E

You might experience a short delay while Dreamweaver determines which version of Word created the HTML file. If Dreamweaver can't determine the version, select the version from the pop-up menu in the Clean Up Word HTML dialog box.

Using External Editors

Enter the extensions for files you want to open in Code view instead of Design view.

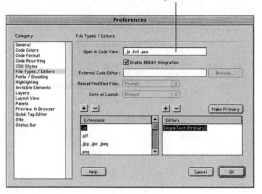

3.28

You can use any text editor as an external editor, although Dreamweaver offers specific support for BBEdit on the Macintosh platform and HomeSite on Windows. An external editor enables you to take advantage of features such as stripping control codes and automated code generation. You also can indicate which editors to use for other file types, such as GIFs and JPEGs.

1. Choose Edit→Preferences to display the Preferences dialog box.

2. Select File Types / Editors from the Category list on the left **(3.28)**.

3. Macintosh users can click the Enable BBEdit Integration check box to use BBEdit as the external editor. Macintosh users must uncheck the Enable BBEdit Integration check box to specify an alternative external editor.

4. Click the Browse button next to the External Code Editor box to choose a text editor.

 **O T E**

If you do not indicate an external editor in the Preferences dialog box, Dreamweaver prompts you to select one if you try to launch an external editor.

Using External Editors continued

5. Select from the Reload Modified Files pop-up menu to indicate what you want Dreamweaver to do when a file has been modified outside Dreamweaver **(3.29)**.

6. Select from the Save on Launch pop-up menu to indicate whether Dreamweaver should always save the current document before launching the editor, never save the document, or prompt you before saving **(3.30)**.

7. Click an extension in the Extensions list, and then click the plus sign icon on the Editors side to choose a program to edit files with a particular extension. Click the Make Primary button to choose the primary editor when more than one is specified. If you want to add an extension that isn't already listed in the Extensions list, click the plus sign icon above that list. Click the minus sign buttons to remove Extensions and Editors.

8. Click OK.

9. Choose Edit→Edit with (editor name) to edit your HTML file using the external editor. Click the Edit button in the Property inspector to edit objects on your page, such as GIFs and JPEGs, in an external editor.

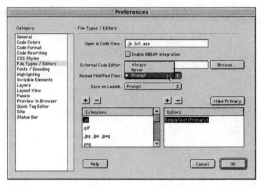

3.29

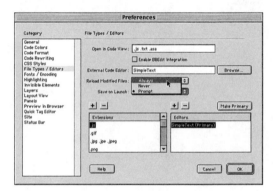

3.30

CHAPTER 4

In this chapter, you will learn how to...

Specify a Typeface

Edit the Font List

Set the Basefont Size

Change the Default Text Color

Specify Text Color Using the Property Inspector

Avoid Multiple Font Tags in Your HTML

Add Comments

Find and Replace Text and HTML Code

Power Search Your Code with Regular Expressions

Dreamweaver provides a comprehensive choice of attributes in the Property inspector to format text. Even though the <font> tag, used to format text properties, is likely to be deprecated in the near future in favor of the more flexible Cascading Style Sheets, the use of this tag will go on for as long as users still have older browser versions. This

CREATING AND EDITING TEXT

chapter covers the formatting of text, including the following:

- **Typeface usage**—Specifies groups of font faces to cover the possible fonts used by visitors to your Web pages.

- **Absolute and relative type styles**—Formats the appearance of the text using type style options, such as bold, italic, and underline.

- **Changing text size**—Though limited, more options are available for type size than the default text sizes used by HTML tags.

- **Changing text color**—Specifies color for text, either by using Dreamweaver's Web-safe color panel or your system color panel or by selecting a color from your screen.

Dreamweaver also enables you to find and replace instances of HTML code or page content. Using Dreamweaver's unique search engine, you can search for regular expressions that enable you to be very specific about the text strings for which you are searching. Specifics about paragraph formatting appear in Chapter 5, "Working with Paragraph Elements and HTML Styles." See Chapter 14, "Working with Cascading Style Sheets," for extensive coverage of using style sheets in Dreamweaver.

Specifying a Typeface

In HTML code, one of the attributes of the `<font>` tag is the capability to specify a series of typefaces for your text. Because the availability of a particular typeface depends largely on the fonts that are installed on the user's computer, specifying a number of typefaces creates a selection list of fonts that has a good chance of matching at least one of the user's fonts (Table 4.1). The browser first tries to use the first font listed, followed by the second, and then the third, and so forth. If none of the fonts in the list are available on the user's computer, the default browser font is used instead.

In the Property inspector, click the downward pointing arrow to the right of the Default Font field to select a typeface group (4.1).

Table 4.1 Default Typefaces

Windows	Macintosh
Arial	Chicago
Arial Black	Courier
Arial Narrow	Geneva
Arial Rounded MT Bold	Helvetica
Book Antiqua	Monaco
Bookman Oldstyle	New York
Century Gothic	Palatino
Century Schoolbook	Times
Courier	Arial*
Courier New	Courier New*
Garamond	Times New Roman*
Times New Roman	
Verdana	
*Fonts are included on most Macintosh systems	

4.1

 **O T E**

When you create new font lists, the generic font families are available at the bottom of the list. Generic font families include cursive, fantasy, monospace, sans-serif, and serif.

Editing the Font List

You also can edit the font list by selecting
Text→Font→Edit Font List.

4.2

When you apply a font group to text in your
document, the font list is included in the FACE
attribute of the <font> tag, like this: <FONT
FACE="helvetica,arial,san-serif">. For this
reason, the font groups are not removed from
the existing HTML code when you remove
them from the font list in Dreamweaver.

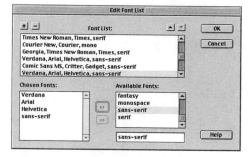

4.3

Scroll to the very bottom of the font list
in the Edit Font List dialog box to select
the generic fonts. The generic fonts rec-
ognized by browsers are cursive, fantasy, monospace, sans-serif, and serif.

Edit the font list to create your own
customized groupings of fonts. This
feature is especially useful if you are
creating pages for an intranet and
you have some control over the
fonts that are available on users'
computers.

1. In the Property inspector,
   select Edit Font List from the
   Font pop-up menu (4.2).

2. When the Edit Font List dialog
   box is displayed, click the plus
   sign (+) in the upper-left corner to add a new list of fonts to
   the scrolling list in the Font
   List window (4.3).

3. Select a font from the scrolling
   list of Available Fonts and then
   click the move button (<<) to
   move the font to the Chosen
   Fonts window. You can add
   any number of fonts using this
   method.

4. If you want to remove fonts
   from the Chosen Fonts window, click the font name, and
   then click the move button
   (>>) to remove the font.

5. Click the up and down arrows
   in the upper-right corner
   above the Font List window to
   rearrange the order of the
   fonts. The fonts appear in the
   menus in the order in which
   they are depicted in the Edit
   Font List window. Click OK.

Setting the Basefont Size

By default, the basefont size is 3. You can, however, change this value so the text on your Web page is based on a size other than 3. Unfortunately, Dreamweaver doesn't offer a way to change the basefont size from within the interface, but you can edit the HTML code, adding a simple tag to make the change.

1. Press F10 to display the HTML Source window if it isn't already displayed onscreen.

2. Locate the <body> tag at the top of the HTML source code. The <body> tag might contain some other attributes for background color and a background image, for example.

3. Insert the basefont tag directly after the <body> tag **(4.4)**, and then save your changes.

4. Press F10 to hide the HTML Source window. Because Dreamweaver does not support the basefont tag, the size change is apparent only when you view the document in a browser **(4.5)**.

N O T E

To resize text, click and drag to select the text you want to resize, and then select an absolute or a relative size from the Size pop-up menu in the Property inspector.

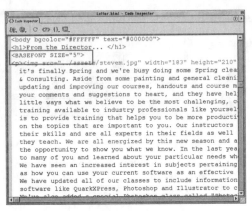

4.4

The text as depicted in Dreamweaver when the basefont tag is inserted, changing the size of the text to 5.

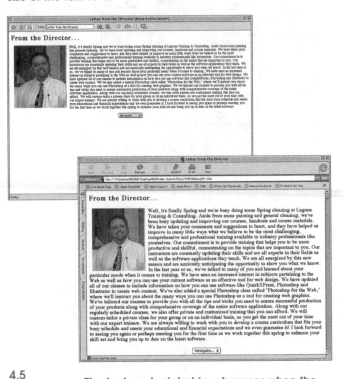

4.5

The text as depicted in a browser when the basefont tag is inserted, changing the size of the text to 5.

Changing the Default Text Color

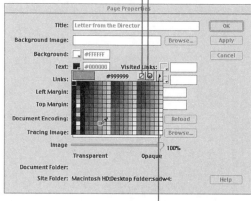

4.6

Click the Default Color icon to remove any color specification from the color field and return to the default color.

Click the Color Panel Menu to select the color display for the color panel.

4.7

Click the Color Wheel icon to select a color from any of your system's built-in color models.

In Dreamweaver, you can specify color by using a variety of color models. Color is typically specified as a hexadecimal value in HTML source code, although color names are acceptable for browsers that support this convention—in particular, Netscape and Internet Explorer version 3 or higher. Dreamweaver enables you to select your colors visually from color panels or by sampling a color anywhere on your computer screen. By default, the text in your document is set to black, but you can change the default text color by editing the page properties.

1. Select Modify→Page Properties to display the Page Properties dialog box **(4.6)**.

2. Click the swatch to the right of the word "Text" in the Page PPage Properties dialog box once to display the color **(4.7)**.

3. Position the eyedropper cursor over a desired color and click to select a color from Dreamweaver's color panel. Click OK to save your changes.

 N O T E

Click anywhere onscreen to sample a color when the color panel is open. You can click to sample colors outside the Dreamweaver application as well.

Specifying Text Color Using the Property Inspector

Using Dreamweaver's visual method of selecting color, text can be colored using hexadecimal values or, if you choose, using color names. Dreamweaver automatically inserts the hexadecimal color value in the color field when you select a color using the Dreamweaver color panel options.

4.8

Click a color swatch with the eye-dropper cursor to select a color.

4.9

1. Click and drag to highlight the text you want to affect.

2. If you know the hexadecimal value for the color you want, enter the value directly into the color field located just to the left of the bold (B) button in the Property inspector. You also can enter a color name, such as teal, in which case the color name is inserted into the HTML code (4.8).

3. To select a color from the Web-safe color panel instead, click the color swatch in the Property inspector to display the Web-safe color panel (4.9).

T I P

You can create Web-safe colors by dithering two or three of the Web-safe colors. Visit www.colormix.com and use the excellent (and free) color mixer to create thousands of colors from the 216 Web-safe colors.

The Macintosh system color picker

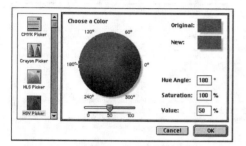

The Windows system color picker

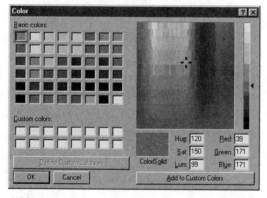

4.10

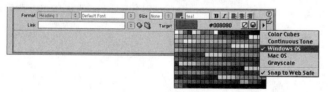

4.11

4. Position the eyedropper cursor over a color cell and click to select the color or choose from the following options:

- Click the square icon with the red diagonal line through it, located in the upper-right corner of the color panel, to reset the color to the default value.

- Click the Color Wheel icon in the upper-right corner of the color panel to select colors using your System color picker (4.10).

- Click the Color Panel menu to select an alternative color panel. Color Cubes is the default Web-safe color panel. Continuous Tone is also a panel containing Web-safe colors and is presented in the order the colors appear on the color wheel. Windows OS and Mac OS display the respective 256-color panels for these systems and are not Web-safe. Grayscale displays a panel of the 256 gray levels and also is not Web-safe. Select Snap to Web Safe to cause colors you select from Windows OS, Mac OS, or Grayscale to snap to the nearest Web-safe color (4.11).

Avoiding Multiple Font Tags in Your HTML

When you specify font information, such as color, size, and typeface, the `<font>` tag indicator is visible in the lower-left corner of the Document window, along with the `<body>` tag and any other tags applicable to the selected text. If you want to change the attributes of text that has been previously formatted, the best way to select the text is to click the `<font>` tag in the status area at the bottom of the Document window. This step enables you to select exactly the text that was formatted last time. If you try to reselect the text by clicking and dragging, you are likely to end up with multiple `<font>` tags for the same text in your HTML code **(4.12)**.

1. Click anywhere within a text area you previously formatted for typeface, color, or size— you should see the blinking cursor within the text.

2. Click the `<font>` tag in the lower-left corner of the Document window **(4.13)** to highlight the previously for-matted text. Make any changes to size, color, or typeface.

 **O T E**

If your Web page already has multiple `<font>` tags, use the Clean Up HTML com-mand in the Commands menu to combine nested `<font>` tags and remove any redun-dant tags.

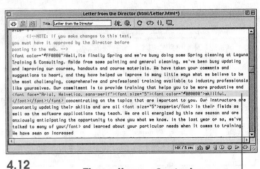

4.12

These three `<font>` tags can be condensed into the single tag `<font face="Arial, Helvetica, sans-serif", size="5" color="#000000">`.

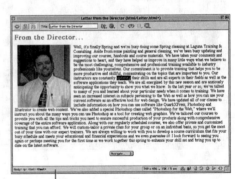

4.13

To select the previously formatted text, click this `<font>` tag.

Adding Comments

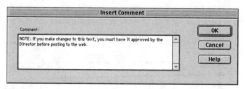

4.14

You do not see the text on your Web page in the Document window, but an icon appears when you have Invisible Elements turned on. Select View→Visual Aids→Invisible Elements to turn invisible elements on and off.

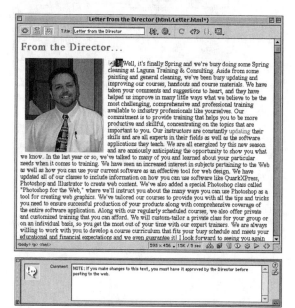

4.15

Comment text

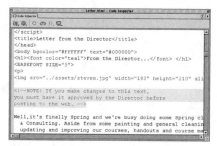

4.16

Comment text can be helpful when multiple sections are coded similarly or if it is likely that someone besides you will be editing the HTML source code in the future. You also might want to use comment text to include copyright information and other pertinent information about the editing of the HTML code, such as date, time, and operator, at the top of the document.

1. Position your cursor in the Document window where you want the comment text to be inserted.

2. Select Insert→Invisible Tags→Comment to display the Insert Comment dialog box **(4.14)**.

3. Enter the comment text and click OK. To view the comments, simply click the Comment icon in the Document window; the text is displayed and highlighted in the Property inspector as well as in the HTML Inspector **(4.15)**.

 O T E

*To find the comment text in the HTML source code, look for text inside the <!-- --> tag **(4.16)**. You also can use the comment tag around portions of HTML code that you want to turn off temporarily. Additionally, you can edit the HTML code for the comment by clicking the Quick Tag Editor icon on the right side of the Property Inspector.*

Finding and Replacing Text and HTML Code

Dreamweaver's powerful search engine enables you to locate a text instance or HTML source code sequence in your document and optionally replace it with new text. You can even search through all the files on your site or all the files in a particular directory. This feature can be invaluable when you need to make a global change on your Web site.

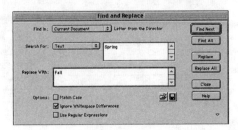

4.17

4.18

1. Select Edit→Find and Replace to display the Find and Replace dialog box (4.17).

2. Select the documents you want to search in the Find In pop-up menu (4.18). You can search the current document, all documents in your Web site, all documents within a particular directory, or the documents currently selected in the Site window.

3. For a basic search, select one of the following from the Search For pop-up menu (4.19):

   ● **Text**—Searches for text instances in the Document window.

4.19

In this example, Dreamweaver finds all text tagged with the `<font size="6">` tag, which does not include a color attribute and is within the table header `<th>` tag within the `<table>` tag. The Action Set Attribute changes the size to 5.

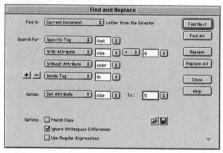

4.20

In this example, Dreamweaver finds the text **Fall Special** when it is formatted as red text and changes the text to **Spring Special**.

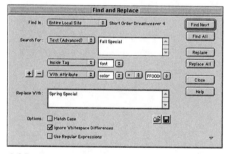

4.21

● **Source Code**—Searches through the HTML source code for the specified text instance.

● **Specific Tag**—Searches for a particular HTML tag with optional attributes. Select the tag and attributes from the pop-up menus and specify multiple attributes by clicking the plus sign icon (+). In this case, the search will find all the text formatted with the specified tag and attributes **(4.20)**. Select an action to perform on the code that is found from the Action pop-up menu.

4. To perform a more complex find and replace, select Text (Advanced) from the Search For pop-up menu. You can restrict the search to the text within specific tags and containing specific attributes **(4.21)**, or you can widen the search criteria. Click the minus (–) button to reduce the search criteria; click the plus (+) button to include more attributes for a specific HTML tag.

 I P

You can perform a find by choosing Edit→Find and Replace in either the Document or Site window.

Finding and Replacing Text and HTML Code continued

5. The three check boxes at the bottom of the Find dialog box help broaden or restrict the scope of the search. These include

- **Match Case**—Select this option to find only exact matches to capitalization.

- **Ignore Whitespace Differences**—Select this option to ignore any extra whitespace, especially in the HTML source code.

- **Use Regular Expressions**—Select this option to enable the use of special descriptors to further refine your text. (See the next section, "Power Searching Your Code with Regular Expressions," for specific information about when and how to use them.)

6. Click the Find Next button to find the first or next instance that meets the specified criteria. If you click the Find All button, the Find and Replace dialog box expands to display a scrolling list of all found instances (4.22). You can double-click these instances to highlight the text within the Document window.

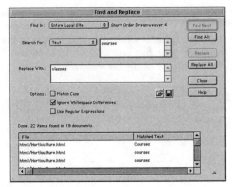

4.22

 I P

HTML code often contains a lot of extra whitespace, which is used to format the code so it is more easily readable.

 **O T E**

Press (Command-F)[Ctrl+F] to display the Find and Replace dialog box. Press (Command-G)[F3] to find the next instance of what you specified in the Find and Replace dialog box.

Power Searching Your Code with Regular Expressions

Certain characters, such as *, ?, \w, and \b, can be treated as expression operators in your search when you select the option Use Regular Expressions in the Find dialog box. Regular expressions are patterns used to describe certain character combinations within the text of your Web page or within the HTML source code. Sometimes you need to actually search for one of the special characters used as a regular expression. In this case, you can escape the character with the backslash (\) followed by the character. For example, if you want to find can*, search for can* and be sure the Use Regular Expressions check box is checked. If you do not include the escape sequence in this example, you will find *cane, candle, candy,* and *cancel* as well as can*. Table 4.2 depicts the character sequences used as regular expressions along with examples of how to use them.

Table 4.2   Regular Expressions

Type This	To Find This	Example
^	Beginning of a line.	^N matches "N" in "New York is..." but not in "I Heart New York."
*	The preceding character 0 or more times.	ut* matches "ut" in "cut," "utt" in "cutter," and "u" in "hum."
+	The preceding character 1 or more times.	ut+ matches "ut" in "cut" and "utt" in "cutter," but matches nothing in "hum."
?	The preceding character 0 or 1 time.	st?on matches "son" in "Johnson" and "ston" in "Johnston," but nothing in "Appleton" or "tension."
.	Any single character except new line (line feed).	.ate matches "mate" and "late" in the phrase "the first mate was late."

Power Searching Your Code with Regular Expressions continued

Table 4.2 continued

Type This	To Find This	Example
x|y	Either x or y.	FF0000|0000FF matches "FF0000" in BGCOLOR="#FF0000" and "0000FF" in FONT COLOR="#0000FF."
{n}	Exactly n occurrences of the preceding character.	o{2} matches "oo" in "zoom" and the first two os in "mooooo", but matches nothing in "movie."
{n,m}	At least n and at most m occurrences of the preceding character.	F{2,4} matches "FF" in "#FF0000" and the first four Fs in #FFFFFF.
[abc]	Any one of the characters enclosed in the brackets. Specify a range of characters with a hyphen (for example, [a-f] is equivalent to [abcdef]).	[e-g] matches "e" in "bed," "f" in "folly," and "g" in "guard."
[^abc]	Any character not enclosed in the brackets. Specify a range of characters with a hyphen (for example, (^a-f) isequivalent to (^abcdef)).	[^aeiou] initially matches "r" in "orange," "b" in "book," and "k" in "eek!"
\b	A word boundary (such as a space or carriage return).	\bb matches "b" in "book" but nothing in "goober" or "snob."
\B	A non-word boundary.	\Bb matches "b" in "goober" but nothing in "book."
\d	Any digit character; equivalent to (0-9).	\d matches "3" in "C3PO" and "2" in "apartment 2G."
\D	Any non-digit character; equivalent to (^0-9).	\D matches "S" in "900S" and "Q" in "Q45."
\f	Form feed.	
\n	Line feed.	
\r	Carriage return.	
\s	Any single whitespace character, including space, tab, form feed, or line feed.	\sbook matches "book" in "blue book" but nothing in "notebook."
\S	Any single non-whitespace character.	\Sbook matches "book" in "notebook" but nothing in "blue book."
\t	A tab.	
\w	Any alphanumeric character, including an underscore; equivalent to (A-Za-z0-9_).	b\w* matches "barking" in "the barking dog" and both "big" and "black" in "the big black dog."
\W	Any nonalphanumeric character; equivalent to (^A-Za-z0-9_).	\W matches "&" in "Jake & Mattie" and "%" in "100%."

CHAPTER 5

In this chapter, you will learn how to...

Enter Paragraph Breaks

Enter Line Breaks

Create an Unordered List

Change Unordered List Properties

Create an Ordered List

Change Ordered List Properties

Insert Special Characters

Add a Horizontal Rule

Create Customized HTML Styles

The Property inspector in Dreamweaver is used to select the various formatting options for paragraphs. Some tags, such as the Heading tags, <h1> for example, automatically create a paragraph when the closing tag is inserted in the HTML source code. For continuous text, you must specify the line and paragraph breaks by using the <br> or <p> tag. Besides affecting the way text looks onscreen, you also can affect the paragraph text by

WORKING WITH PARAGRAPH ELEMENTS AND HTML STYLES

specifying formatting for definition lists, bulleted and numbered lists, text alignment, and indents. You can use the preformatted text option to utilize the HTML <pre> tag to align text vertically using the browser's default monospace font. The horizontal rule tag, although not a paragraph formatting option, is included in this chapter because it is widely used to create divisions among formatted paragraph text.

Using the HTML Styles panel, you can define customized styles that format text using standard HTML formatting commands. For example, you can create HTML styles named subhead1 and subhead2, each with specific formatting that includes typeface, size, color, and format. This feature is very helpful if you're working on a large Web site in which text is consistently formatted a particular way and works in concert with Dreamweaver templates and library items to maintain a uniform look and feel for your Web site (see Chapter 19, "Creating Templates and Libraries").

Entering Paragraph Breaks

Two basic HTML tags create line breaks and paragraph breaks: The <br> tag breaks lines without adding extra space, and the <p> tag inserts an additional blank line after each paragraph.

1. Position your cursor in the Document window where you want to insert a paragraph break.

2. Press the (Return)[Enter] key to insert a paragraph break (5.1).

In HTML code, the paragraph is preceded by the <p> tag and ends with the </p> tag.

5.1

Entering Line Breaks

The line break (<br>) does not insert additional line space. The break tag also is used to clear the vertical space an image occupies using the clear attribute in the HTML source code.

1. Position your cursor in the Document window where you want to insert a line break.

2. Press (Shift-Return) [Shift+Enter] (5.2).

Select View→Visual Aids→Invisible Elements to see the break tags in Layout view.

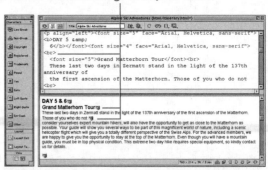

5.2

 O T E

By default, the break tags are set to be invisible, even when the invisible elements are turned on. Select Edit→Preferences to display the Preferences dialog box; select Invisible Elements, click the check box next to Line Breaks (5.3), and click OK.

5.3

Creating an Unordered List

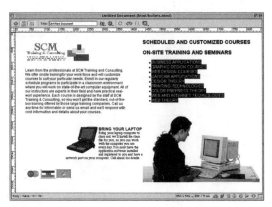

5.4

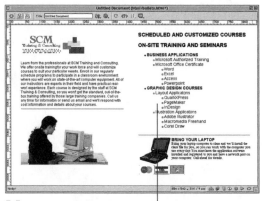

5.5

The open square is displayed in Netscape on the Macintosh, whereas the solid square is displayed in Internet Explorer on the Mac and all browsers in Windows. Dreamweaver displays an open box on the Macintosh, but a solid box in Windows.

An unordered list is typically referred to as a *bulleted* list. Unordered lists also can contain multiple levels of nesting, in which case you can specify the type of bullet character to use and the level of indent to use.

1. Click and drag to select the text from which you want to create an unordered list.

2. Select Text→List→Unordered Lists or click the Unordered List button in the bottom-right corner of the Property inspector (5.4).

3. Select Text→Indent to create an additional level for the unordered list. The open bullet is used for the second level of indent, and the square is used for the remaining levels of indent by default (5.5).

4. Select Text→Outdent to return to a previous indent level in the unordered list.

5. Press (Return)[Enter] twice to end the unordered list.

 I P

You can format text as an unordered list while you type it by choosing Text→List→Unordered List before you begin typing.

Changing Unordered List Properties

To change the type of bullet used in the unordered list edit the list properties. Only three characters are available for unordered lists—discs, circles, and squares. If you want to create nested unordered lists, you can indicate a different character for each level.

1. Position the cursor in the list where you want to change the bullet type used.

2. Select Text→List→Properties to display the List Properties dialog box **(5.6)**.

3. Select Bulleted List from the List Type pull-down menu.

4. Select a bullet style from the Style pull-down menu. The style you select will apply to all bullets in the current level.

5. Select a bullet style from the New Style pull-down menu if you want to change the bullet style from the current line forward. This change, however, does not affect bullets preceding the current line.

6. Click OK to change the bullet character **(5.7)**.

5.6

5.7

 O T E

Click within the first level (no indent) to change all the first-level bullet types or the bullet type from that point forward. If your cursor is positioned within an indented level, only the bullets in that level are affected.

Creating an Ordered List

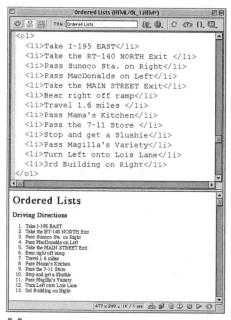

5.8

5.9

5.10

The default ordered list is a numbered list. Ordered lists can be nested within each other to create an outline format in which you specify the order for each level of nesting **(5.8)**.

1. Click and drag to select the text from which you want to create an ordered list.

2. Select Text→List→Ordered List or click the Ordered List button in the bottom-right corner of the Property inspector to create the ordered list from your selected text **(5.9)**.

3. Select Text→Indent to create additional levels for the ordered list. Numbers are used for all levels by default **(5.10)**.

4. Select Text→Outdent to return to a previous indent level in the ordered list.

5. Press (Return)[Enter] twice to end the Ordered List.

 I P

You can format text as an ordered list while you type it by choosing Text→List→ Ordered List before you begin typing.

 I P

Press (Command-Option-])[Ctrl+Alt+]] to indent text, ordered lists, and unordered lists. Press (Command-Option-[)[Ctrl+Alt+]] to outdent text, ordered lists, and unordered lists.

Changing Ordered List Properties

Edit an ordered list's properties when you want to choose a specific order, such as capital letters, lowercase letters, numbers, or roman numerals. When nesting ordered lists to create an outline format, specify a different ordering sequence for each level.

1. Position the cursor in the list where you want to change the ordering style.

2. Select Text→List→Properties to display the List Properties dialog box (5.11).

3. Select Numbered List from the List Type pull-down menu.

4. Select an ordering format from the Style pull-down menu (5.12). The style you select will apply to all list items in the current level.

5.11

You can specify upper- and lowercase roman numerals and letters, as well as numbers in the Style pull-down menu.

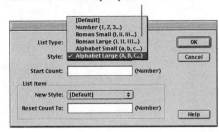

5.12

  I P

Remember that indented lists are actually individual ordered lists embedded in the current ordered list.

(T) I P

When you create a numbered list, the period is automatically inserted after the number and the numbers are aligned on the right so the periods align.

5.13

5.14

5. Enter a number value in the Start Count field to start numbering from a number other than 1. If you are changing a lettered list, enter the number that corresponds to the letter in the alphabet. For example, if you want your list to start with the letter K, enter **11** in the Start Count field **(5.13)**.

6. Select an ordering format from the New Style pull-down menu for the list item if you want to change the ordering format from the current line forward **(5.14)**. This change does not affect line items preceding the current line.

7. Enter a number value in the Reset Count To field to change the numbering order from the current list item forward. Click OK.

(N) O T E

You can remove all formatting of ordered lists and unordered lists by clicking the outdent button in the Property inspector until all levels of indent are removed.

(T) I P

Ordered lists and unordered lists can be formatted with Cascading Style Sheets. See Chapter 14, "Working with Cascading Style Sheets," for instructions on how to customize lists.

Inserting Special Characters

Dreamweaver automatically inserts the codes for special characters if you know the key sequences for your particular operating system and type them into the Document window. The Characters Objects panel contains some of the most commonly used special characters, as well as an option to display a more extensive character map, where you can select accented and less common characters.

5.15

1. Select Window→Objects to display the Objects panel if it isn't already onscreen.

2. Click the menu at the top of the Objects panel and select Characters to display the Characters Objects panel (5.15).

5.16

3. Click to select the desired special character from the Characters Objects panel or click the Insert Other Character (the last button, labeled Other) to display an extended character map (5.16).

5.17

(N) O T E

5.18

If you're using a Macintosh computer, you can find the key combinations that insert special characters using Key Caps, located under the Apple menu (5.17). Windows users can access the Character Map to find special character key combinations. Click the Start menu, and then select Programs→ Accessories→System Tools→Character Map to display the Character Map (5.18).

Adding a Horizontal Rule

The default horizontal rule extends from left to right and is embossed.

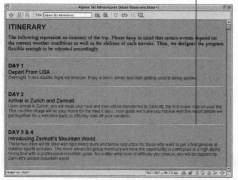

5.19

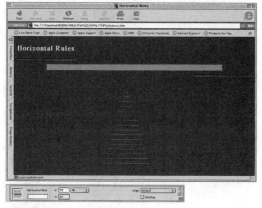

5.20

Horizontal rules occupy their own line from the left margin to the right margin. The standard horizontal rule is an embossed-looking rule in the background color with a dark shadow on the top and left and a highlight on the right and bottom.

1. Position your cursor in the Document window where you want to add the rule.

2. Click the Horizontal Rule icon in the Objects panel to insert the rule at the cursor (5.19).

3. Select Window→Properties to display the Property inspector if it isn't already visible.

4. Click the horizontal rule within the Document window to highlight it. Adjust the attributes for the rule (Table 5.1) in the Property inspector (5.20).

Table 5.1   Setting Horizontal Rule Attributes

Option	Result
Width	Specifies the length of a rule. You can enter a pixel value in this field, or select % from the pull-down menu and enter a value that is the percentage of the browser window width.
Height	Specifies the thickness of a rule in pixels. The default height is 1 pixel, with a 1-pixel shadow and highlight.
Align	Selects an alignment option from the Align pull-down menu. The default alignment for horizontal rules is centered.
Shading	Checks the Shading check box to achieve the embossed-looking rule. If you uncheck this box, the rule appears solid.

 O T E

You can specify a color for the horizontal rule in the HTML source code by using either a hexadecimal color, such as `<hr color="#FF3333">`, or a color name, such as `<hr color="red">`. Microsoft's Internet Explorer is the only browser that supports using the color attribute with the horizontal rule tag. When you specify a color for the horizontal rule, shading is turned off and the rule appears solid in the browser.

Creating Customized HTML Styles

With the HTML Styles panel, you can define your own customized HTML styles. All the formatting options for the styles are selected from a single dialog box. You specify all the standard HTML formatting options you're accustomed to, and then apply multiple formatting features at one time by simply selecting the style from the HTML Styles panel. You can create paragraph styles that apply to entire paragraphs of text and selection styles that apply only to the selected text.

1. Select Window→HTML Styles to display the HTML Styles panel (5.21).

2. Click the plus (+) icon in the bottom-right corner of the HTML Styles panel to create a new HTML style. All style options are presented in the Define HTML Style dialog box (5.22).

Dreamweaver comes with some pre-installed HTML styles. You can modify any of these except the Clear Paragraph Style and Clear Selection Style Option. These two are not actually HTML styles, but instead enable you to remove HTML style formatting from text.

5.21

 I P

To edit an existing HTML style, double-click the style in the HTML Styles panel.

 I P

If you want to create an HTML style based on some text you've already formatted on your Web page, simply select the formatted text, and then click the plus (+) icon in the lower-right corner of the HTML Styles panel to create a new style with your formatting.

5.22

5.23 Check the Apply check box to automatically apply HTML styles when
they're selected. If you leave this box
unchecked, you must click the Apply
button to apply HTML styles to text.

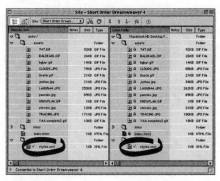

5.24

3. Assign a name to your new
HTML style and specify the
formatting options for your
style; then click OK. Notice
that the paragraph styles and
selection styles have corresponding icons to the left of
the style name in the HTML
Styles panel (5.23).

4. To share your HTML styles
with other users, select
Window→Site Files to open the
Site window and open the
Library folder (5.24). The file
named styles.xml contains all
the styles for your site. This file
can be edited, checked in and
out, and shared with other
users working on your site.

 O T E

*You can use Clear Paragraph Style and
Clear Selection Style to remove paragraph
formatting regardless of whether you used
the HTML styles to format the text or the
Property inspector.*

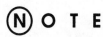 O T E

*For information on creating a remote site
and using Dreamweaver's Check-In/Check-
Out function, refer to Chapter 2, "Setting
Up Your Site in Dreamweaver."*

CHAPTER 6

In this chapter, you will learn how to...

Import Images

Set Image Properties

Resize an Image

Edit Images

Redefine an Image Source

Specify a Low Src

Add and Changing the Color of Image Borders

Set Image Alignment

Wrap Text Around Images

Specify a Background Image

Insert Animated GIFs

Create Web Photo Albums

Dreamweaver enables you to import images and graphics in three file formats accepted by most browsers: GIF, JPEG, and PNG. The Graphic Interchange Format (GIF) is most commonly used for images and graphics that can be limited to a maximum of 256 colors and is best suited for artwork, illustrations, and any image with large areas of flat color. The Joint Photographic Experts Group (JPEG) format is used for

WORKING WITH GIF, JPEG, AND PNG IMAGES AND GRAPHICS

photographic images because it offers a full range of RGB colors and maximum file compression. The Portable Network Graphic (PNG) format is continually gaining support from the latest browser versions and is the native format of Fireworks files. The format you choose for your images should be decided on an image-by-image basis, with the objective of creating the smallest possible file size while retaining acceptable image quality.

Using Dreamweaver's Site window, you can easily manage your graphics and images and even replace an image globally throughout your site. When working with images and graphics, the Property inspector offers a link to an external image-editing application that you specify in Dreamweaver's preferences.

Importing Images

Dreamweaver imports and previews GIF, JPEG, and PNG files. Inserting an image into your Web page is as simple as clicking the Image object in the Common Objects panel and locating an image file to import. When you have a site created in Dreamweaver, you can use the Point-to-File icon to select graphics or simply drag an image from the Site window onto your Web page. To access an image that is not part of your site, click the folder icon next to an image field in the Property inspector and locate the file. Dreamweaver then prompts you to copy the file to your site if you select an image outside the site root folder.

1. Select Insert→Image to display the dialog box to select an image source (6.1).

2. Click the name of the file you want to import. On the Mac, click the Show Preview button to display a preview of the image. Using Windows, click the Preview Images check box to display the image preview.

The dimensions of the image (in pixels) and the size of the file are displayed along with the amount of time necessary to download the image at the connection speed indicated in the Status Bar preferences.

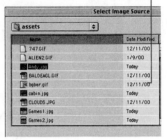

6.1

 I P

To duplicate an image, hold down the (Option) [Ctrl] key and drag the image in the Document window.

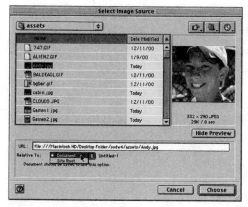

6.2

6.3

3. Click the pull-down menu and indicate whether the image is to be relative to the particular HTML document or to the Site Root folder (6.2). If you choose to make the image relative to the document, a dialog box prompts you to relocate the file to a location within the Site Root folder if it isn't already in that folder. If you select Site Root, the path of the file is indicated from the Root folder forward. If the file is outside the Site Root folder, you are prompted to copy the image to a location within the Site Root folder.

4. Click (Choose)[Select] to import the specified image. Click the image in the Dreamweaver Document window to edit the image properties in the Property inspector (6.3).

Ⓝ O T E

If you import an image before saving the file, the path is specific to its location on the hard drive of your computer regardless of whether you choose to make it relative to the document or to the Site Root: `file:///C|/scans/web/andy.jpg` *on Windows and* `file:///scans/web/andy.jpg` *on the Mac OS. The good news is that after you save the Dreamweaver file, all absolute addresses are changed to relative addresses.*

Setting Image Properties

InDreamweaver, image properties are set using the Property inspector. When you import an image into the Dreamweaver Document window, the `<img>` tag is inserted into the HTML source code. The top half of the Property inspector contains the basic image attributes, such as width, height, image source, link, alignment, and alternate text. The lower half of the Property inspector contains additional attributes along with buttons to edit the image and create an image map.

1. Select Window→Properties to display the Property inspector if it is not onscreen **(6.4)**.

2. Enter a name for the image in the first field in the upper-left corner of the Property inspector if you want to reference this image later using a script.

3. Enter alternative text in the Alt field to accommodate users who have the images turned off in their browsers or perhaps are using text-only browsers. The Alt text is also the text that appears on the Web page when an image does not load **(6.5)**. Windows users will see a tag containing the Alt text when the cursor hovers over an image in a Web browser **(6.6)**. The Alt text also displays when the image is loading.

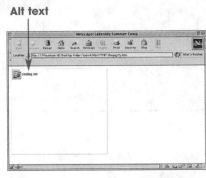

6.4

Alt text

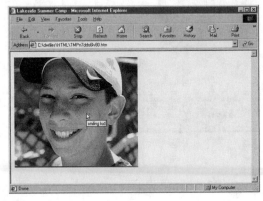

6.5

6.6

Resizing an Image

You also can click and drag one of the three anchor points that appear to the right, bottom, and lower-right corner of the image when it's selected. Hold down the Shift key while dragging to maintain the aspect ratio of the image while resizing.

6.7

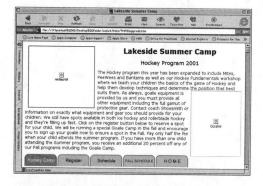

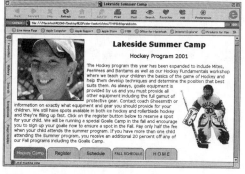

6.8

You can resize an image in two ways after it's placed in the Document window—with the Property inspector or manually with the selection handles. If you have to significantly resize an image, you should perform this function in an image-editing program, such as Photoshop or Fireworks.

1. Click to select the image you want to resize; then select Window→Properties to display the Property inspector.

2. Type new width and height values in the Property inspector (6.7).

3. Click the Reset Size button in the Property inspector to restore the original dimensions of the image.

Ⓝ O T E

An image can be included on your Web page without the width *and* height *attributes, but there is a very good reason for including the width and height even if the image is not resized. When a Web page is loaded into your browser window, the information on the page is displayed linearly—in the order in which it appears in the HTML source code. If you specify the width and height of the images on your Web page, the browser reserves the spaces for the images on the page and loads the text first. This technique gives the user a chance to start reading the content of the page while the images are loading* (6.8).

Editing Images

Dreamweaver does not provide a method of editing imported images directly, but you can launch an image-editing program directly from Dreamweaver to accomplish this task. When you click the Edit button in the lower-right corner of the Image Property inspector, the selected image opens in the image-editing software specified in the External Editors preferences.

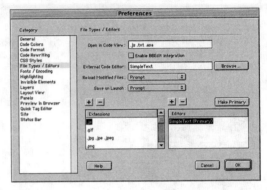

6.9

1. Select Edit→Preferences to display the Preferences dialog box (6.9).

2. Select File Types/Editors from the Category list on the left.

3. Select an extension from the Extensions list. If an extension for the file type you want to specify is not in the list, click the plus sign icon above the Extensions list to add it (6.10).

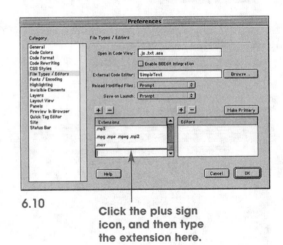

6.10

Click the plus sign icon, and then type the extension here.

(T) I P

You can edit an extension in the Extensions list by double-clicking it. If you want to include more than one extension as a single list item, separate the extensions by a space.

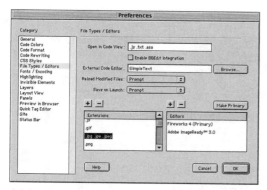

6.11

The image editing software, Adobe ImageReady 3.0 in this case, loads independently from Dreamweaver.

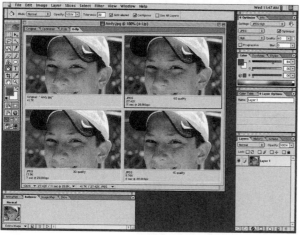

6.12

4. Click the plus sign icon over the Editors list to select the program you want to launch to edit files with the specified extension(s) (6.11). You can add more than one program to the Editors list.

5. The first application you specify for an extension is automatically designated the primary application. To change the primary application, select the application in the Editors list that you want to make the primary editing application and click the Make Primary button. Click OK to close the Preferences dialog box.

6. To edit an image, select the image in the Document window and click the Edit button in the Property inspector (6.12).

 I P

Hold down the (Command)[Ctrl] key and double-click an image to launch the external editor for that image.

 O T E

Dreamweaver's built-in integration with Fireworks 4 makes editing images easier than ever and offers many features to increase your productivity. See Chapter 7, "Round-Trip Graphics Editing with Fireworks," for detailed information.

Redefining an Image Source

When you first import an image into the Document window, the path to the source file is inserted in the Src field in the Property inspector. If you want to replace the existing image with another, you can redefine the source location of the file. The new image then replaces the current image and the Property inspector is updated to reflect the new image file size. You can redefine the source of an image in the Design view of the Document window in four ways:

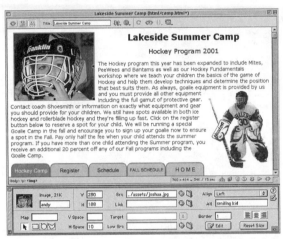

6.13

- Type a new filename in the Src field in the Property inspector (6.13).

- Double-click the image in the Document window and locate the new image file.

- Click the Folder icon to the right of the Src field in the Property inspector to locate a file on your hard drive.

- Click and drag from the Point-to-File icon in the Property inspector onto a file in the Site window (6.14).

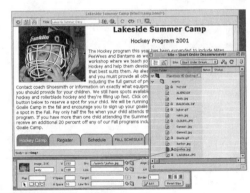

6.14

 I P

Hold down (Option)[Ctrl] and drag an image to make a duplicate copy of it on the Web page.

Specifying a Low Src

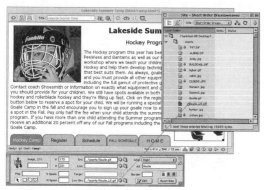

6.15

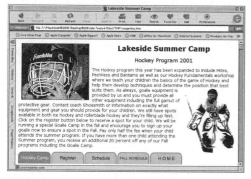

6.16

The low src file displays for the length of time it takes the full-size or full-color image to download. You must preview the Web page in a browser to see the low src image load and, depending on its size, the image might load too quickly from your local hard drive to see the transition.

The `lowsrc` attribute enables you to specify a low-resolution image that loads prior to the high-resolution image. Low src files are typically black and white, dithered renditions of the high-resolution image. You can use the `lowsrc` attribute to display a graphic with a much smaller file size while an image is downloading. If you specify the width and height for the image, the space allotted to the image on the Web page will be accurate even if the low src file is smaller.

1. Click the image in the Design view of the Document window to select it.

2. In the Property inspector, type a pathname for the low src file in the Low Src field or click the Folder icon to the right of this field to locate the file on the hard drive. You also can click and drag from the Point-to-File icon onto the file in the Site window (6.15).

3. Preview the file in a browser to see the low src file load prior to the full-resolution, full-color image (6.16).

 I P

Create a low src image with text that says "Please Wait… Image Loading," or something to that effect for large images on your Web page that you want the user to wait to see.

Adding and Changing the Color of Image Borders

The `border` attribute creates a border
around an image in the default text
color specified in the Page
Properties dialog box. Enter a value
in the Border field in the Property
inspector to indicate a border in pixels. When an image is used as a link,
a default border in the link color is
displayed around the image, unless
the border value is set to 0.
Dreamweaver sets the border value
of images to 0 initially.

1. Click an image in the
   Document window to select it.

2. Enter a pixel value in the
   Border field of the Property
   inspector **(6.17)**.

3. To change the color of the border, be sure the image is still
   selected; then, select
   Text→Color to display the
   color picker **(6.18)**.

4. Select a color and click OK.

6.17

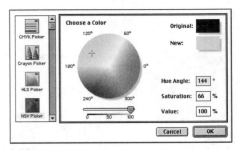

6.18

**The font tag is inserted
around the image tag.**

6.19

 **O T E**

*When you change the color of the border
around an image, the `<font>` tag is inserted
around the image in the HTML code with
the `color` attribute set to the color you indicated in the color picker **(6.19)**. Some
browsers—Internet Explorer for Windows in
particular—do not display the border color
unless you change the default text color.*

Setting Image Alignment

6.20

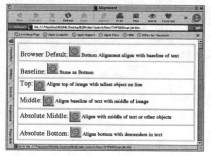

6.21

Image alignment is the key to how your images interact with the other elements on your Web page, including text. Aside from the typical left, right, and center horizontal alignment options, seven vertical alignment options are used for inline images. When you import an image, it is initially treated as an inline image that aligns with the baseline of the text (6.20). The vertical alignment options always treat the graphic as an inline graphic and align the image with the line of text where it resides (6.21). Figure 6.21 depicts the various vertical alignment options.

1. Click the image in the Design view of the Document window to select it.

2. Select an alignment option from the Align pull-down menu in the Property inspector.

 I P

You can have multiple images side by side with different vertical alignment options to create a staggered effect.

 I P

When aligning images with text that is all capital letters, do not use the absmiddle *or* absbottom *alignment attributes because these take the descenders of the text into account.*

Wrapping Text Around Images

When you select left or right alignment for images, text automatically wraps around the images. If you specify left alignment for one image and right alignment for another image that is inserted right next to the first, the text flows between the two images. Images can be inserted within paragraphs with left or right alignment, which results in the images aligning on the right or left and text flowing around the images at that point in the paragraph.

1. Click the image you want to modify in the Document window.

2. Select an alignment option from the Align pull-down menu in the Property inspector.

3. Specify a pixel value for V Space and H Space to affect the text outset (**6.22**). Horizontal space is added to the left and right of an image, whereas vertical space is added at the top and bottom of the image.

 **N O T E**

*To see where an image is positioned within the paragraph, select View→Visual Aids→Invisible Elements to display the image icons. You can click and drag these icons around to reposition the associated image within the text (**6.23**).*

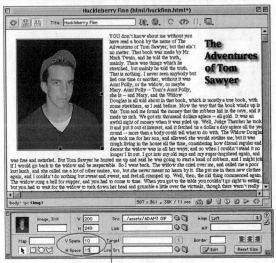

6.22

The H Space value is set to 15 pixels, and the V Space value is set to 10 pixels.

The image icons show you where the image is inserted in the HTML code.

6.23

Specifying a Background Image

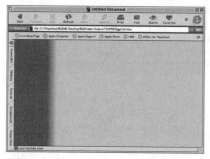

6.24

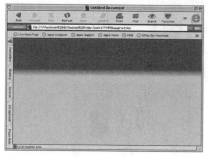

6.25

Background images are specified in the Page Properties dialog box. When you specify a background image smaller than the browser window, the background image is tiled to fill the window area. The tiling feature can be used to your advantage when creating background images because you can create images that are quite small in size, resulting in smaller file sizes.

1. Select Modify→Page Properties to display the Page Properties dialog box.

2. Click the Browse button to the right of the Background Image field to locate an image for the background of your Web page.

 O T E

Aside from using small square images to tile a background image, you also can use horizontal or vertical bars. In this first example, a 1KB image that is 1 pixel tall by 1200 pixels wide is used to create the sidebar effect **(6.24)**. *In the second example, the 1KB image is 1 pixel wide by 1200 pixels tall* **(6.25)**.

 I P

A variety of Web sites offer free tiled background images. Visit www.WebGraphicsArchive.com for links to background images and textures.

Inserting Animated GIFs

Animated GIFs are imported into Dreamweaver in the same way as stationary images. Because animated GIFs are actually a number of GIFs played in rapid succession, these files can become quite large. The key to creating effective animated GIF files is twofold: First, try to keep the number of colors to a minimum and keep the overall dimensions of the image small as well. Second, try to limit the number of frames used to create animation. Limiting the number of frames might mean sacrificing some of the smoothness during animation playback—a factor that could be even more exaggerated when the image is viewed remotely, depending on the user's processing power. To insert an animated GIF, select Insertfilmage or click the Image button in the common Object panel (6.26). See Chapter 7, "Round-Trip Graphics Editing with Fireworks," for details on creating animated GIFs.

You can create animated GIFs with Macromedia Fireworks (as shown here), Adobe ImageReady, and others. Visit www.animatedgifs.com or www.iconbazaar.com to download some nifty animated GIFs.

6.26

N O T E

A number of Web sites offer free animated GIFs for use on your Web pages, and many talented artists will create GIF animations to your specifications for a fee. Search for animated GIFs in any search engine on the Web or check out a few of my favorite sites. A1 Icon Archive has more than 300,000 free Web site graphics at www.freegraphics.com. Another nifty site is www.iconbazaar.com.

Creating Web Photo Albums

6.27

6.28

You can easily create a Web photo album using Dreamweaver in concert with Fireworks. You must have Fireworks installed for this command to work. When you select the Create Web Photo Album command in Dreamweaver, a dialog box appears, prompting you for information on how you want to build the Web pages for your photo album. Indicate the folder that contains the images for your photo album and a folder that is to contain the converted images and HTML files—Dreamweaver along with Fireworks does the rest.

Put all the images you want your photo album to contain in a single folder. Be sure the files are in a format that is supported (.gif, .jpg, .jpeg, .png, .psd, .tif, or .tiff) **(6.27)**.

2. Create a folder for the Web photo album files. This folder will contain both the HTML files and image files.

3. In Dreamweaver, select Commands→Create Web Photo Album to display the Create Web Photo Album dialog box **(6.28)**.

4. In the Photo Album Title field, enter a title to appear at the top of each Web page. Enter a subhead in the Subheading Info field. Type any other information to appear below the title and subhead in the Other Info field.

Creating Web Photo Albums continued

5. Click the Browse button to the right of the Source Images Folder field and locate the folder that contains your images. Click the Browse button to the right of the Destination Folder field and locate the folder that will receive the Web pages and images.

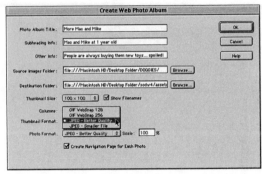

6.29

6. Select a thumbnail size from the Thumbnail Size pop-up menu, and then click the Show Filenames check box if you want the filenames to appear below the thumbnail images. Indicate how many columns of thumbnails you want in the Columns field.

7. Select a file format for the thumbnails and photos from the pop-up menus for Thumbnail Format and Photo Format, respectively (6.29). Type a value in the Scale field if you want to reduce the size of the images.

8. Check the check box for Create Navigation Page for Each Photo if you want each image to appear on a separate Web page with navigation links labeled Back, Home, and Next. If you leave this option unchecked, the thumbnails will link to the images instead of a Web page with navigation links.

6.30

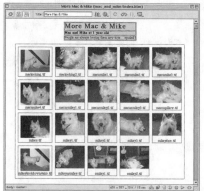

6.31

Title   **Filename**   **Navigation links**

6.32

9. Click OK and Fireworks launches, displaying a Batch Progress dialog box (6.30).

10. When the Album Created dialog box appears, click OK. Dreamweaver displays the first page of your Web photo album, named and titled the same as the title you assigned (6.31).

11. Preview the page in a browser. Each of the images on the thumbnail page is a link to a separate HTML page containing the larger image (6.32).

T I **P**

Create and apply a template to the HTML files created for your photo album. See Chapter 19, "Creating Templates and Libraries," for information on creating and applying templates.

CHAPTER 7

f you're using Dreamweaver 4 and Fireworks 4 together, you can round-trip images and any HTML and JavaScript code between the two applications. You can edit any graphic in Dreamweaver using Fireworks with the option of either editing the GIF or JPEG files or editing the original Fireworks PNG file. Any changes made in Fireworks are automatically updated in Dreamweaver. Dreamweaver includes two objects that insert Fireworks

ROUND-TRIP GRAPHICS EDITING WITH FIREWORKS

HTML—including all the code and graphics—to create rollover images and navigation bars. You also can use Dreamweaver's Optimize Image command to load the Fireworks Export Preview dialog box and optimize images instantly within Dreamweaver.

Dreamweaver and Fireworks share many of the same file-editing features, such as link changes, image maps, table slices, and behaviors. The two applications can provide a streamlined workflow, saving you precious production time. When you use the optimization features, changes made to the Dreamweaver image also are made to the external image file, as well as the Fireworks PNG file when it's used. Graphics created in Fireworks can be exported as a Dreamweaver library item and are automatically accessible when placed in the Dreamweaver library folder. If you're sharing files between Dreamweaver and Fireworks, the information about the files, stored in Design Notes, is accessible in both applications as well

Setting Fireworks as Your Default Image Editor

The External Editors preference in Dreamweaver enables you to specify which application is used to edit the objects on your Web pages, including images such as JPEGs and GIFs. To achieve round-trip graphics editing with Fireworks, you must set Fireworks as the primary editor for GIF, JPEG, and PNG files.

1. In Dreamweaver, select Edit→Preferences to display the Preferences panel; then select File Types / Editors from the Category list (7.1).

2. Select a Web file extension from the Extensions list (.gif, .jpg, or .png).

3. In the Editors list, select Fireworks 4 and click the Make Primary button. If Fireworks 4 does not appear in the Editors list, click the plus (+) button and locate the Fireworks 4 application on your hard drive.

4. Perform steps 2 and 3 to set Fireworks as the primary editor for all three image formats (.gif, .jpg, and .png).

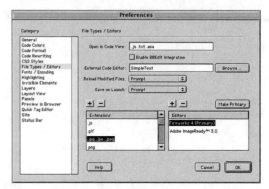

7.1 **You can use earlier versions of Fireworks as the primary image editor in Dreamweaver 4, although some round-trip editing features are not available. Fireworks 3 does not fully support the launch and edit of placed tables and slices. Fireworks 2 does not support the launch and edit of source PNG files for images placed in Dreamweaver.**

Setting Fireworks Launch and Edit Preferences

The Launch and Edit preferences for Fireworks on the Mac.

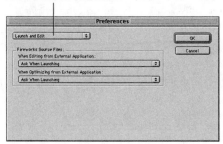

7.2

The Launch and Edit preferences for Fireworks on Windows.

7.3

 **O T E**

When you export a Fireworks file to a Dreamweaver site, Fireworks writes a Design Note that contains information about the location of the Fireworks PNG source file, each image in a slice file, and each HTML file that handles slices. When you edit a Fireworks image from Dreamweaver, the Design Note is used to locate a source PNG for that file. To ensure that the Fireworks PNG source files are always available for images on your site, save the Fireworks PNG file in your Dreamweaver site along with the exported GIF or JPEG.

Fireworks saves files in the Portable Network Graphics (PNG) format by default. When you launch Fireworks to edit an image placed on a Dreamweaver Web page, Fireworks opens the original PNG file when it's present and prompts you to locate it when it cannot be found. You can specify how you want Fireworks to open images when they're being edited in an external application, such as Dreamweaver or Director, by setting the Launch and Edit preferences in the Preferences dialog box in Fireworks.

1. In Fireworks, select Edit→Preferences to display the Preferences dialog box, and then (select Launch and Edit from the pop-up menu (7.2))[click the Launch and Edit tab (7.3)].

2. Select from the pop-up menus to determine when you want Fireworks to open the original PNG file. Select Always Use Source PNG when you want Fireworks to use the original PNG file for the Dreamweaver image. Select Never Use Source PNG if you want Fireworks to open and edit the actual image file, such as JPEG or GIF. Select Ask When Launching if you want Fireworks to prompt you before opening the original PNG file.

Optimizing Fireworks Images

You can modify the optimization settings for an image that was saved from Fireworks, as well as images saved from another image editing program, using the Fireworks Export Preview dialog box from within Dreamweaver. You must have enough memory to launch both Dreamweaver and Fireworks because the optimization dialog box comes from Fireworks even though you don't actually edit the image within Fireworks.

1. Click an image to select it in the Dreamweaver Document window.

2. Select Commands→Optimize Image in Fireworks.

3. If you set the Fireworks Launch and Edit preferences to Ask When Launching, a dialog box appears prompting you to locate the original PNG file or proceed without it (7.4). This dialog box also appears whenever the originating PNG cannot be found.

4. In the Optimize dialog box, enter the optimization settings, and then click Update (7.5).

Click No if you don't have the original PNG source file or if you only want to edit the image file.

Click Yes if you want to edit the original PNG source file.

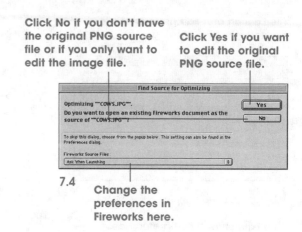

7.4

Change the preferences in Fireworks here.

Customize the optimization.

Preset optimizations.

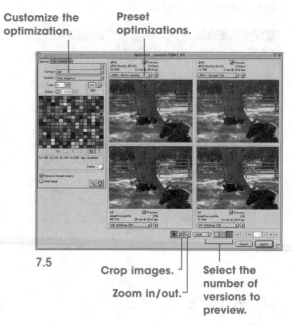

7.5

Crop images.

Zoom in/out.

Select the number of versions to preview.

T I P

The updated image is saved over the existing image and is updated in Dreamweaver as well.

Resizing Fireworks Images

Constrain the image proportions.
Enter the scaling percentage.

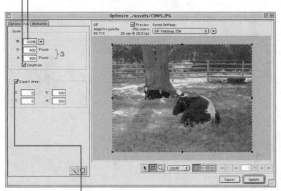

7.6

Export a specific area of the image.

7.7

Drag inside the selection area to adjust the cropping area and reveal hidden areas.

Use the optimization dialog box to resize Fireworks images that are placed on a Dreamweaver page. You also can select a specific area of the image to be exported.

1. Click an image to select it in the Dreamweaver Document window.

2. Select Commands→Optimize Image in Fireworks to display the Optimize dialog box.

3. Click the File tab in the upper-left corner of the Optimize dialog box to display the file export settings (7.6).

4. To scale the image, enter a scale percentage or width and height values.

5. To export a selected area of the image, click the Export Area check box and drag the handles along the dotted border that appears around the image (7.7).

6. Click the Update button to update the image in Dreamweaver.

If you open an image from the Dreamweaver Site window, the Fireworks integration features are not implemented. Open images from the Dreamweaver Document window to take advantage of Fireworks integration.

Editing Fireworks Animations

Use the Optimize dialog box to edit animation settings for Fireworks animations, such as animated GIFs. Customize animation controls— such as Frame Delay, which determines the speed of the animation, and Disposal Method, which determines what appears behind a frame when it is removed—to make way for a new frame.

Frame delay in 100ths of a second

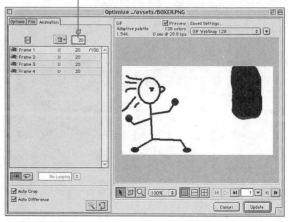

7.8

1. Click an animated image to select it in the Dreamweaver Document window.

2. Select Commands→Optimize Image in Fireworks to display the Optimize dialog box, and then click the Animation tab in the upper-left corner.

3. Click the frames in the frames list and specify the frame delay in the field under the clock icon (7.8).

4. Click the trash can pop-up menu to select a disposal method for the selected frame (7.9).

Change the frame disposal method.

7.9 Loop animation.   Play once.

**O T E**

Click the Auto Crop check box in the Optimize dialog box to crop each frame as a rectangular area, so only the image area that differs between frames is output. Click the Auto Difference option to output only the pixels that change between frames.

Editing Images with Fireworks

7.10

Fireworks logo

Location of the Fireworks PNG file

Edit in Fireworks

Indicates editing of a Dreamweaver image

Save PNG and update image in Dreamweaver

7.11

Use Fireworks to edit Fireworks-generated images and tables placed in a Dreamweaver document. The Property inspector in Dreamweaver displays the Fireworks logo when a Fireworks image is selected and identifies the image with the words FW Image. A second Src attribute is also added to the Property inspector, showing the path of the originating PNG file. Make changes to a Fireworks-generated image in Fireworks, and the image is automatically updated in Dreamweaver. Links, image maps, text in text slices, and other edits made in Dreamweaver are preserved in Fireworks.

1. In Dreamweaver, select Window→Properties to display the Property inspector if it isn't already onscreen.

2. Select the image you want to edit in Fireworks (7.10).

3. Click the Edit button in the Property inspector to launch Fireworks and edit the original PNG file for the selected image (7.11).

4. Make any necessary changes in Fireworks; then click the Done button in the upper-left corner of Firework's Document window to save the changes and return to Dreamweaver.

Editing Fireworks Tables and Slices

In Fireworks you can slice a file into discrete pieces to save and optimize the slices individually, enabling you to keep the file sizes small for faster downloading. When you export the slices to an HTML file for Dreamweaver, Fireworks creates a table from the sliced images. You always can open the original PNG source file in Fireworks to make changes to the entire layout, and then regenerate an HTML file for Dreamweaver. In Dreamweaver 4, you now can edit the individual slices in Fireworks and update the existing Dreamweaver document.

1. In Dreamweaver, select Window→Properties to display the Property inspector if it isn't already onscreen.

2. If you want to edit the entire Fireworks table, select the table in the Dreamweaver Document window and click the Edit button in the Property inspector.

3. If you want to edit a slice in the table, click in the table cell that holds the image slice and click Edit in the Property inspector (7.12).

4. Edit the table image in Fireworks and click the Done button in Fireworks to update the Dreamweaver table (7.13).

Slice image in a table cell

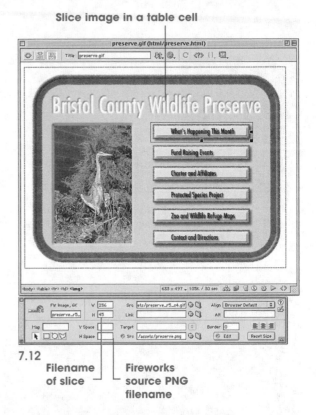

7.12

Filename of slice **Fireworks source PNG filename**

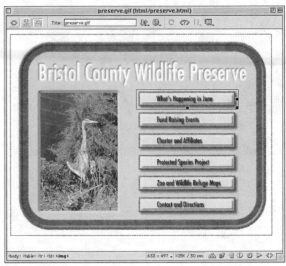

7.13

Placing Fireworks HTML into a Dreamweaver Document

7.14

If you want to delete the imported Fireworks HTML document, select Delete File After Insertion.

If you open the HTML file generated by Fireworks, instructions for inserting the image and its associated JavaScript commands are included as comments in the file.

7.15

If you create images in Fireworks that contain Fireworks behaviors or JavaScript code, you must include this code in your Dreamweaver file. For example, you can create rollovers in Fireworks and import the image into Dreamweaver, but the rollovers will not work unless you also import the HTML from Fireworks.

1. In Dreamweaver, select Insert→Interactive Images→Fireworks HTML or click the Insert Fireworks HTML button in the Objects panel.

2. When the Insert Fireworks HTML dialog box appears, click the Browse button and navigate to locate the HTML file created by Fireworks when the image was exported (7.14).

3. Click OK.

 O T E

The Fireworks HTML code is placed in the Dreamweaver document, along with any associated image files and JavaScript (7.15).

 O T E

When you export an image from Fireworks, you are offered the opportunity to generate the necessary HTML code into a separate HTML file. This is the file that will be used to insert the HTML code into the Dreamweaver document.

CHAPTER 8

In this chapter, you will learn how to...

Link to Local HTML Pages

Link to Remote HTML Pages

Link to Images

Create E-mail Links

Link with Image Maps

Insert Named Anchors

Link to Named Anchors

C reating hypertext links is an integral part of Web site creation because these links are the primary method of navigation between Web pages on a site or to pages on other sites. HTML enables you to create links using images, text, and image maps via the anchor tag (<a>). Whatever appears between the <a> tag and the </a> tag becomes a link, with the exception of the named anchor where a location is marked as a place to link to.

CREATING LINKS

The links on your Web pages should be considered during the planning stages, when you're developing the hierarchy of your Web pages. A uniform interface for your Web site requires the creation of graphic elements to act as links that appear in the same place on every Web page. Your Web site can contain many sections that require their own graphic elements to facilitate linking—each adding time to the graphic development stage.

Although the temptation to create links to other sites is great, you should avoid sending the user to another site, perhaps losing him forever. Create a links page for your site or include pertinent links at the bottom of pages so that the user hears what you have to say before jumping to another site. A popular method of linking to other sites is to create a new browser window to display that site. True, this method keeps your site open in the browser as well, but many users don't realize they're in a new window and hence might not return to the window containing your Web site. In this chapter I'll show you the various methods of creating links on your Web page, links to named anchors, links to images, and e-mail links and how to create image maps to link from various zones on a single image.

Linking to Local HTML Pages

Dreamweaver enables you to link to files using the Point-to-File icon, available wherever you can create links. With the Point-to-File icon, you simply click the icon and drag to point to the file you want to link in the Site window. Refer to Chapter 2, "Setting Up Your Site in Dreamweaver," for specific information on defining the Site window.

8.1

1. Click an image to select it, or select some text you want to make into a hypertext link.

2. Select Windows→Properties to open the Property inspector.

3. If you have defined a site, choose Site→Open Site to display the Site window for the previously created site. (Refer to Chapter 2 for information on setting up the Site window.)

4. To create a link using the point-to-file method, click and drag on the Point-to-File icon to the right of the Link field in the Property inspector. Drag until the cursor is over a file in the Site window to which you want to link, and then release the mouse button (8.1).

**O T E**

After you have selected some text and created a link, you can later edit the link by clicking anywhere inside the linked text. You don't have to select all the link text to change the link.

If you have a folder in your root directory for images and graphics, such as **GIF**, **JPEG**, and **PNG** files, and you are linking to a GIF image outside the root folder, copy the file to that folder when prompted.

8.2

8.3

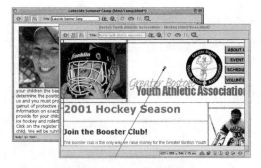

8.4

5. To create a link to a file outside your site, click the Folder icon to the right of the Link field in the Property inspector. Dreamweaver prompts you to copy the file to the site root folder (8.2). If you choose to follow this prompt, you must locate the folder to which you want to copy the file within your site.

6. To create a link using a previously defined link, click the arrow to the right of the Link field in the Property inspector and choose a link. Dreamweaver remembers all the links you created in the current session and displays them in a list (8.3).

 I P

If the file resides in the same folder as the current HTML file, simply type the name of the file, without any path information, into the Link field of the Property inspector.

 **O T E**

You can use the Point-to-File icon to link to another Web page that is open in Dreamweaver. Position the Document window so you can see both files, and then click and drag with the Point-to-File icon. When you drag over the other Web page, it comes to the front and inserts the link in the Link field of the Property inspector **(8.4)**.

Linking to Remote HTML Pages

When linking to remote HTML pages, you must enter the entire URL for the Web site, including any directories and specific Web pages.

1. Click an image you want to use as a link, or select some text you want to use as a hypertext link.

2. Type the URL in the Link field in the Property inspector (8.5).

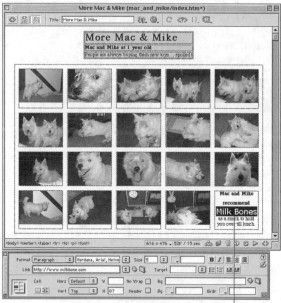

8.5

 N O T E

A File Transfer Protocol (FTP) site is simply a collection of files that reside on some remote server (8.6). The only difference between the way you access FTP sites and ordinary Web pages is in the URL address. Instead of using the http:// prefix you typically use for a Web page, FTP sites have the ftp:// prefix and usually begin with ftp.

 N O T E

To link to a specific file on a remote site, you must enter the path information of the URL in the Link field. For example, http://www. macromedia.com/products/dreamweaver or http://www.apple.com/products/imac/ about.html. When you link to a Web site without indicating any directories or HTML filenames, the site's home page is loaded, usually named index.html or home.html, depending on the server.

When entering the URL address for an HTML file on a remote site, you must always include the http:// portion of the address.

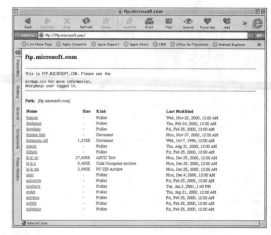

8.6

Linking to Images

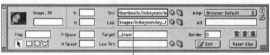

8.7

Thumbnail images are linked to larger images so the user can choose which image to view.

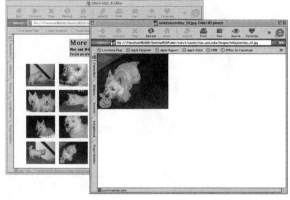

8.8

If your site will contain image files—a common practice for Web sites created by artists and photographers who are presenting their work online, or in the case of an online catalog containing a large number of images—it is in the best interest of your site visitors to place a small image on the Web page, called a *thumbnail image*, that acts as a link to a larger version of the same file. The thumbnail image gives the visitor the option of selecting which large file to download rather than waiting for each file on the site to download.

1. Select a thumbnail image on your Web page (8.7).

2. In the Property inspector, enter the link information for the image—link to the larger file, either on your Web site or on a remote site, with a URL (8.8).

 I P

If you have defined a site within Dreamweaver, you can use the Point-to-File icon in the Property inspector to select an image file by dragging it onto the image file in the Site window.

 I P

If you want to give your audience the opportunity to browse through the large image files, place these files on HTML pages with link buttons to either view the images in sequence or return to the thumbnail page.

Creating E-mail Links

E-mail links give the user a simple way to send e-mail to a predetermined e-mail address. Usually, the e-mail address is entered on the Web page and is made into a link that, when clicked, opens the default e-mail program on the user's computer.

1. Select an object or some text to create the e-mail link.

2. In the Property inspector, type **mailto:** followed by the e-mail address to which you want the user to send mail (8.9). When the user clicks on the mail link, the mail form pops up with the e-mail message already addressed (8.10).

3. To create an e-mail link from scratch when the link text does not yet exist, click the E-mail Link button in the Common Objects panel to display the Insert Email Link dialog box (8.11).

4. Enter the link text in the Text field and the e-mail address in the E-Mail field; then click OK.

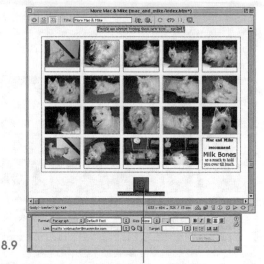

8.9

An icon of a mailbox is also a popular method of indicating that an e-mail address is available.

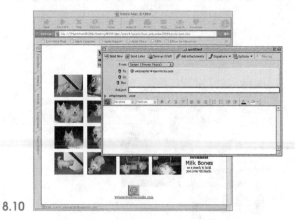

8.10

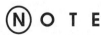O T E

When you include an e-mail link on your Web page, the end user must have a mail program installed on her computer. If you want to get specific information from a user, use an HTML form. See Chapter 13, "Creating and Customizing Forms."

When you enter an e-mail link, do not include the double slashes, such as those used for FTP and HTTP links.

8.11

Linking with Image Maps

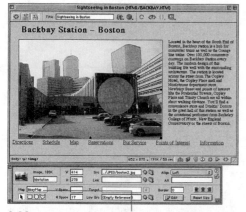

8.12

Map names can contain letters and numbers only, without spaces. Map names also cannot start with a number.

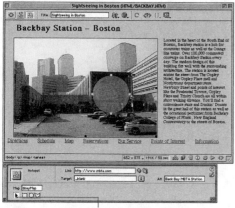

8.13

Use the Pointer tool to select and move the map coordinates.

Image maps are used to create links for multiple zones on a single image. By indicating rectangular, circular, or polygon-shaped zones, you can create multiple links for one image. Dreamweaver makes creating an image map very simple by providing the Map option in the Property inspector when an image is selected.

1. Select an image and type a name for the map in the Map field of the Property inspector. You can name the map anything you want, and you must include a name to create an image map (8.12).

2. Use the rectangle, circle, or polygon tools located under the map name in the Property inspector to create the zones you want to make into hot spots.

3. After you click and drag with one of the drawing tools, the options for Link, Target, and Alt are displayed in the Hotspot Property inspector and the selected areas are highlighted in the image (8.13).

4. Enter the link pathname or URL address for the selected zone, along with the Target and Alt text information. Perform this step for each zone created on your image.

Inserting Named Anchors

Named anchor tags are used to mark a place in a document that can be accessed by another link somewhere else on the page or on another page. Simply insert named anchors somewhere on your Web pages and then link to them with standard linking techniques.

1. Position your cursor in the Dreamweaver Document window to indicate where you want to create a named anchor.

2. Select Insert→Invisible Tags→Named Anchor or click the Named Anchor button in the Invisible Objects panel to display the Insert Named Anchor dialog box (8.14).

3. Type in a name for your anchor. Click OK after you assign a name.

4. Select View→Visual Aids→Invisible Elements to see the Anchor icons in the Document window (8.15).

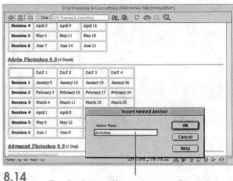

8.14

Try to keep the names of your named anchors short and easy to remember because you must refer to them later.

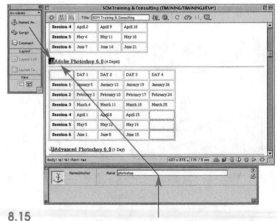

8.15

You can change the name of an anchor by clicking its icon in the Document window and changing the name in the Property inspector.

Anchor tags are ideal either for pages that contain an index at the top of a page with the content further down the page or for taking a user back to the top of a page. You also can use named anchors to mark a specific point on a page that you link to from other Web pages.

Linking to Named Anchors

8.16 You can click and drag the Point-to-File icon located to the right of the Link field onto the Anchor icon in the Document window. If you hover over the arrows of the scrollbar, you can scroll the window while using the Point-to-File icon.

8.17 If the file exists on a remote server, enter the URL followed by any subpaths followed by the named anchor reference—for example, http://www.scmtraining.net/descriptions.html#photoshop.

You can access the named anchors in your document by linking to them in the same document or from other documents. Named anchors are used to link to specific places on a Web page. An example is when you are linking to a page that contains many topics but want to direct the user to a specific topic on the page. Another common use of named anchors is to create an index of sorts at the top of a Web page that links to areas further down on the same page.

1. Click an object or select some text to use as the link to an existing named anchor.

2. Type the # symbol followed by the named anchor's name in the Link field of the Property inspector **(8.16)**. You must include the # symbol to link to named anchors.

3. To link to a named anchor within a remote file, type the address of the remote file followed by the name of the named anchor—remember to include the # symbol **(8.17)**.

 I P

You can use the Point-to-File icon to link to a named anchor on another Web page. Open both pages in Dreamweaver and drag from the Point-to-File icon in one document onto the named anchor in another.

©HAPTER 9

In this chapter, you will learn how to...

Insert a Rollover Image

Insert a Navigation Bar

Use the Set Nav Bar Image Behavior

Insert Flash Buttons

Modify Flash Buttons

Insert Flash Text

Modify Flash Text

Create and Edit Jump Menus

Dreamweaver provides a variety of objects in the Objects panel that enable you to incorporate interactive images, such as rollover images, navigation bars, Flash buttons, and jump menus. With the exception of Flash buttons and Flash text, the interactive images you can add to your pages with Dreamweaver are a combination of images, such as GIFs and JPEGs, and JavaScript code. Creating a navigation bar for your Web pages

INSERTING INTERACTIVE IMAGES

is a simple matter of clicking an object in the Objects panel. Use the Insert Navigation Bar dialog box to select images for the up, over, and down states of each button in the navigation bar, and then assign URLs to each button.

Dreamweaver 4 includes two new objects in the Objects panel to insert Flash buttons and Flash text. Macromedia's Flash is a vector-based application that can create complex images and interactions that are relatively small in size compared to their bitmap counterparts in JPEG and GIF files. With the new Flash buttons and Flash text in Dreamweaver 4, adding professional interactivity to your Web pages has never been easier.

Inserting a Rollover Image

Dreamweaver enables you to create a rollover by simply selecting two files—an image that initially appears on the page and another image that is swapped with the first when the cursor is passed over the first image. Rollovers require the use of JavaScript's Swap Image and Swap Image Restore functions. In Dreamweaver, the JavaScript is automatically written for you and implemented in the <img> tag's attributes. To create a rollover, you need two images of the same dimensions that represent the two stages of the rollover animation.

1. Select Insert→Interactive Images→Rollover Image to display the Insert Rollover Image dialog box (9.1).

2. Enter the path in the Original Image field or click the Browse button to locate the image.

3. Enter the path in the Rollover Image field or click the Browse button to locate an image.

4. Rollover images always are treated as linked buttons. Enter the path of the file the button will link to in the When Clicked, Go to URL field or click the Browse button to select a file. If you leave this field blank, the rollover still acts like a button, but clicking it has no effect.

Enter an image name in the Image Name field. Dreamweaver inserts an image name for you because JavaScript requires the image to be named to create the rollover. You can change this name to anything you want.

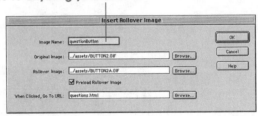

9.1

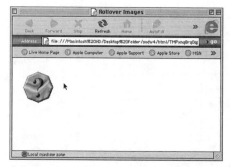

9.2

9.3

5. Check the Preload Rollover Image check box if you want the rollover button to be loaded into memory when the page is loaded on the user's browser. This option prevents a delay when the user rolls over the button. Click OK when you have entered all the data.

6. Preview the Web page in a browser to see the rollover effect **(9.2)**. Notice that the cursor changes to the Hand icon, indicating that this button has a link **(9.3)**. Click the button to display the linked HTML page.

(N) O T E

Rollover images are treated just like inline graphics, so you can set the attributes for the rollover in the Property inspector.

(T) I P

When you create images to use as rollovers, be sure the images are of the same dimension and crop the images close to avoid extra space around the edges. The rollover effect occurs when the cursor enters the rectangular area the image occupies, so extra space around the image results in the rollover effect occurring when the user simply gets close to the image. This condition occurs even if you use GIFs with the outside area set to transparent.

Inserting a Navigation Bar

When the navigation bar is created, images are specified that represent the various states of the buttons in the navigation bar. For example, create an image that will be a specific button in its initial state (the way it looks when you first view the page). Then create images for the way the button looks when the mouse is over it and when it is clicked. You can edit the navigation bar after creating it and use behaviors in the Behaviors panel to change the buttons in the navigation bar.

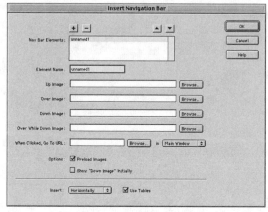

9.4

1. Select Insert→Interactive Images→Navigation Bar or click the Navigation Bar object in the Common Objects panel to display the Insert Navigation Bar dialog box (9.4).

2. Assign a name to the element (button) you're describing; then click the Browse buttons to set the Up, Over, Down, and Over While Down images. Specify the URL to which the image links when clicked (9.5).

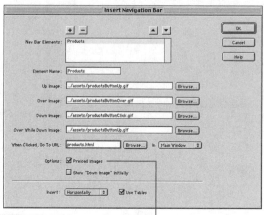

9.5

Check the Preload Images check box to load all the images when the page loads.

If you create a horizontal navigation bar and don't place the images in a table, the images that make up the navigation bar can wrap around each other when the browser window is resized.

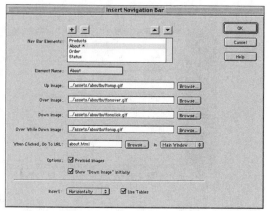

9.6

3. Click the plus (+) button to add additional elements to the navigation bar (9.6).

4. Click OK to generate the navigation bar on your Web page (9.7). Preview the page in a Web browser to test the buttons (9.8).

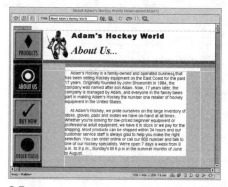

9.7

The Over image is displayed when you move the cursor over the buttons.

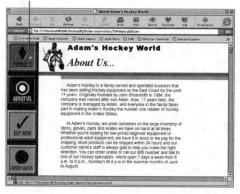

9.8

 I P

When you create your images for the navigation bar, offset the images by moving them down and to the right a few pixels to create the illusion of a button being depressed for the Over and Down images. Leave some white space around the images to accommodate this.

The Over While Down image is displayed for this button when the cursor moves over it because the button is in the Down state initially.

 O T E

After you have created your navigation bar, select Modify→Navigation Bar to make any changes to the images. You cannot change the navigation bar from vertical to horizontal or vice versa or select the Table feature when editing a navigation bar.

Using the Set Nav Bar Image Behavior

Use the Set Nav Bar Image behavior to turn an image into a navigation bar image or to change the display and actions of images in an existing navigation bar. The Basic tab of the Set Nav Bar Image dialog box enables you to create or update navigation bar images, to change which URL is attached to a button, and to select a different window to display the indicated URL. The Advanced tab of the Set Nav Bar Image dialog box enables you to change the swap images of other navigation bar buttons, as well as any other image on the page.

1. Select Window→Behaviors to open the Behaviors panel if it isn't already onscreen.

2. Select one of the images in a navigation bar to display the Set Nav Bar Image actions in the Behaviors panel **(9.9)**.

3. In the Behaviors panel, double-click the Set Nav Bar Image action you want to edit to display the Set Nav Bar Image dialog box **(9.10)**.

4. In the Basic tab of the Set Nav Bar Image dialog box, make any necessary changes to the button states of the currently selected button.

5. In the Advanced tab, select a button state from the pop-up menu, and then select one of the images in the Also Set Image list box **(9.11)**.

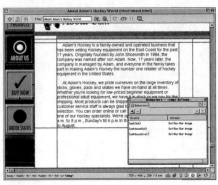

9.9

Basic tab **Advanced tab**

9.10

This example sets the state of the Products, About, and Status buttons to Over when the Order button is in the Down state.

9.11 **Asterisks appear next to images with changes.**

Inserting Flash Buttons

9.12

The text you enter for the button does not appear in the sample button. Click the Apply button to see the button on your Web page.

9.13

The Flash Button object in the Common Objects panel enables you to insert predesigned Flash buttons. Flash buttons are vector-based graphics that can be resized without affecting the image quality, unlike the JPEG and GIF images used in the Navigation bar elements. Flash buttons also are created using Macromedia Flash, which can incorporate many of the special effects available in Flash.

1. Select Insert→Interactive Images→Flash Button or click the Flash Button object in the Common Objects panel to display the Insert Flash dialog box (9.12).

2. Select a button style from the Style list and type the text you want to appear in the button in the Button Text field (9.13).

3. Specify a font size and select the font you want for the text inside the button.

4. Enter a URL in the Link field or click the Browse button to the right of the Link field to select a file on your site. Use the Target pop-up menu to specify a frame or window to display the linked URL.

Inserting Flash Buttons continued

5. Specify a background color for the Flash button in the BG Color field.

6. You can change the name of the SWF file in the Save As field (9.14). Click OK to insert the button on your Web page (9.15).

Click Get More Styles to launch your browser and connect to Macromedia's Exchange pages.

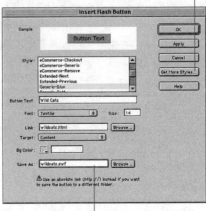

9.14

Save your buttons in the same directory as the Web page to ensure that all browsers will correctly display the Flash buttons.

You can resize Flash buttons by dragging the handles.

9.15

 **O T E**

You must save your document in your site prior to inserting Flash buttons. If you want to use document-relative paths for the SWF files, save the files in the same directory as the HTML page they are on.

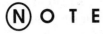 **O T E**

Flash buttons must be saved with the .swf extension to work correctly on your Web pages. Macromedia Flash creates files for the Web in the Shockwave format (swf). When you insert Flash buttons in Dreamweaver, you are actually creating a Shockwave format file (swf) from a Flash Generator template file (.swt extension).

Modifying Flash Buttons

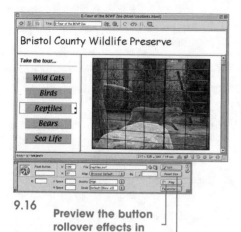

9.16

Preview the button rollover effects in Dreamweaver.

Set the button to its original size.

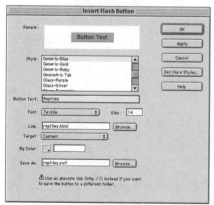

9.17

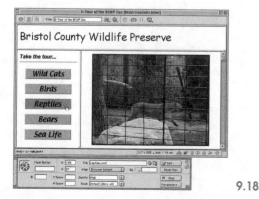

9.18

Using the Property inspector, you can modify some of the properties of Flash buttons, such as the HTML attributes width, height, and Bg color. Use the Insert Flash Button dialog box to change the Flash characteristics of your buttons.

1. Select Window→Properties to display the Property inspector; then select a Flash button in your document (9.16).

2. Click the Edit button in the Property inspector to display the Insert Flash Button dialog box (9.17). Make the desired changes and click OK.

 O T E

If you want to preview your Flash buttons within Dreamweaver, click the Play button in the Property inspector when you have a Flash button selected. Position your cursor over the Flash button to see the rollover effect; click the button to see the click effect (9.18). Click the Stop button in the Property inspector to turn off the button preview.

 I P

To learn how to create your own button templates, go to http://www.macromedia.com/ support/dreamweaver/insert_media.html.

Inserting Flash Text

The Insert Flash Text object in the Common Objects panel enables you to insert text in the font, size, and style that you want. Because Flash embeds the font in the Flash movie, you don't have to worry about the user having the font you want installed on his system. The Flash Text object is also a great way to make text buttons that change color when you roll over them.

1. Select Insert→Interactive Images→Flash Text or click the Insert Flash Text object in the Common Objects panel to display the Insert Flash Text dialog box (9.19).

2. Select a font from the Font pop-up menu, and then enter the font size in points in the Size field.

3. Use the style buttons to set the bold and italic attributes, as well as the text alignment.

4. Set the text color in the Color field and a rollover color, if desired, in the Rollover Color field.

Type text in here.

Make the text change color when you roll over it.

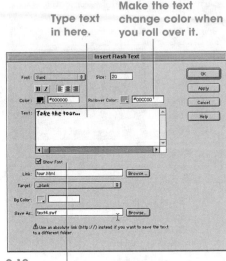

9.19

Display the text in the specified font within this dialog box.

 **O T E**

The Font field in the Insert Flash Text dialog box displays only TrueType fonts installed on your system.

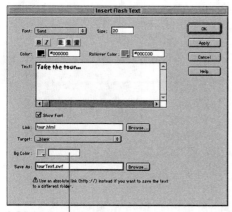

9.20   **Set a background color for the Text field if you want the text to appear on a field of color.**

5. Type the text you want in the Text field. Click the Show Font check box if you want the text in the Text field to display in the specified font.

6. If you want the text to act like a button, enter a URL in the Link field and a frame or window in the Target field.

7. Assign a sensible name for the Flash Text object in the Save As field; then click OK (9.20).

Site-relative links are not accepted for Flash buttons and Flash text because browsers do not recognize them within Flash movies. If you use a document-relative link, be sure to save the SWF file in the same directory as the HTML Web page.

Modifying Flash Text

Using the Property inspector, you
can modify some of the properties
of Flash Text, such as the HTML
attributes width, height, and Bg
color. Use the Insert Flash Text dialog box to change the Flash characteristics of your text.

1. Select Window→Properties to
   display the Property inspector;
   then select a Flash text image
   in your document **(9.21)**.

2. Click the Edit button in the
   Property inspector to display
   the Insert Flash Text dialog box
   (9.22). Make the desired
   changes and click OK.

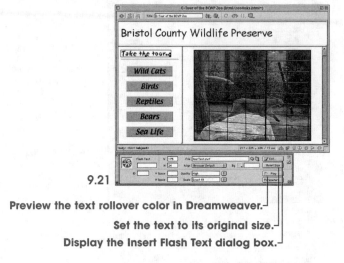

9.21

Preview the text rollover color in Dreamweaver.
Set the text to its original size.
Display the Insert Flash Text dialog box.

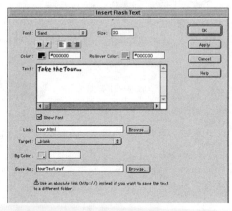

9.22

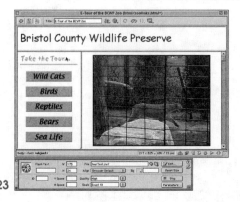

9.23

NOTE

*If you want to preview your Flash text
within Dreamweaver, click the Play button
in the Property inspector when you have a
Flash text image selected. Position your cursor over the Flash text to see the rollover
effect **(9.23)**. Click the Stop button in the
Property inspector to turn off the Flash text
preview.*

Creating and Editing Jump Menus

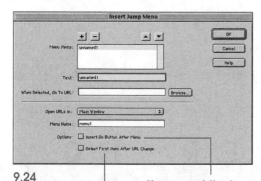

9.24

Check the Insert
Go Button After
Menu option if you
want the option of
linking to the URL
currently dis-
played in the
jump menu.

If you want the jump menu to
always display the same thing
when the page is loaded, click the
check box to Select First Item After
URL Change. Create a menu selection prompt by placing a user
instruction at the top of the list,
such as "Choose One" or
"Select...."

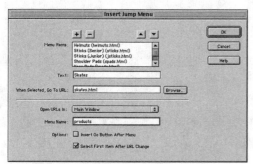

9.25

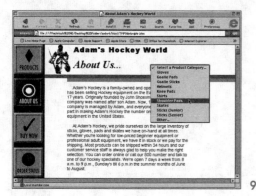

9.26

A *jump* menu is a pop-up menu
with a list of choices that link to
another document or file. You can
create links to Web pages on your
site, remote Web pages, e-mail links,
links to graphics, links to sounds,
and links to any other content that
can be opened in a browser. The
jump menu behaves just like a standard pop-up menu, except that the
selection that is made takes the site
visitor to a specific URL. You can
optionally include a Go button that
enables the site visitor to go to the
menu choice currently visible.

1. To insert a jump menu on your
   page, select Forms from the
   Objects panel menu to display
   the Form objects and click the
   Jump Menu object. The Insert
   Jump Menu dialog is displayed (9.24).

2. Enter the Menu Items by typing the names in the Text field;
   then specify the link information for the menu choice in the
   When Selected, Go To URL
   field (9.25).

3. Click OK, and then preview
   your page in a browser to test
   the jump menu (9.26).

 I P

*Use the List Values button in the Property
inspector to add and remove menu items
after the jump menu is created.*

CHAPTER 10

In this chapter, you will learn how to...

Insert Tables

Set Table Properties

Insert, Delete, and Move Rows and Columns

Span and Split Rows and Columns

Insert Table Data from Outside Sources

Use the Built-In Table Formatting Feature

Sort Table Data

Tables are a part of the HTML code that is supported by most browsers at this writing. Therefore, tables are a safe way to lay out your Web page so that the largest number of users can view it the way you intend. Aside from being useful in creating the overall layout of your Web pages, tables also can act as inline images in the sense that they can be aligned like images and even have text run around them. Tables also can be embedded

BUILDING TABLES

inside other tables, which comes in handy when you're using tables to lay out your Web pages. See Chapter 11, "Designing Pages in Layout View," for more information on using tables to lay out your Web pages.

You can format tables in a number of ways, depending on whether you have selected a table cell, a table row, or the entire table. You can specify background images and background colors for individual cells, rows, or the entire table. Think of each table cell as a separate HTML page on which you can include text, images, links, buttons, and any of the large variety of plugin image types available. Table cells also can be locked to maintain a static width and height, giving you precise control over the space on your Web pages. You can also use the Insert Tabular Data command to build a table from a delimited text file.

Inserting Tables

If you are going to use tables to control the layout of your Web page,
start with a blank document and
insert a table, or switch to the
Layout View and create layout
tables and layout cells (see Chapter
11). If you are inserting tables as
part of your page content, insert
them at the blinking cursor. Use the
Property inspector to control the
attributes of the table after it's
inserted.

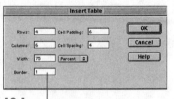

10.1 **Set the table border to
0 to create a table
without borders.**

1. Select Insert→Table, or click
   the Table button in the
   Common Objects panel, to display the Insert Table dialog
   box (10.1).

2. Specify the number of rows
   and columns for your table as
   well as the overall width of the
   table in either exact pixel
   dimensions or as a percentage
   of the browser window width.

3. Enter a value for the border
   width in the Border field.

4. Enter pixel values in the Cell
   Padding and Cell Spacing
   fields to control the text inset
   and distance between the cells,
   respectively.

5. Click OK to insert the table
   into your Web page. Click and
   drag the handles of the table to
   resize it or click inside the first
   field and begin entering data
   (10.2).

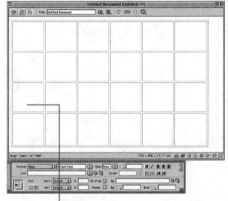

10.2 **Treat each table cell like a separate HTML file in which you can
insert background images, insert
inline images, format text,
change the background color,
and create links. Some of these
features are not supported in earlier browser versions, so be sure
you preview your pages in a variety of browsers and versions to
ensure your pages will be viewed
correctly.**

Setting Table Properties

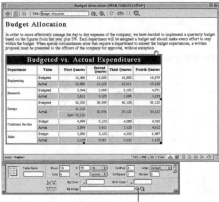

10.3   You can use the Point-to-File icon to point to a file in the Site window, or click the Folder icon to locate a background image.

10.4   If you have a difficult time selecting the entire table, click anywhere inside the table and then click the <table> tag in the lower-left corner of the Document window.

After you have inserted a table in your document, use the Property inspector to modify the table's attributes. When you select the entire table, the Property inspector contains the options for the whole table (10.3). Position the cursor just above or just below the table until the (Hand)[Move] icon appears, and then click to select the entire table. The top half of the Property inspector contains all the options you specified when you inserted the table, along with the align options for the table. You don't have to name your table unless you plan to reference it with JavaScript or Dreamweaver's Behaviors later.

1. Indicate a background image for the entire table in the Bg Image field (10.4).

2. Indicate a background color either by clicking the Bg Color swatch or by entering a color value in the Bg Color field.

3. Indicate a border color either by clicking the Brdr Color swatch or by entering a color value in the Brdr Color field.

4. You can change the row width and column height by clicking and dragging the divider lines in the Document window.

 I P

The border color attribute yields different results in different browsers, so be sure you preview your page in multiple browsers.

Formatting Tables

You can format entire rows and columns at the same time by first selecting a row or column and then modifying the attributes in the Property inspector.

1. Click and drag to select a range of cells in your table, or position your cursor over a column or to the left of a row and click when you see the large black arrow (10.5).

2. Use the Property inspector to format the contents of the selected row or column.

3. When a table is selected, four small icons appear in the lower-left corner of the Property inspector. Click along the table edge to select the table.

4. Click the upper-left icon in the lower-left corner of the Property inspector to reset the row heights after you have changed them. Click the upper-right icon to reset the column widths after you've changed them.

5. Click the lower-left icon in the lower-left corner of the Property inspector to set all table widths to pixels. Click the lower-right icon to set all table widths as percentage values (10.6).

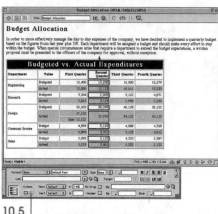

10.5 Indicates an entire column is selected.

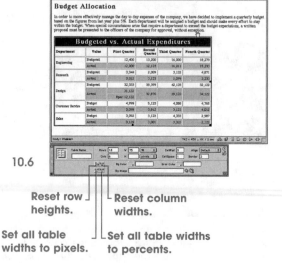

10.6

Reset row heights.

Reset column widths.

Set all table widths to pixels.

Set all table widths to percents.

Inserting, Deleting, and Moving Rows and Columns

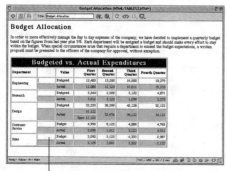

10.7

A new column is inserted to the left of the column containing the cursor, and the cursor is positioned in the new column.

10.8

To delete rows or columns, choose Modify→Table→Delete Row or Modify→Table→Delete Column.

You can use two methods to insert rows and columns into a table. The first method inserts a single row or column, whereas the second method enables you to insert multiple rows or columns. When inserting a single row or column, rows are inserted above the row the active cell is in and columns are inserted to the left of the column the active cell is in.

1. Click inside a cell of your table.

2. Choose Modify→Table→Insert Row or Modify→Table→Insert Column to insert a new row above the current row or a new column to the left of the current column (10.7).

3. To insert multiple rows or columns at the same time, choose Modify→Table→Insert Rows or Columns to display the Insert Rows or Columns dialog box (10.8).

4. Indicate the number of rows or columns you want to add and where the new columns or rows are to be inserted in the table. Click OK.

ⓃO T E

To move or copy table rows and columns, select a row or column; choose Edit→Copy or Edit→Cut; click where you want to insert the row or column; and choose Edit→Paste. Columns are pasted to the left of the current column, and rows are pasted above the current row.

Spanning and Splitting Rows and Columns

When working with tables, you might need to merge table cells together to span multiple columns or rows. Likewise, you also might find it necessary to split existing columns and rows to create new ones. Span columns when you want to add a heading to your table that is included within the table or if you want to have two or more columns under a single heading. In the HTML code, when you span rows, the content for the column with the rowspan attribute is in the first row of the rows being spanned.

1. Click and drag to select a row of cells; type the letter M to merge the cells into a single cell (10.9).

2. Insert some rows into your table and merge the cells in a single column to span two rows (10.10).

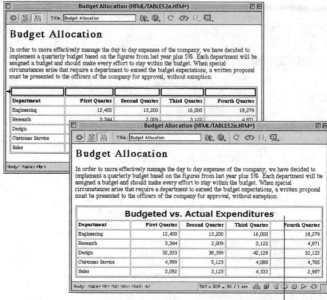

10.9

Here the heading spans the columns of the entire width of the table to give a clean, balanced look to the table.

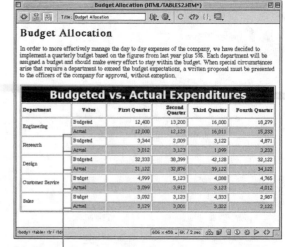

10.10

Here an additional row was added for each department, and then the two rows were merged for the cell containing the department name. Text is vertically centered in table cells by default.

Ⓝ O T E

When splitting rows, the new table cells are added above the selected row or cell. When splitting columns, the new table cells are added to the left of the selected row or cell. If you want to add rows or columns to the bottom or right of the table, respectively, add rows or columns to the entire table using the Table Property inspector.

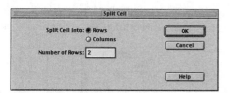

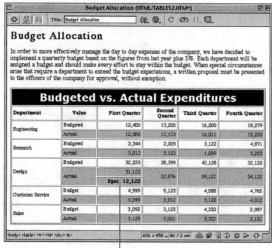

10.11

Here you see that the First Quarter Actual cell has been split into two cells to indicate a special budget allowance.

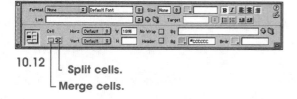

10.12 └ **Split cells.**
└ **Merge cells.**

3. Click inside a cell and choose Modify→Table→Split Cell to split an individual cell into rows or columns. Indicate the number of rows or columns in the Split Cell dialog box **(10.11)**.

 I P

Click the icon in the lower-left corner of the Property inspector (under the word "Cell") when you have selected multiple cells to merge into one cell. You must have the Property inspector expanded to use this option. Click the icon to the right of the Merge Cell icon to split individual cells into rows and columns **(10.12)**.

 I P

If you have an entire row or entire column selected, the Merge and Split icons appear under the words Row or Column, respectively, in the Property inspector.

Inserting Table Data from Outside Sources

Dreamweaver can import tab-, comma-, semicolon-, and colon-delimited text as well as any delimiter you specify to create a table. All spreadsheet and database programs provide a method to export files to some form of delimited text file—usually tab or comma delimited. When Dreamweaver imports the table data, an HTML table is automatically generated, based on the arrangement of the data in the imported file.

1. Export the table data from a spreadsheet or database program to a delimited text file (10.13).

2. In Dreamweaver, select Insert→Tabular Data or click the Tabular Data button in the Common Objects panel to display the Insert Tabular Data dialog box. Enter the name of the delimited text file in the Data File field or click the Browse button to locate the file (10.14).

Here a spreadsheet is exported from Microsoft Excel as a tab-delimited text file.

10.13

10.14

10.15

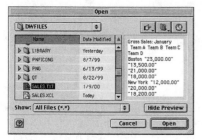

10.16

Select a delimiter.

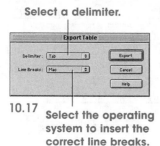

10.17   **Select the operating system to insert the correct line breaks.**

3. Choose the delimiter that corresponds to the data file from the Delimiter pull-down menu. Specify your preference for the other table formatting options and click OK to place the table in the Document window **(10.15)**.

I P

Macintosh users can click the Preview button in the Open dialog box to see a preview of the delimited text file **(10.16)***.*

**O T E**

To export your Dreamweaver table data to a delimited text file that you can open in other programs, such as Microsoft Excel and Lotus 1-2-3, click anywhere inside your table and select File→Export→Export Table **(10.17)***.*

Using the Built-In Table Formatting Feature

You can quickly format tables in Dreamweaver using the Format Table command. Select from a variety of preset table formats.

1. Click to select a table in the Document window, and then select Commands→Format Table to display the Format Table dialog box (10.18).

2. Select a basic format from the scrolling list on the left, or specify your own criteria for the table's format.

3. Click the Apply button to preview the table formatting on your table in the Design view of the Document window.

4. Click OK when you're satisfied with the table format and make any further edits using the Property inspector (10.19).

Enter color names or hexadecimal color values in color fields.

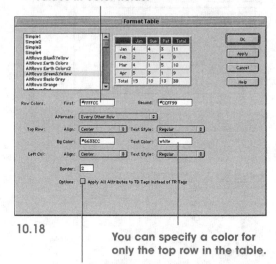

10.18

You can specify a color for only the top row in the table.

Check here if you want to include the table formatting codes in each TD (cell) tag instead of the TR (table row) tags.

10.19

 **N O T E**

If you click the Apply button in the Format Table dialog box, the format of the table will remain changed, even if you click the Cancel button. Type (Command-Z)[Ctrl+Z] to undo the table formatting.

 I P

Visit the companion site for this book at www.sodw.net for information on how to add your own table formats to the scrolling list in the Table Format dialog box.

Sorting Table Data

![Tabular Data window showing a table with columns Team A, Team B, Team C, Team D and rows for Boston, New York, Portland, Providence with dollar amounts, some rows highlighted]

10.20

![Sort Table dialog box with Sort By Column 1, Order Alphabetically Ascending, Then By Column 2, Order Numerically Ascending, and Options to Sort Includes First Row and Keep TR Attributes With Sorted Row]

10.21

![Tabular Data window showing the sorted table with Boston, New York (Manhattan), Portland, Providence rows and dollar amounts]

10.22

The background color of the rows moves with the sorted rows because Keep TR Attributes With Sorted Row is checked in the Sort Table dialog box.

After you have imported or created a table, you can sort the data in the table. The table cannot contain any row or column spans and every row and column in the table will be affected, with the exception of the first row, which you can choose to exclude.

1. Click to select a table in the Document window (10.20).

2. Select Commands→Sort Table to display the Sort Table dialog box (10.21).

3. Indicate the type of sort you want. You can specify one sub-sort from the Then By pull-down menu.

4. Click the Apply button to see the results of the sort or click OK to apply the sort (10.22).

 I P

The Sort Table command cannot be applied to tables that contain rowspan or columnspan data.

 I P

When you click the Apply button, the table data is permanently changed and will not revert to its original state if you click Cancel in the Sort Table dialog box. You can undo the sort by typing (Command-Z)[Ctrl+Z].

CHAPTER 11

The Dreamweaver Layout view is the easiest way to set up your page layout. Most Web pages today are created using tables to constrain the content to a static layout. Creating tables as a design structure for Web pages has always been a tedious process—that is, until now. Using Dreamweaver's Layout view, you easily can draw table cells, customize the cell and its content, and even move the cell around until you're happy with

DESIGNING PAGES IN LAYOUT VIEW

its placement. Layout view uses tables as an underlying structure, but it provides two tools—the layout table and layout cell—which enable you to draw boxes on the page and rearrange them. You can switch easily from the Standard view to the Layout view and back again to build tables that control the format of your Web pages.

When you switch to Layout view, you can use layout cells to block off areas of the page. Dreamweaver automatically creates a layout table to hold the layout cells. A layout table can have many layout cells, and more complicated pages can contain more than one layout table. Using multiple layout tables you can isolate parts of your Web page, creating permanent holding places for your page content. The layout cells can grow and shrink to accommodate the content, but they will not affect layout cells in other layout tables on the same page. You also can nest layout tables inside other layout tables, adding even more flexibility to the layout and design of your Web pages.

Drawing Layout Cells and Layout Tables

To create layout cells and tables, you first must switch from Standard view to Layout view. If you create a layout cell first, a layout table that is the width of your Document window is automatically inserted as a container. Your layout cells always reside inside a layout table. If you want to control the size and position of the layout table, start by first creating a layout table, and then add layout cells to the layout table.

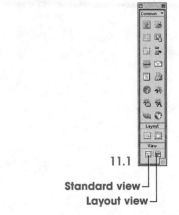

11.1

Standard view⌐
Layout view⌐

1. Switch to Layout view by clicking the Layout View button in the lower-right corner of the Objects panel (11.1).

2. Click the Draw Layout Table button in the Layout category of the Objects panel. The mouse pointer changes to a plus sign (+). Drag to create a layout table in the Document window (11.2).

3. Use the Property inspector to precisely set the width and height of the layout table, set the background color, and insert cell-padding and cell-spacing values (11.3).

Select layout table.
Drag to move lay-
out table.

Width of layout
table

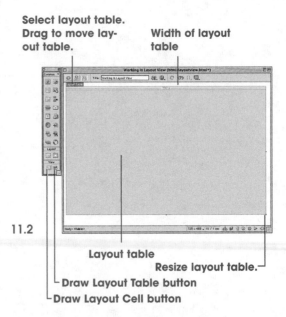

11.2

Layout table

Resize layout table.⌐

└ Draw Layout Table button
└ Draw Layout Cell button

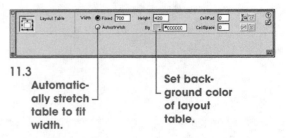

11.3

Automatic-
ally stretch
table to fit
width.

Set back-
ground color
of layout
table.

Layout cell width   **Layout cell**

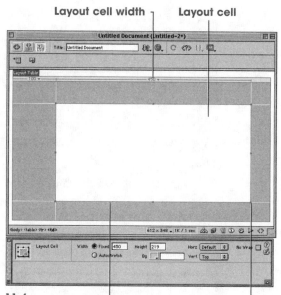

11.4

Drag the edges of the layout cell between the handles to move the layout cell.

Drag handles to resize the layout cell.

11.5

4. Click the Draw Layout Cell button in the Layout category of the Objects panel; then drag to create a layout cell inside the layout table. Use the Property inspector to set the attributes for the layout cell **(11.4)**.

5. Click inside the layout cell and add content as you would to any Web page. Add more layout cells to the table to better control the overall layout. Switch back to Standard view to see the table **(11.5)**.

(T) I P

Hold down the (Command)[Ctrl] key to draw multiple layout cells and layout tables. Hold down (Option)[Alt] while drawing layout cells and layout tables to temporarily disable snapping to other layout cells and layout tables.

Drawing a Nested Layout Table

You can insert multiple nested tables by adding layout tables inside existing layout tables. The rows and columns of the outer table do not control the nested tables, which gives you more control over the layout than in previous versions of Dreamweaver.

1. Switch to Layout view if you are currently in Standard view.

2. Click the Draw Layout Table button in the Layout category of the Options panel and drag inside the Document window to create the parent table.

3. Click the Draw Layout Table button again and drag inside the parent table to create a nested table (11.6).

11.6

Nested tables cannot be larger than the table that contains them.

The main layout table is always positioned in the upper-left corner of the page.

11.7

A new layout table was drawn around the existing layout table to create the black border.

T I **P**

You can draw a layout table around existing layout cells or layout tables. Click the Draw Layout Table button in the Layout category of the Objects panel, and then drag to create a layout table around existing layout cells or layout tables. The new layout table will enclose the existing layout cells or layout tables (11.7). Preview your page in a Web browser to see the page without all the table lines (11.8).

11.8

Formatting Layout Tables

Clear Row Heights

Make Cell Widths Consistent

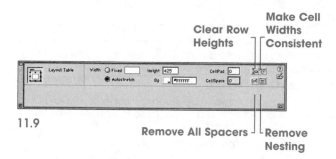

11.9

Remove All Spacers ┘ └ **Remove Nesting**

Use the Property inspector to control the format of layout tables. Most of the options should be familiar to you if you have created standard HTML tables.

1. Click along the layout table edge or on the layout table tab to select the layout table.

2. Select Window>Properties to display the Property inspector if it isn't already onscreen (11.9).

3. Set the attributes for the table in the Property inspector (Table 11.1).

If you click an autostretch column, the Make Column Fixed Width option is available here instead.

Autostretch column—Column dividers

11.10

11.11

The last column is designated as the autostretch column.

(N) O T E

When you select Autostretch for your table in the Property inspector, one of the columns in your table is designated as the autostretch column. A zigzag line in the column header of the layout table indicates the autostretch column. Click the column dividers at the top of the layout table to set the column that will autostretch (11.10). In the browser, the column designated as the autostretch column will stretch, leaving the other columns intact (11.11).

Formatting Layout Tables continued

Table 11.1   Layout Table Formatting Options

Property	Description
Width	Select Fixed and type a width to create a static table. Select Autostretch if you want your table to always fit the width of the browser window.
Height	Specify the height in pixels in the text field.
CellPad	Cell padding controls the amount of space between the content of a layout cell and the cell wall. All the layout cells in a layout table are affected by this setting.
CellSpace	Cell spacing is the amount of space between the layout cells.
Clear Row Heights	Removes any extra row space and collapses the table. If the table is empty, the entire table collapses.
Make Widths Consistent	If your table contains fixed-width cells, click the Make Widths Consistent button to automatically set the width of each cell to match the content within the cell.
Remove All Spacers	If you selected Autostretch for your table, spacer images (a transparent GIF file) might have been inserted in the table. Click the Remove All Spacers button to remove the spacer images. See "Using Spacer Images in Layout Tables" in this chapter for more information.
Remove Nesting	If the selected layout table is nested inside another layout table, the Remove Nesting button is available in the Property inspector. Click the Remove Nesting button to transfer the contents of the nested layout table to the parent layout table, eliminating the nested table but preserving its contents.

Using Spacer Images in Layout Tables

You can insert and remove spacer images in specific columns or remove all spacer images in the page.

11.12

11.13

Spacer images are transparent GIF images that do not appear in the browser window but are used to control spacing in autostretch tables. The spacer images are inserted by Dreamweaver when you choose to create an autostretch table, essentially locking the widths of all table columns except the column designated as the autostretch column. Spacer images are typically 1 pixel by 1 pixel transparent GIFs. When you insert a spacer image in a column or make a layout table autostretch, a dialog box appears prompting you to set up the spacer image file. You can set a spacer image using the Layout View preferences, explained later in this chapter in the section titled "Setting Layout View Preferences."

1. Check the Autostretch radio button in the Property inspector for a layout table, or click a column header and select Add Spacer Image from the Column Header menu (11.12).

2. If a spacer image has not yet been associated with the current site, a dialog box appears prompting you to either create a new spacer GIF or select an existing one (11.13). If you select Create a Spacer Image File, Dreamweaver creates a 1-pixel-by-1-pixel transparent GIF file and prompts you to save the file in your site somewhere.

Using Spacer Images in Layout Tables continued

3. When you check the
Autostretch radio button in the
Property inspector for a layout
table, an additional option
appears in the dialog box
(11.14). Select Don't Use Spacer
Images for Autostretch Tables
if you want your table columns
to compress to fit the content.
Empty columns will collapse
to a small width or disappear
altogether when this option is
selected (11.15).

11.14

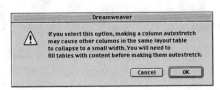

11.15

*Dreamweaver inserts the spacer images at
the bottom of the table in a new row that is 1
pixel in height. Use the Code View window
to locate the spacer images in the table by
scrolling to the bottom of the table.*

*Spacer images only have to be 1 pixel by 1
pixel because the width of the spacer image
is controlled by the width attribute of the
<img> tag—for example, <img height="1"
width="229" src="spacer.gif">.*

Setting Layout View Preferences

Dreamweaver will
create a spacer
image for you if
you don't already
have one.

A spacer image is
defined here for
the entire site.

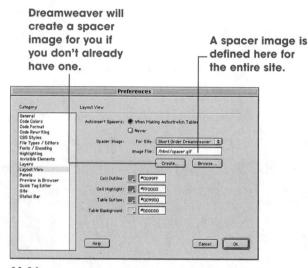

11.16

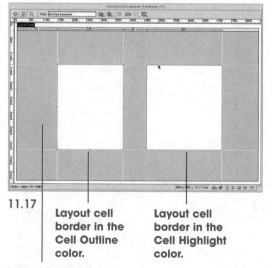

11.17

Layout cell
border in the
Cell Outline
color.

Layout cell
border in the
Cell Highlight
color.

Layout table border in
the Table Outline color.

The Layout View preferences enable
you to set specific guidelines for creating tables with layout tables and
layout cells.

1. Select Edit→Preferences; then
   select Layout View from the
   Category list to display the
   Layout View preferences
   (11.16).

2. The default for Autoinsert
   Spacers is to automatically
   insert them when making
   autostretch tables. Click the
   Never radio button if you
   don't want spacer images
   inserted in autostretch tables.

3. Click the For Site pop-up menu
   to define a spacer image for
   specific sites.

4. Click the Create button to have
   Dreamweaver create a spacer
   image for you, or click Browse
   to locate an existing spacer
   image.

5. Select a color for the Cell
   Outline, Cell Highlight, and
   Table Outline. Layout cells
   appear in the Cell Outline
   color and change to the Cell
   Highlight color when selected.
   Layout tables appear in the
   Table Outline color and do not
   change color when selected
   (11.17).

6. Select a color for the Table
   Background.

CHAPTER 12

In this chapter, you will learn how to...

Create Frames

Specify Frame Properties

Select Framesets

Save Frames and Framesets

Target with Links

Create NoFrames Content

Use JavaScript Behaviors with Frames

Frames enable you to subdivide the browser window into multiple frames, with each containing its own HTML documents. Frames are implemented as a separate HTML document that uses the HTML `<frameset>` tags to describe the columns and rows that are frames. Therefore, when you create a frames document in Dreamweaver, you're actually creating a single HTML file that describes the framesets and multiple HTML documents that describe the content of each frame.

CREATING FRAMES

Dreamweaver 4 enables you to build the Web pages for frames right in the frame itself, unlike most other Web design applications, which require you to create the Web pages separately. The capability of building the Web pages in the frames enables you to easily create links between frames with the Point-to-File icon as well as drag and drop images and text from one frame into another. In Dreamweaver, you build the NoFrames content in a separate Document window even though the HTML code goes in the frameset HTML file. Switch back and forth from the framesets to the NoFrames content with a simple menu command. The Property inspector contains all the attributes for frames, enabling you to name and target frames, turn borders on and off, inset frame contents, and control the display of scrollbars. When you save the frameset file, you are prompted to save the individual frame content for any unsaved frames.

This chapter shows you how to use these features to quickly create professional-looking frames pages that will appeal to your site visitors.

Creating Frames

Frames are created by splitting the Web page horizontally, vertically, or both. After you split the Web page to create a frame, you can split that frame into other frames as well.

1. Create a new document; then, select Modify→Frameset and select Split Frame Up, Split Frame Down, Split Frame Left, or Split Frame Right. After you've created a frame, click and drag the divider line to resize the frame (12.1).

2. Click inside an existing frame and select Modify→Frameset to split the frame into additional frames. Click and drag the divider line to size the frame.

3. Select File→Save Frameset to save the frameset as an HTML document. Name this file as you would any other HTML document—be sure to include the .html or .htm extension.

4. To create your frame content from scratch, simply click inside a frame and create the content as you would for any other Web page (12.2). Select File→Save and save the frame contents as an HTML file.

Click the Frames Objects to create and split frames.

You can click and drag to reposition the frame dividers.

12.1

12.2

Deciding whether to use frames as a way to format your Web pages depends on the audience you want to reach because only versions 3 and later of both Netscape and Explorer support frames. Many Web page developers offer an alternative Web site built from tables for browsers that do not support frames.

Specifying Frame Properties

12.3

12.4

Use the Property inspector to specify the way you want your frames to behave. When you click inside a frame, you are editing an HTML page, so the Property inspector displays the standard character properties. To specify the properties for the frames, use the Frames panel to select the individual frames.

1. Select Window→Frames to display the Frames panel and click the frame you want to edit (12.3).

2. Select Window→Properties to display the Property inspector if it isn't already onscreen. In the Property inspector, type a name for your frame in the Frame Name field. You use these names later to target the individual frames (12.4).

3. By default, frames have an embossed border that surrounds the entire page and divides the frames. Select No from the Borders pull-down menu in the Property inspector if you want to turn off the borders. Select a border color by clicking the Border Color swatch or by entering a color value.

 I P

You can specify how both frame and frameset borders appear in a document. When you set border options for a frame, the frameset border is overridden.

Specifying Frame Properties continued

4. The default scrolling method is set to Auto for all browsers. When Auto is selected as the scroll method, scrollbars appear if the content exceeds the depth of the frame, but they do not appear if the content fits. Select Yes to always display scrollbars or No to never display them **(12.5)**.

5. Check the No Resize check box if you want to prevent users from resizing your frames in their browser windows.

6. Specify a Margin Width and Margin Height value in pixels. The margin values determine how far from the borders of the frame the content is displayed **(12.6)**.

Scroll set to Yes.   Scroll set to No.

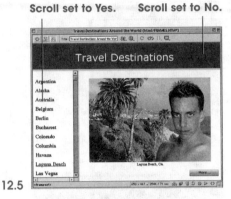

12.5

The margin width of this frame is set to 50 pixels, and the margin height is set to 20 pixels.

12.6

 **O T E**

You can target a frame with a link as long as you first name the targeted frame in the Property inspector. For example, your Web page can contain a frame that lists the information available on your site as hypertext links. When you click the links, the linked document is displayed in a frame to the right of the frame containing the links **(12.7)**.

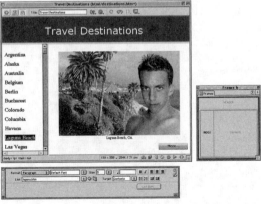

12.7

Selecting Framesets

When borders are turned off, Dreamweaver displays dashed divider lines to show the divisions of the frames. These dashed lines do not appear in the browser.

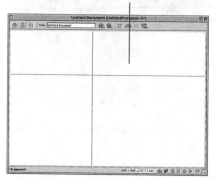

12.8

12.9 You can specify a frameset's dimensions as precise pixel values, percentages of the available space, or proportionally, which divides the remaining space equally. Browsers always create frames based first on the pixel dimensions followed by the percentage values and the proportional frames.

Framesets describe the rows and columns of your Web page. In the example seen in the last task in Figure 12.6, the page is divided into two rows, and then the second row is divided into two columns. Because a frameset can be a row that contains columns or a column that contains rows, selecting and editing the framesets is necessary if you want to edit the width, height, and border attributes of framesets. For example, even though a frame's border can be turned off, the frameset still has its own border, which also must be turned off if you want to eliminate all borders.

1. Click along the outside border to select the dominant frameset—rows in this example. A dotted line appears around the Document window when the frameset is selected (12.8).

2. The Property inspector displays the attributes for the frameset. Set the options for the borders of the frameset. Click in the thumbnail picture on the right side of the Property inspector to select the available rows or columns and specify the width or the height, depending on whether you have a column or a row selected. The thumbnail picture displays the rows and columns in equal proportion (12.9).

Saving Frames and Framesets

The frameset file is the one that is opened in the browser and therefore should contain the title that displays at the top of the browser window. Within the frameset HTML file, each frameset is described along with the default content for the frames (12.10). Saving your frames document is actually a multistep process. You must save each HTML page contained in the frames as well as the frameset.

The content of each frame is saved as a separate HTML file.

12.10

1. Select Window→Frames to display the Frame panel.

2. Click the outside border in the Frame panel to select the frameset.

3. Select Modify→Page Properties to display the Page Properties dialog box and type a title for your Web page (12.11).

4. Select File→Save Frameset to save your frameset information as an HTML file.

5. Click inside a frame and select File→Save to save that frame's contents as an individual HTML file. Repeat this process for all the frames in the frameset.

12.11

Select File→Save All to save all the HTML files in the frames as well as the frameset. When you select File→Preview in Browser, you are prompted to save any unsaved files.

Targeting with Links

12.12

Select _blank from the Target pull-down menu to display the link document in a new blank browser window. Select _parent to open the linked document in the parent frameset of the current frame. Select _top to open the link in the outermost frameset of the current document, replacing all frames. Select _self to display the link contents in the same frame as the link.

12.13

When you have created frames and given them names, you can target the frames to hold the content of any links you create. In the HTML source code, the target attribute is added to the <anchor> tag to specify which in frame to display the HREF file. When you don't specify a target for your links, the linked document or file is displayed in the same frame as the link.

1. Click an image or select some text to use as a link.

2. In the Property inspector, enter a link address in the Link field.

3. Click the arrow to the right of the Target field in the Property inspector and select the frame in which you want the linked file to appear (12.12).

Take advantage of frames to present the user with a uniform interface to browse your site. In Figure 12.13, clicking a button in the top frame displays a list in the left frame. You can then make a selection from the list on the left and display the contents of the link in the bottom-right frame (12.13).

Creating NoFrames Content

The `<noframes>` tag is automatically inserted in the HTML source code when you create frames. Alternative page content is inserted between the `<noframes>` and `</noframes>` tags for browsers that do not support frames.

1. Select Modify→Frameset→Edit NoFrames Content to display the page that will appear when a browser does not support frames.

2. Create an alternative Web page that does not contain frames with the same basic content as the page that contains frames (12.14). You also might include a brief message indicating that a browser that supports frames is necessary—if you select this option, provide some links for users to update their browser software (12.15).

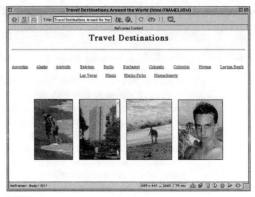

12.14

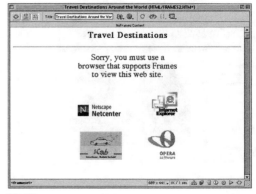

12.15

 O T E

To use an existing HTML page as your NoFrames page, copy the HTML source code of the page you want to use as the NoFrames page and paste it between the `<noframes>`/`<body>` tags and the `</body>`/`</noframes>` tags in the HTML inspector or your external HTML editor. Do not, however, include the `<html>` and `</html>` tags.

Using JavaScript Behaviors with Frames

12.16

The null link causes the text to act like a hypertext link without actually linking to anything. The link in this case is handled by a behavior.

A number of JavaScript behaviors can be applied to frames. Most Web developers use frames to design pages that are dynamic, changing content within a single browser window. You can use the Set Text of Frame behavior to change the content of a frame. Use the Go to URL behavior to change the content of a single frame or multiple frames at the same time. You also can use Dreamweaver's Navigation Bar and Jump Menu behaviors to create links that target frames. See Chapter 9, "Inserting Interactive Images," for instructions on creating navigation bars and jump menus.

1. Open or create a frameset document and ensure that all frames are named. You need a frame you can target with changing content. Create some default content for the target frame so something shows up when the page first loads. In the document used throughout this chapter, a new frame is inserted above the list of travel destinations where the text changes when you roll over a name in the list.

2. Select some text that will be the link that triggers the behavior and type the # symbol in the Link field of the Property inspector to create a null link (12.16).

Using JavaScript Behabiors with Frames continued

3. Select Window→Behaviors to display the Behaviors panel if it isn't already onscreen.

4. Select the text with the null link, and then click the plus (+) symbol in the Behaviors panel to display a menu of behaviors (12.17).

5. Select Set Text→Set Text of Frame from the Behaviors panel to display the Set Text of Frame dialog box. Select a target frame from the Frame pull-down menu. Then type the HTML code and text in the New HTML field and click OK (12.18).

6. Click the down-pointing triangle in the Events column of the Behaviors panel and select onMouseOver.

Behaviors available for a selected object or text are displayed in the Behaviors panel menu.

12.17

Select the frame in which you want to change the content.

Include any HTML code to replace the contents of the target frame.

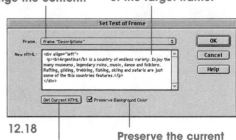

12.18

Click to get the current contents of the target frame for this behavior.

Preserve the current background color of the frame, which is set in the Page Properties of the current frame contents.

 I P

Create frames by clicking and dragging. Create a new document and select View→Visual Aids→Frame Borders. Drag from any of the borders to create the frame divisions. To delete a frame, simply drag the frame's border to the edge or onto another border.

Select a target frame for the URL. You can assign multiple URLs to multiple frames at the same time.

Enter a URL or click the Browse button to select a file from your site.

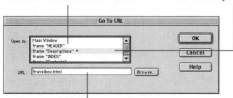

12.19

Asterisks appear next to the frames with URLs.

12.20

7. With the same text still selected, click the plus (+) symbol in the Behaviors panel and select Go to URL to display the Go to URL dialog box (12.19).

8. Select the same frame you used for the Set Text of Frame behavior and set the URL to the HTML file you created as the default file for the target frame. Click OK and set the Event for this behavior to onMouseOut (12.20).

ⓃO T E

You can assign multiple behaviors that use the same event for a single object. For example, create more than one onMouseOver and onMouseOut event to change the contents of multiple frames when you roll over an image or some text. If you want to have some text appear in the status bar at the bottom of the Web browser, use the Set Text of Status Bar action in the Behaviors panel.

©HAPTER 13

F orms enable you to gather information from visitors of your Web site. Online surveys, mailing lists, password protection, and online shopping are all prime candidates for the use of forms. After the fields in a form are filled in, the data is sent to a form-handling program that resides on the Web server. Common Gateway Interface (CGI) scripts are commonly used, although a form handler can be programmed in many other

CREATING AND CUSTOMIZING FORMS

programming and scripting languages. The script processes the information it receives from your form and does something with it. The script might create database records, build a Web page to display as a result of the form entries, or send e-mail containing the contents of the form.

In Dreamweaver the form objects are added to the Web page using the Objects panel, and their attributes are specified in the Property inspector. Using the Forms Objects panel, you begin by inserting the Form object. The Form object inserts <form> and </form> in the HTML code and creates an invisible bounding area where all the form fields are added. Each form field is described using the Property inspector. Include the Submit button inside the form's bounding area and you have a functioning form.

This chapter provides you with tasks that will enable you to easily create and edit forms for your site, as well as provide information on how to handle the form data submitted by your site visitors.

Creating a Form

In the HTML source code, forms are always enclosed between the <form> and </form> tags. The Forms Objects panel contains all the form objects you need to build a form. Form elements are added inline with text and are affected by the width of the browser window just like paragraph text.

1. Select Window→Objects to display the Objects panel if it isn't already onscreen.

2. Select Forms from the pull-down menu at the top of the Objects panel (13.1).

3. Click the Form button in the Forms Objects panel to create the bounding box for your form (13.2).

4. If you don't see the red dotted line, select View→Visual Aids→Invisible Elements.

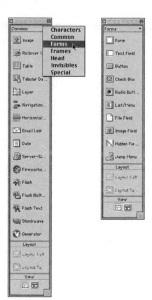

13.1

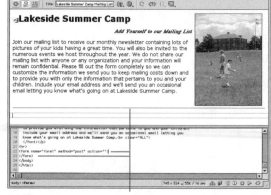

13.2

This red, dashed bounding box extends the width of the page and represents the opening and closing form tags in the HTML code.

T I P

For maximum control over the layout of your form, consider creating the form in tables using layout tables and layout cells in the Layout view. See Chapter 11, "Designing Pages in Layout View," for more information on working in Layout view.

The system administrator or Internet
service provider can help you with
the location of form-handling scripts.

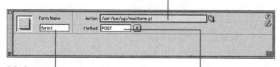

13.3

Most servers
require the POST
method, but check
with your system
administrator or ISP
to be sure.

Assign a name to
your form if you want
to address it with
JavaScript later.

13.4

A typical CGI script written in Perl. This script
forwards the form data to an e-mail address,
and then responds to the user with a new
HTML file thanking him for the input.

5. In the Property inspector, enter
the path of the form handler
script in the Action field or
click the Folder button to
locate a script on your site
(13.3).

6. Select POST or GET from the
Method pull-down menu,
depending on which method
your server supports.

 O T E

*CGI scripts are usually written in a script-
ing language, such as Perl (13.4). If you are
creating a basic mail form, most likely the
system administrator or Internet service
provider has an existing script you can use.
To learn more about CGI scripts, visit
www.cgi101.com or www.w3.org.*

 I P

*You can learn about CGI and download
some sample scripts at www.cgi101.com.*

Inserting Text Fields

The text field can be a single line of text or multiple lines with a scroll-bar attached. You can control the maximum length of a text field, control the maximum number of characters a user can enter, and specify text that initially appears in the field. Text fields also are used to create password fields in which the characters typed are echoed onscreen as bullets or asterisks.

1. Click inside the red dotted bounding box in the Document window, created when you click the Form button in the Forms Objects panel.

2. Click the Text Field button in the Forms Objects panel to add a text field (13.5).

3. Double-click the text field to display the Property inspector if it isn't already on your screen.

4. In the Property inspector, replace the default name with a name that describes the input (13.6). Be sure to use a name that correctly describes the input data.

 I P

Click the Password radio button in the Property inspector to make a single-line text field a password field. The password field is echoed onscreen as asterisks in Windows and as bullets on the Macintosh.

13.5

13.6

The name you type here is passed along with the form data to identify the contents of each field, just like a field name in a database.

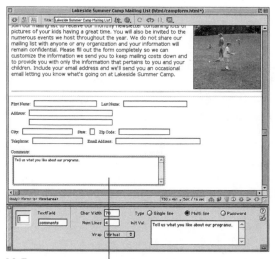

13.7   **A multiline text field is typically used for input, such as comments, descriptions, and special instructions.**

Table 13.1   Wrap Settings

Setting	Description
Default	Uses the browser default—sometimes wrap, sometimes not.
Off	Turns off text wrap for all browsers. All text entered remains on one line, which more or less defeats the purpose of a multiline text box.
Virtual	Wraps the text without adding hard returns to the text. This setting is the preferred method in most cases.
Physical	Inserts hard returns at the end of each wrapped line of text.

5. Enter a character width for the field to indicate the length of the field on the Web page. Enter a value for Max Chars to limit the number of characters a user can enter. If the Char Width value is set to a number lower than the Max Chars value, the text scrolls to the right when the user exceeds the width of the field. If you want the field to contain an initial value, type the desired text into the Init Val field.

6. Select a text field and click the Multi Line radio button in the Property inspector to create a multiline field with a scrollbar (13.7). In addition to the width of the field, you can specify the number of lines in the Num Lines field of the Property inspector to set the height.

7. The default wrap settings for multiline text boxes vary from browser to browser. Some browsers automatically wrap the text, whereas others do not. Select from the Wrap pull-down menu in the Property inspector to indicate how the multiline text box will wrap (Table 13.1).

 I P

You should use the Virtual option for wrapping text in a multiline text box when the data will be delivered as an e-mail message.

Inserting Radio Buttons and Check Boxes

Radio buttons and check boxes are used when you want to offer options and enable users to simply click to make a selection. To offer a number of choices but accept only one of those choices, use the radio button. To let the user make multiple choices, use the check boxes.

1. Click the Check Box button to insert a check box in the Document window.

2. In the Property inspector, assign a name to the check box in the CheckBox Name field. This name should describe the field, and each check box must have a unique name (13.8).

3. In the Checked Value field, type the information you want the form to return when the check box is checked.

4. To insert a radio button, click the Radio button in the Forms Objects panel. Radio buttons typically are used in groups, and all the radio buttons in the group must have the same name but different field values (13.9).

T I P

If you want a check box or radio button to be selected when the form is initially displayed, click the Checked radio button in the Property inspector. Only one radio button can be initially checked.

13.8
The Checked Value field of the Property inspector contains the word Yes for the check box named group 1 next to Male 6-10. Therefore, the form will return the value group1=Yes when this check box is checked.

13.9
When creating radio buttons, create a single radio button and assign it a name in the Property inspector. (Option-Drag)(Ctrl+Drag) this radio button to create the other instances in the group. Now you can simply change the Checked Values for each button because they will all be named the same.

Creating Lists and Menus

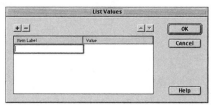

13.10

**The first item in the list is
selected. Type an Item
Label and use the Tab key
to move from field to field.**

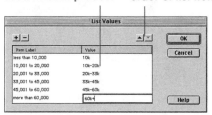

13.11

**If you leave the
Value fields blank,
the Item Label is
used in both places.**

**Click to change the
order of list items.**

13.12

A *Menu* is a pop-up menu that offers multiple choices. Only one item can be selected from a menu, and the menu always displays one item. *Lists*, on the other hand, can be displayed with multiple options showing and can accept multiple choices, as well. In both cases, you determine what's displayed and which values are sent to the handler script.

1. Click the List/Menu button in the Objects panel to add a list or menu to your form document. The same button is used to add both lists and menus.

2. In the Property inspector, click the Menu radio button and assign a name to this menu (13.10).

3. Click the List Values button in the Property inspector to display the List Values dialog box (13.11). Click the plus sign (+) or click inside the Item Label field to begin adding list values (13.12). The Item Label column is the text that is displayed in the menu for the user. The Value column is the information that is sent to the handler script when a particular choice is made.

(T) I P

Be sure to tell the user he/she can make multiple selections by including some text, such as "select all that apply."

Creating Lists and Menus continued

4. After you create the list values, select one of the values in the Initially Selected list in the Property inspector. The Initially Selected menu item is displayed as the default entry in the menu **(13.13)**.

5. To create a list box, click the List/Menu button in the Objects panel. Click the List radio button in the Property inspector and assign a name to your list.

6. Click the List Values button in the Property inspector to create a list of items the same way you created the list for menus in step 3.

7. Enter a Height value in the Property inspector to determine how many of the choices will be visible at one time. Check the Allow Multiple check box to enable the user to make multiple selections by using the Shift key and the (Command)[Ctrl] key **(13.14)**.

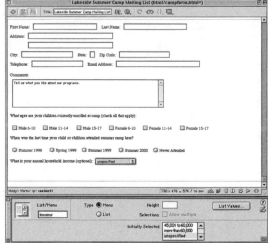

13.13

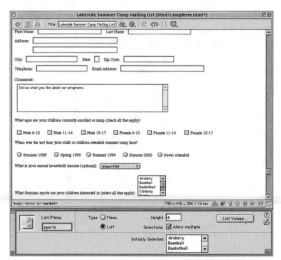

13.14

N O T E

Holding down the Shift key and making multiple selections highlights all the items between the selected item and the one you Shift-click. Holding down the (Command) [Ctrl] key enables you to make noncontiguous selections.

Adding File Fields

Insert the enctype attribute in the <form> tag.

13.15   **Set the Method to POST.**

13.16

File fields enable users to upload files from their hard drives to the Web server location specified in the `action` attribute of the `<form>` tag. The File field looks similar to a text field, but it also contains a Browse button to enable the user to locate a file. The `method` attribute in the `<form>` tag must be set to POST when you include a File field, and you should manually edit the HTML code to insert the `enctype` attribute in the `<form>` tag.

1. Click the red dotted line that is the form outline and set the Method field to POST in the Property inspector.

2. Select Window→Code inspector to display the Code inspector panel and locate the `<form>` tag. Insert the attribute `enctype="multipart/form-data"` in the `<form>` tag (13.15).

3. Position the insertion point inside your form and click the Insert File Field button in the Forms Objects panel (13.16).

4. Enter a name for the File field in the Property inspector and indicate the width of the field, and the maximum number of characters allowed.

Ⓣ I P

Confirm with your server's administrator that anonymous file uploads are allowed before using the File field.

Inserting Hidden Fields

Hidden fields hold static data you don't want the user to see, but do want to send to the handler script along with the user input. This data could be information—such as the URL of the page, a form name, a form version, or an e-mail address— or variable data, such as an e-mail recipient when using a generic handler script.

1. Click the Hidden Field button in the Forms Objects panel. An invisible object on the Web page represents the hidden field. Select View→Visual Aids→Invisible Elements to see the object on the page (13.17).

2. In the Property inspector, assign a name to the hidden field and enter the text you want to send to the handler script in the Value field.

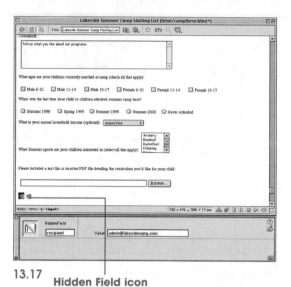

13.17 **Hidden Field icon**

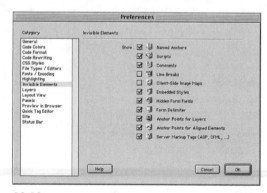

13.18

 **O T E**

If the hidden fields do not appear onscreen, even with invisible elements turned on, select Edit→Preferences, and select Invisible Elements form the Category list. Check the check box for Hidden Form Fields (13.18).

Adding Submit and Reset Buttons

13.19

13.20

You can use three types of buttons in your form. The Submit button sends the form data to the handler script on the Web server. The Reset button resets and empties the form fields. The third type of button is a blank button you can use with behaviors, JavaScript, or other active content scripts. See Chapter 16, "Using Behaviors," for more information on using the blank button.

1. Click the Insert Button button in the Forms Objects panel. The Submit button is inserted by default (13.19).

2. In the Property inspector, assign a name to the button. It's okay to leave the Submit button named Submit.

3. Type the text you want your button to display in the Label field.

4. Click the Action radio button next to Submit Form in the Property inspector.

5. Insert another button and click the Reset Form radio button. Assign a field name and Label (13.20).

(N)O T E

When the user clicks the Submit button, the form data is sent to the handler script you indicated previously in the action *attribute of the* <form> *tag.*

Inserting Graphic Buttons in Forms

Image fields are used in place of the Submit button when you want to use an image to act as the Submit button. You also can use any other image, including Flash buttons, to perform Form operations, such as resetting the form, validating individual fields, or validating the entire form. However, you must use Dreamweaver's behaviors to attach JavaScript functions to images unless you're using an Image field as a Submit button.

1. Click the Image Field button in the Forms Objects panel and locate an image on your hard disk to insert as an Image field (13.21).

2. Using a graphic image as a Reset button is a bit more complicated, requiring you to edit the HTML code and add a bit of JavaScript code. Insert an image using the Insert Image button in the Common Objects panel.

3. With the image still selected, set the link to # in the Property inspector; the # symbol represents a null link. When you insert the # symbol in the Link field, the anchor tag <a href="#"> is inserted in front of the image tag in the HTML code and the closing anchor tag, </A>, is inserted after the image tag in the HTML code.

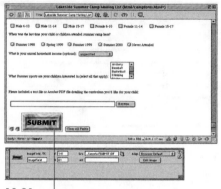

13.21

The Property inspector displays choices for the display of the image, but it does not enable you to specify any links or form properties.

This is the default form name for forms in Dreamweaver. If you gave your form a different name, replace this text with your form name.

The null link makes the image act like a button and inserts the anchor tag around the image.

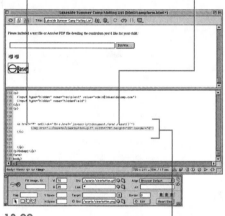

13.22

The code for the image is highlighted when you select the image in the Design view.

4. Select View→Code and Design to split the Document and display both the Design view and Code view. Select the image you are using as a Reset button and the code is highlighted in the Code view (13.22).

5. Edit the anchor tag in the Code view to read as follows:

```
<a href="#"
onClick="this.href='javascript:
document.form1.reset()'">
```

6. Preview your form in a browser to test the Reset button image.

O T E

You can become familiar with JavaScript a little bit at a time by including small commands like the one used for the reset image. You will find this little snippet of JavaScript code and a wide array of developer support at www.irt.org.

I P

A Reset button isn't necessary for most forms and can create problems if you position the Reset button next to the Submit button. Users have been known to accidentally click the Reset button, erasing all the data entered in the form. If you want to include a Reset button, consider placing it at the top of the page or using an image that clearly distinguishes it from the Submit button.

Inserting a Jump Menu

A *jump menu* is a form tool that enables you to create a pop-up menu with choices that link to URLs. You can use the jump menu as a standalone form without including the Submit button.

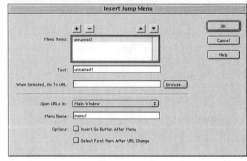

13.23

1. Click the Jump Menu object in the Forms Objects panel to display the Insert Jump Menu dialog box **(13.23)**.

2. Click the plus icon to add menu items and the minus icon to remove menu items. Enter the text you want to appear in the jump menu in the Text field and the URL you want the menu choice to link to in the URL field **(13.24)**.

3. If you're using Frames, select the frame window in which you want the URL to display from the Open URLs In pull-down menu. The default choice is Main Window, which will replace the current browser window contents with the URL.

Click the up/down arrows to rearrange the menu items in the list.

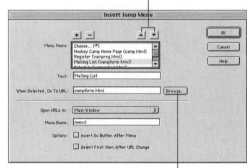

13.24

Click the Browse button to locate a file on your hard drive.

**O T E**

If you include the Go button with the jump menu, the Go button is useful to go only to the item currently selected in the jump menu. If you're somewhat HTML savvy, remove the onchange attribute for the jump menu; then you will be able to make a selection followed by the Go button to jump to a URL.

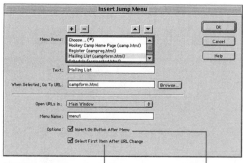

13.25

Check this box to jump back to the first item in the list after a selection is made.

Check this box to insert a Go button to the right of the jump menu.

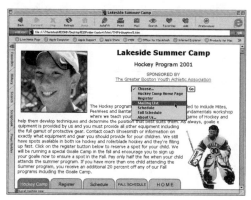

13.26

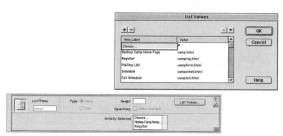

13.27

4. Assign a name to the menu if you want to control the jump menu with JavaScript. The default menu name is inserted here because the jump menu is actually a Form object that can be handled by a remote script **(13.25)**.

5. Preview the Web page in a browser to test the links in your jump menu **(13.26)**.

6. To edit the jump menu, select it in the Document window and click the List Values button in the Property inspector **(13.27)**.

 I P

Include a menu choice at the top of the list, such as Choose or Select. Set the link to #, and check the Select First Item After URL Change check box to always display the first item in the list. You will not need the Go button in this case because the first item will always display and does not link to a URL.

 I P

If you want to include divider lines in your jump menus, insert a string of dashes as one of the list items and set the link to #.

Validating Form Data with Behaviors

The Validate Form behavior enables you to perform a limited amount of form validation before the form is posted to the Web server. This action checks the contents of text fields to ensure that the user has entered the correct type of data. You can attach this action to individual text fields with the onBlur event to validate the fields as the user leaves the field. You also can attach this action to the entire form with the onSubmit event, which validates multiple fields at once when the Submit button is clicked. If you attach the action to the form, any invalid data prevents the form from being submitted until the fields are corrected.

1. Select Window→Behaviors to display the Behaviors panel; then click any text field in your form (13.28).

2. Click the + button in the Behaviors panel and select the Validate Form action to display the Validate Form dialog box (13.29).

3. Select a field from the Named Fields list. If you want to validate only the selected field, click that field in the list. Click the Required check box if the user cannot leave this field empty. Check a radio button to specify the criteria for acceptance of the data. Click OK.

The Last Name field is selected.

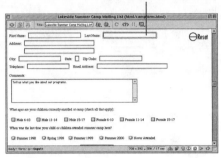

13.28

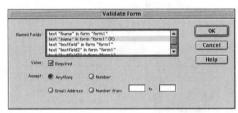

13.29

13.30

The onChange event reports an error only if the content of the field changes and requires the user to type something into the field. The onBlur event occurs whether or not the user has typed in the field and is the best choice when checking for empty fields.

The Tab key was pressed to leave this field empty.

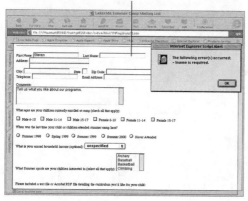

13.31

4. The onBlur event is indicated as the event in the Behaviors panel because you had a single field selected when choosing the Validate Form behavior. You can choose a different event, such as onChange, by clicking the triangle to the right of the event name (13.30).

5. Preview the form in a browser. In this example, when you enter the wrong data in the selected field, an error dialog box appears in the browser when you try to leave the field (13.31).

When you select the entire form, the onSubmit event is used instead of the onBlur event that results when a single field is selected.

The criteria for the Validate Form behavior are specified in parenthesis next to the Form field in the Validate Form dialog box.

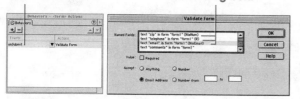

13.32

(N)OTE

To validate multiple fields when the form is submitted, click the <form> tag in the lower-left corner of the Document window before creating the Validate Form action. When the dialog box appears, specify all the validation criteria for all the fields in the list (13.32).

CHAPTER 14

In this chapter, you will learn how to...

Create Custom Style Classes

Redefine HTML Tags

Define CSS Selectors

Set CSS Type Attributes

Set CSS Background Attributes

Set CSS Block Attributes

Set CSS Box Attributes

Set CSS Border Attributes

Set CSS List Attributes

Set CSS Positioning Attributes

Set CSS Extensions Options

Export and Linking Style Sheets

I n Dreamweaver, Cascading Style Sheets are referred to as *CSS Styles*. CSS Styles are a group of formatting attributes that enable you to specify precisely how text and paragraphs are formatted and enable you to specify unique HTML attributes, such as positioning, special effects, and mouse rollovers. CSS Styles can be defined at the top of a Web page in the `<head>` section or in a separate document.

WORKING WITH CASCADING STYLE SHEETS

When the styles are defined in a separate document, they can be applied to multiple Web pages, enabling you to change the formatting of an entire Web site by simply changing the external style sheet document.

In Dreamweaver you use the CSS Styles panel to manage and define styles. Using Cascading Style Sheets, you can redefine the existing HTML tags in a document. You also can create custom styles, called *classes*, which you apply by selecting text and choosing a style in the CSS Styles panel. CSS *Selectors* are a third type of style that enables you to define how links appear, as well as how text appears when a specific combination of tags exists. Each of these is covered in detail in the following pages. Some of the CSS style attributes appear differently in Microsoft Internet Explorer 4.0 and Netscape Navigator 4.0, and some are not currently supported by any browser.

Creating Custom Style Classes

The simplest way to take advantage of styles is by using elements called classes. You can use classes to create multiple instances for a single style or to apply some formatting to an existing HTML tag. Styles and classes can be applied to a selection of text or to an entire paragraph. Styles are created and applied using the Styles panel.

1. Select Window→CSS Styles to display the CSS Styles panel (14.1).

2. Click the New Style button at the bottom of the Styles panel to display the New Style dialog box (14.2).

3. Select Make Custom Style (class) by clicking the radio button; then give a name to this class.

4. Select This Document Only to create the style sheet in the <head> section of the current document (14.3). External style sheets are discussed later in this chapter in the section "Exporting and Linking Style Sheets."

Select style sheet options from the panel's Options menu.

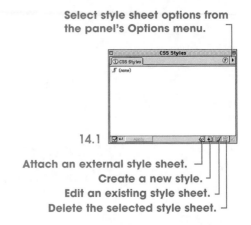

14.1

Attach an external style sheet.
Create a new style.
Edit an existing style sheet.
Delete the selected style sheet.

14.2

Select whether to create an external style sheet or include the styles in the <head> section of this document.

Class names cannot contain any spaces or special characters.

14.3

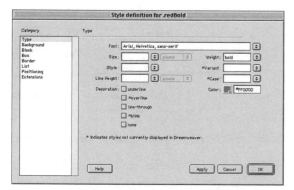

14.4   **Change one or many of the type characteristics. In my example, I am simply changing the typeface, setting the weight to bold and the color of the text to red.**

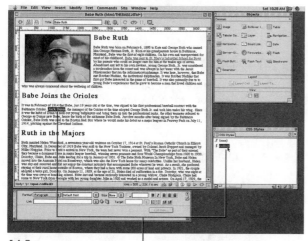

14.5   **Position your cursor within a paragraph and select the class from the CSS Styles panel to apply the class to the entire paragraph.**

5. Click OK to display the Style Definition panel, and then click Type in the Category list to the left. Specify the type settings for your class; then click OK to save the Style class (14.4). The class is displayed in the CSS Styles panel.

6. Click and drag to select some text in the Document window, and then click your style in the CSS Styles panel to format the selected text (14.5). You can apply this class to any text regardless of the HTML tag used to format it.

 I P

Ctrl-click)[Right+click] anywhere in the Document window and select CSS Styles→Edit Style Sheet to edit the styles.

 O T E

Inspect the HTML code to see how the Style class was handled in the <head> section of your document. When the class is applied to a selection of text, the <span> HTML tag is used—for example, <span class= "redBold"> some red text</span>. When the class is applied to an entire paragraph, the class attribute is added to the paragraph tag, such as this: <p class="redBold">. If you apply the class to a heading, the class attribute is added to the heading tag, such as this: <h1 class="redBold">.

Redefining HTML Tags

Styles are commonly used to redefine the standard HTML tags, such as <h1>, <h2>, <body>, and <p>. By redefining the standard HTML tags, you can specify precisely the formatting you want for the tags and include many features that are not available in the standard HTML code. Similar to classes, the styles used to redefine HTML codes are included in the <head> section of the HTML source code between the <style type="text/css"> and </style> tags.

1. Select Window→CSS Styles to display the CSS Styles panel, and then click the New Style button to display the New Style dialog box (14.6). Select Redefine HTML Tag and select an HTML tag from the Tag pop-up menu.

2. Select This Document Only to include the style in the <head> section of this document; then click OK to display the Style Definition panel (14.7).

14.6

Select measurement units from the pop-up menus.

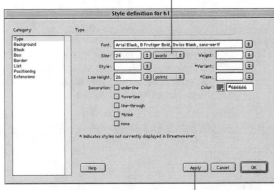

14.7

Click the Apply button at any time to preview your specifications on your Web page in the Document window.

Select a CSS Style from the pop-up menu.   **Browsers that support the selected style**   **Version of Cascading Style Sheets (CSS1 or CSS2)**

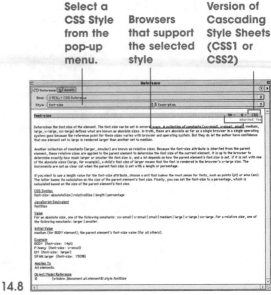

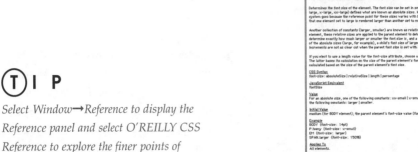

14.8

(T) I P

Select Window→Reference to display the Reference panel and select O'REILLY CSS Reference to explore the finer points of Cascading Style Sheets (14.8).

Notice how the comment tags surround the style definitions. This practice prevents older browsers that do not support CSS from displaying the style codes on the page.

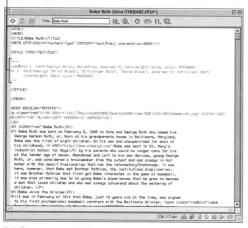

14.9

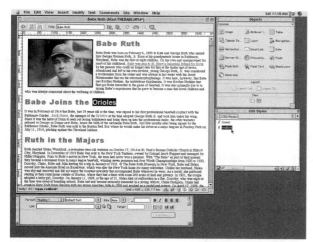

14.10

3. Change type properties as necessary, and then click OK.

4. Inspect the HTML source code to see the code that was added to your Web page at the top of the file in the <head> section (14.9).

 O T E

When you use style sheets to redefine an HTML tag, the style is applied whenever that tag is used within the document. If you make any changes using standard HTML codes, the HTML overrides the attribute in the style sheet. For example, if you define a style that makes all the heading 1 text red, and then select a word and change the color to blue, the blue color overrides the red defined in the style sheet.

 O T E

You also can apply classes to modify the styles you defined for the HTML tags. Select a class from the Styles panel to apply the class to either a selection of text or an entire paragraph of text (14.10). All other formatting described in the style remains; only the attributes specified in the class change.

Defining CSS Selectors

CSS Selectors are referred to as *pseudoclasses* because they are a cross between a custom style and a redefined HTML tag. CSS Selectors affect the anchor tag (<a>) used to create hypertext links. The pop-up menu for Use CSS Selector offers four choices that pertain to the anchor tag and its link colors. You also can use CSS Selectors to create combinations of tags that use the specified style only when the tags are in the indicated sequence.

1. Select Window→CSS Styles to display the CSS Styles panel, and then click the New Style button at the bottom of the CSS Styles panel to display the New Style dialog box.

2. Select Use CSS Selector by clicking its radio button. Select a Selector from the pop-up menu (14.11), or type the tag combination you want to format (14.12).

3. Click the radio button for This Document Only to add the style to the <head> section of the current document; then click OK to display the Style Definition panel (14.13).

 **O T E**

The a:hover choice in the CSS Selector pop-up menu is a CSS Level 2 specification and is supported only by Internet Explorer 4.0 and above for Windows at this writing.

Select the anchor tag attributes you want to format from the pop-up menu.

14.11

Type the sequence of HTML tags you want to format. In this example, the style is applied when text is formatted as bold italic.

14.12

14.13 **Set the Type Decoration for a CSS Selector that defines the a:link, a:hover, a:active, or a:visited anchor tag attribute to None to eliminate the underline from your hypertext links.**

This hypertext link was formatted with a CSS Selector that changed the color and font. The None text decoration was included to eliminate the underline.

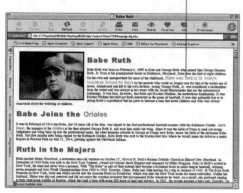

14.14

14.15   The formatting applied to the style is displayed when you highlight a style.

4. When the Style definition panel appears, specify the text formatting for your CSS Selector and click OK.

5. Select some text and format the text using the HTML sequence you defined in the CSS Selector. If you defined any of the anchor tag attributes, such as a:link, preview the page in a browser to see the effect (14.14).

 O T E

To edit existing styles, click the Edit Style Sheet button (to the left of the trash can icon) at the bottom of the CSS Styles panel to display the Edit Style Sheet dialog box (14.15). Select a style and click the Edit button to modify the style attributes.

 I P

The order of the HTML tags makes a difference when you are defining a pseudoclass with the CSS Selector. If, for example, the italic tag (<i>) precedes the bold tag (<b>) in the HTML source code, but you define the bold tag to precede the italic tag in the CSS Selector, the style then has no effect on the text.

Setting CSS Type Attributes

When you define a style—whether it's a class, HTML tag redefine, or CSS Selector—the left side of the Style Definition panel lists eight categories. Click the Type category to specify the CSS type attributes (14.16). Asterisks identify the options that do not display in the Dreamweaver Document window but do display in Web browsers. (Table 14.1) describes the attributes available in the Type category.

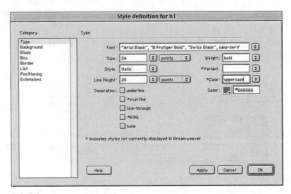

14.16

Table 14.1   CSS Type Attributes

Attribute	Description
Font	Choose from the pop-up menu to select some predefined font groups, or enter a font name. You can enter a number of fonts separated by commas to increase the likelihood of an end user having the desired installed font.
Size	You can choose relative sizes, such as small, medium, and large, from the Size pop-up menu, or enter a numeric value. When you enter a numeric value, you can select the measurement units from the pop-up menu (points is the default, although pixels produces more consistent results between Macintosh and Windows platforms).
Style	Indicate one of three type styles—normal, oblique, or italic. Oblique is used to slant a typeface when an italic face is not available.
Line Height	Line height is the space between the lines of text, typically referred to as *leading*. The line height is measured from the descenders of the previous line to the descenders of the current line.
Decoration	Decorations include additional text formatting, such as underline, overline, line-through, blink, and none. Blink is supported by Netscape browsers only.
Weight	Weight can be specified as a relative value, such as light, bold, bolder, and boldest. The numeric values represent intensities of boldness, with normal text being about 400 and bold text about 700.
Variant	Variant is used to indicate small caps. *Small caps* are smaller capital letters used in place of the lowercase letters. The small caps option is not wholly supported by Netscape or Explorer at this writing.
Case	Changes text to uppercase, lowercase, or capitalized (initial caps).
Color	Specify the color of the text here. Click the color swatch to select a color from the browser-safe color panel or use any of your system's color panels. You also can type a color name in the color field, such as "aquamarine."

Setting CSS Background Attributes

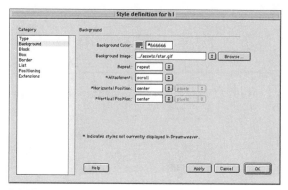

14.17

Click the Background category in the Style definition panel to specify the CSS background attributes **(14.17)**. Ordinarily, you can specify only a single background image and background color for your Web page using HTML tags. The background attributes for styles enable you to set a background image and background color for virtually any HTML element on your page. You also can control the way a background image repeats. Be sure to check your Web page in multiple browsers because the background attributes are not completely supported by all browsers at this writing. Asterisks appear next to options that do not display in the Dreamweaver Document window but do display in Web browsers. **(Table 14.2)** describes each of the available attributes in the Background category.

Table 14.2   CSS Background Attributes

Attribute	Description
Background Color	Click the color swatch to select a background color from the Web-safe color panel or from a panel available on your system. You also can enter a color name, such as "tan," in the Background Color field.
Background Image	Indicate a background image by typing the URL in the field or by clicking the Choose button. Keep in mind that you are setting a background image only for the tag you are defining.
Repeat	Controls the tiling of the background image. Select No-Repeat to display only one instance of the background image. Select Repeat to tile the background image both horizontally and vertically. Select Repeat-X to tile the background image horizontally only. Select Repeat-Y to tile the background image vertically only.
Attachment	Select fixed to keep the background image in place when scrolling the Web page window. Choose scroll if you want the background image to scroll with the Web page.
Horizontal Positioning	Controls how the background image is positioned from left to right on the Web page or between any other elements before and after the styled text.
Vertical Positioning	Controls how the background image is positioned vertically relative to the elements above and below the styled text.

Setting CSS Block Attributes

Use the Block attributes to control things such as word and letter spacing, vertical and horizontal text alignment, and indents (14.18). Asterisks appear next to options that do not display in the Dreamweaver Document window but do display in Web browsers. (Table 14.3) describes each of the available attributes in the Block category of the Style definition panel.

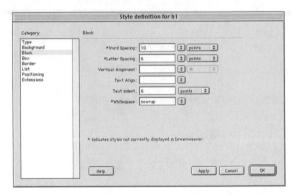

14.18

Table 14.3 CSS Block Attributes

Attribute	Description
Word Spacing	Use positive or negative values to increase or decrease the spacing between words (14.19).
Letter Spacing	Use positive or negative values here to increase or decrease the spacing between the letters of each word (14.19).
Vertical Alignment	Select from baseline, sub, super, top, text-top, middle, bottom, and text-bottom, or indicate a value of your own.
Text Align	Set the text alignment to left, right, center, or justified.
Text Indent	Indents the first line of text by the amount you specify. The browser ignores these indents when text wraps around an image. In Figure 14.15, each paragraph of text has a custom class assigned that indents the first line of text 12 points.
Whitespace	Specify how you want additional spaces to be handled. The default is to collapse all extra spaces into a single space. If you select Pre, the extra space is treated the same way the `<pre>` tag treats it, enabling multiple spaces in a row. The Nowrap option causes your text to stay on a single line and extend beyond the browser window dimensions if necessary. Use the break tag (` `) to manually break lines of text when the Nowrap option is used.

The block attributes in the Style definition panel affect word and letter spacing.

14.19

Setting CSS Box Attributes

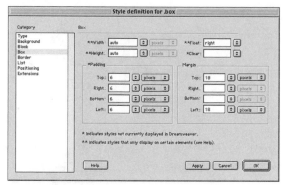

14.20

14.21

The Box attributes in the Style definition panel of Dreamweaver are used primarily for images and control the placement and spacing of the stylized elements (14.20). Many of these attributes emulate the way tables handle alignment and spacing. Some specific rules exist about when you can see these attributes in the Dreamweaver Document window and when you can't. The Float and Clear attributes, for example, only display in the Document window when used on an image. The Margin attributes preview correctly when applied to block elements, such as the <p> tag and heading tags (<h1> through <h6>). (Table 14.4) describes each of the available attributes in the Box category.

Table 14.4   CSS Box Attributes

Attribute	Description
Width	Determines the width of the element being defined. Select Auto if you're not sure of the size of the image or element.
Height	Determines the height of the element being defined. Select Auto if you're not sure of the size of the image or element.
Float	Aligns the element on either the right or left side of the Web page. Any text next to the element wraps around it (14.21).
Clear	When using layers, it determines on which side of the element layers are not allowed. When a layer is encountered, the element with the clear attribute is placed below the layer.
Margin	Determines the amount of space between the element and any surrounding elements. Similar to the vspace and hspace attributes for images, you can control the amount of space separately on each side of the element. 18 pixels of space is indicated for the top and left side of the image (14.21).
Padding	Controls the amount of space between the element and its border when a border is specified. The gray space around the picture in Figure 14.21 depicts a padding value of 6 pixels on all sides.

Setting CSS Border Attributes

You can specify eight styles of borders to surround text, images, or other elements (such as Java applets and Shockwave images). You also can specify a thickness and color for each side of the bordered box (14.22). Asterisks appear next to all the border options, indicating that you must preview the page in your browser to see the effect of the borders. Be forewarned that borders display quite differently in the two major browsers. (Table 14.5) describes each of the available attributes in the Border category of the Style definition panel.

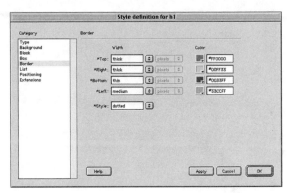

14.22

Table 14.5   CSS Border Attributes

Attribute	Description
Top	Indicate the width and color of the border along the top of the element.
Right	Indicate the width and color of the border along the right side of the element.
Bottom	Indicate the width and color of the border along the bottom of the element.
Left	Indicate the width and color of the border along the left side of the element.
Style	Indicate the kind of border you want to use around your element by selecting it from the pop-up menu. Select from dotted, dashed, solid, double, groove, ridge, inset, and outset. Compare the way Internet Explorer handles the border styles as opposed to Netscape Communicator (14.23).

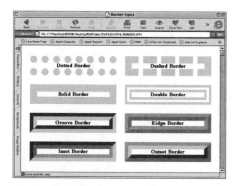

Internet Explorer 5.5 (Mac)

Netscape Communicator 6.0 (Mac)

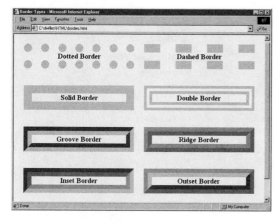

Internet Explorer 5.5 (Windows)

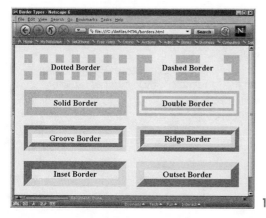

Netscape Communicator 6.0 (Windows)

14.23

 I P

Border attributes specified with CSS do not display in Dreamweaver's Document window. You must preview the page in a browser to see the result of a specified border.

 I P

You can use the Border attributes to create a box around some text. Specify a padding value in the Box category of the Style definitions panel to inset the text from the border.

Setting CSS List Attributes

The CSS List attributes specify the formatting features for ordered and unordered lists. You can specify the order of a list as well as the type of bullet used for bulleted lists (14.24). You can even specify a graphic image to be used as a bullet in place of the standard disc, circle, or square (14.25). List attributes do not show up in Dreamweaver's Document window. See (Table 14.6) for specifics about the various list options.

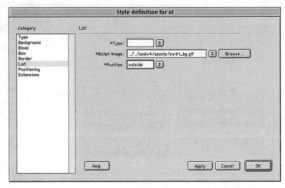

14.24

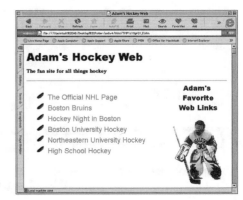

14.25

Table 14.6   CSS List Attributes

Attribute	Description
Type	Select from disc, circle, square, decimal, lowercase roman, uppercase roman, lowercase alpha, and uppercase alpha to specify the list type.
Bullet Image	To use an image in the place of bullets as depicted in Figure 14.25, click the Browse button and locate an image. Bullet images appear on the Macintosh only in Internet Explorer.
Position	Specify whether the list items wrap to the indent of the bullet (default) or to the left margin. Select Inside to include the bullet inside the paragraph of text or select Outside to hang the bullet outside the text.

Setting CSS Positioning Attributes

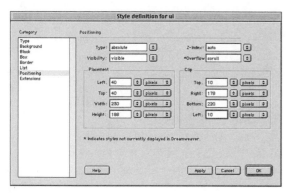

14.26

The CSS Positioning attributes control the position on the page of an element using layers (14.26). See Chapter 15, "Creating Layers," for information on working with layers. If you specify a style that contains positioning information for an element on your Web page, a layer is automatically created for it if it's not already on a layer. The CSS Positioning attributes are detailed in (Table 14.7).

Table 14.7   CSS Positioning Attributes

Attribute	Description
Type	Choose whether the element is to be positioned absolutely or relatively on the page. Select Static to prevent the element from being repositioned.
Visibility	Specify whether the element is visible, is hidden, or inherits the properties of its parent.
Z-Index	Specify the depth of a layer with higher values closer to the top.
Overflow	Indicates how an element is displayed when it is larger than the dimensions of the layer. Select Clip to clip the element to the dimensions of the layer. Select None to display the element regardless of the layer dimensions. Select Scroll to insert scrollbars when the element is larger than the layer.
Placement	Indicate the position of the element by specifying the left and top attributes. Indicate the width and height of the element using the same attributes.
Clip	Clips the element within the layer based on the left, top, width, and height attributes.

Setting CSS Extensions Options

Many of the CSS Extensions options are advanced settings included in CSS2 that are not yet wholly supported by browsers. Use the Extensions category of the Style Definition panel to indicate page breaks for printing, cursor type displayed, and special effects filters (14.27). (Table 14.8) contains the general settings for the CSS Extensions, whereas (Table 14.9) contains specifics about the available filters.

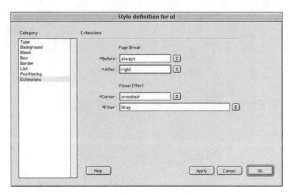

14.27

Sixteen special effects currently are available in the pop-up menu for Filter. The Extension style attributes control features that are not supported by most browsers at this writing. (Table 14.9) contains some specifics about what to enter for the argument values.

Table 14.8 CSS Extensions Attributes

Attribute	Description
Pagebreak	Inserts a page break at a specific point on the Web page when the page is printed.
Cursor	This feature enables you to select from a pop-up list of display cursors. Choices such as E-resize, Ne-resize, and W-resize refer to points on the compass and display arrows pointing in those directions.
Filter	Special effects filters available in the pop-up menu currently are supported by Explorer 4 and later for Windows. At this writing, no support exists for Netscape browsers or Macintosh browsers.

Table 14.9   CSS Filters

Filter	Description and Arguments
Alpha	Controls the opacity value of an image and enables you to specify a blend type. The Opacity value is a value from 0 (transparent) to 100 (opaque). The style values represent the type blend for the image: 0 for uniform, 1 for linear, 2 for radial, and 3 for rectangular.
BlendTrans	Creates a blend transition that makes an image fade in or out over a specified interval of time. Specify a time value in the form seconds.milliseconds.
Blur	Creates a motion blur effect. Specify an integer value other than 0 for Add. Direction is indicated as degrees in increments of 45, with a maximum value of 315. Strength is a positive integer that controls the number of pixels to affect.
Chroma	Indicates transparency for a specific color in an image. The color value must be specified in hexadecimal format (#rrggbb).
DropShadow	Creates a drop shadow for both images and text. Indicate the color value in hexadecimal format. Indicate the x and y offsets using pixel values or OffX and OffY. Set the Positive value to 1 to create a shadow for nontransparent pixels, or set it to 0 to affect the transparent pixels.
FlipH	Flips an image or text horizontally.
FlipV	Flips an image or text vertically.
Glow	Creates a background glow effect for selected text or images. Specify a hexadecimal value for Color and a value between 0 and 100 for Strength.
Gray	Converts color images to grayscale.
Invert	Creates an inverse of a color image.
Light	A spotlight type effect that is used to cast light on areas of an image.
Mask	All the transparent pixels in an image change to the specified color and all other pixels are converted to the background color. Specify a hexadecimal value for Color.
RevealTrans	A transition effect that reveals the image using one of 23 transition types. Indicate a Duration value in seconds.milliseconds. At this writing, further information on the 23 style choices is not available.
Shadow	Creates a shadow effect for text or images. Specify the Color value in hexadecimal format. Indicate a direction by degree with values 0–315 in increments of 45.
Wave	Creates a waveform distortion for images and text. Set the Add value to 1 to combine the original image with the wave effect, and set Add to 0 to display only the wave effect. Indicate the number of waves desired as the Frequency value. Indicate a percentage value for LightStrength. The Phase value controls the angle of the waves using values 0–360. The intensity of the wave is control by the Strength value.
Xray	Converts a color image to grayscale and inverts it to create a X-ray effect.

Exporting and Linking Style Sheets

When you create new styles using the CSS Styles panel, you have the option of creating the styles in the current document or in an external style sheet file. External style sheets enable you to use the same Cascading Style Sheets for multiple Web pages and are saved with a .css file extension. A Web page can be linked to one or more external style sheets.

14.28

External style sheets on the current site appear in the pop-up menu.

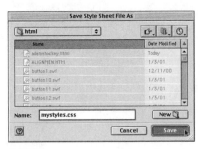

14.29

1. Click the New Style button at the bottom of the CSS Styles panel to display the New Style dialog box.

2. Select an existing external style sheet file from the pop-up menu or select New Style Sheet File to define a new external style sheet (14.28).

3. If you are creating a new external style sheet, click OK and assign a name with the .css extension to your external style sheet file (14.29). If you are adding a new style to an existing style sheet file, click OK and continue defining the new style.

Internal styles in the <head> section of the current document

Styles from the linked external style sheet file

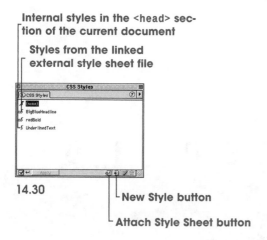

14.30

New Style button

Attach Style Sheet button

4. To attach an external style sheet to the current Web page, click the Attach Style Sheet button at the bottom of the CSS Styles panel and locate the `.css` file on your site. You can tell the difference between the internal and external styles because they have different icons in the CSS Styles panel (14.30).

 O T E

When you attach an external style sheet to your document, the `<link rel="stylesheet" href="mystyles.css" type="text/css">` tag is added to the `<head>` section of your document. Any internal styles you specify will override external styles with the same names. If you attach more than one external style sheet, subsequent external style sheets will override previous external style sheets if they have the same style names within.

 I P

You also can link to external style sheets in the Edit Style Sheet dialog box. Click the Edit Style Sheet button at the bottom of the CSS Styles panel to open the Edit Style Sheet dialog box; then click the Link button.

CHAPTER 15

In this chapter, you will learn how to...

Draw Layers

Set Layer Defaults

Set the Position and Visibility of Layers

Set Background and Clipping Properties for Layers

Nest Layers

Nest Existing Layers

Use Styles with Layers

Align Layers with the Grid and Rulers

Use a Tracing Image

Convert Layers to Tables

Convert Tables to Layers

Layers are part of the CSS specification and are one component of what is known as *Dynamic HTML (DHTML)*, along with Cascading Style Sheets (CSS), VBScript, and JavaScript. DHTML is a blanket term used to describe all the nifty things you can do with CSS, JavaScript, layers, and so on. With CSS you can precisely position elements on your Web page using x and y coordinates, which often is referred to as *CSS-P* (Cascading Style

CREATING LAYERS

Sheet-Positioning). With JavaScript and VBScript for Internet Explorer, you can move elements around on your Web page; that's where the dynamic part comes in. Layers enable you to create containers to hold pretty much anything you would put on a regular Web page, such as images, tables, text, and even plugin features. Aside from the x and y coordinates used to position elements on your Web page, layers have an additional dimension called the *z-index*, which determines an object's location above or below other objects. As with most of the features in Dreamweaver, you use the Objects panel, Layers panel, and Property inspector to create and edit layers.

Layers are not supported by version 3 browsers and earlier. Dreamweaver provides a choice in the File menu to convert files to make them compatible with version 3 browsers. This option converts layers to tables as long as no layers are overlapping or extending off the page. So if you want to use layers but still provide support for version 3 browser users, you can create two pages: one with layers and one with tables.

Drawing Layers

Layers are simply boxes that can hold almost any element you find on a typical Web page. The Layers panel is used to manipulate the layers, make them visible and invisible, and control the z-index position of the layers. Making a layer invisible enables you to turn off the layers you're not currently using, making maneuvering in Dreamweaver easier. You also can use Dreamweaver behaviors to script the appearance or disappearance of layers, so any layers set to invisible when you save the document are initially invisible in the browser as well.

1. Select Window→Objects to display the Objects panel if it is not already onscreen, and then select Common from the Objects panel menu. To select the Layer object, click it once in the Objects panel.

2. Click and drag in the Document window to create a layer (15.1). When the layer is selected, eight anchor points are displayed; you can use them to resize the layer (15.2).

3. Create content for the layer in the same way you would for standard HTML documents. The layer resizes to accommodate any text or image you insert that is larger than the original size of the layer.

The Layer icon is displayed on your page when invisibles are turned on to indicate where in the HTML source code the layer code appears.

Click the Selection tab or anywhere along the top and left borders to select the layer. Click and drag to move the layer.

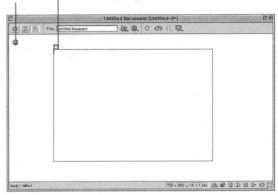

15.1

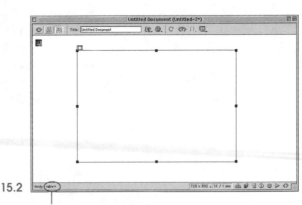

15.2

This layer is defined with the <div> tag. You can click here to select the layer as well.

15.3

Double-click a layer name to edit the name. Click a z-index value once to change it.

15.4

4. Select View→Visual Aids→Layer Borders to show and hide the layer borders **(15.3)**.

5. Preview the Web page in a browser to see how the layers appear without apparent borders **(15.4)**.

I P

To make a layer fit to an image, reduce the size of the layer until it is smaller than the image it contains. The edges of the layer will snap to the edges of the image.

O T E

When specifying a z-index value, the highest values position objects above objects with lower values. For example, a z-index of 3 positions an object above another object with a z-index of 1. Dreamweaver automatically names layers Layer 1, Layer 2, and so on, and assigns appropriate z-index values. These layers can be renamed and a z-index value specified for the layer that determines its position above or below other layers.

I P

Dreamweaver automatically renumbers the z-index values for layers when you rearrange the layers in the Layers panel. The z-index values do not have to be sequential.

Setting Layer Defaults

The Layer defaults determine the size of the layer when you use the Insert→Layer menu command to add a layer to a document. You can specify some default attributes for layers in the Preferences dialog box, which is also where you specify the default HTML tags to use for layers. In the HTML source code, layers are designated using either the <div>...</div> or ... opening and closing tags. The method you use depends on the browser and platform for which you are developing your Web pages. The <div> tag offers the widest support among browsers on all platforms.

1. Select Edit→Preferences to display the Preferences dialog box, and then select Layers from the Category list (15.5).

2. Select the HTML tag you want to use for layers from the Tag pull-down menu.

3. Select a default Visibility from the corresponding pull-down menu (Table 15.1). Most browsers use the Inherit option as their default, which is also the default visibility in Dreamweaver.

 I   P

If you have the Nest When Created Within a Layer option checked, take care not to drag a layer directly onto another layer in the Layers panel because doing so creates a nested layer.

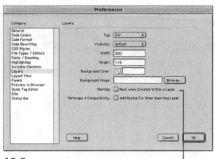

15.5

The Nesting preference determines whether creating a layer within another layer nests the new layer inside the underlying layer.

Table 15.1   Visibility Options

Option	Description
Inherit	Inherits the visibility from the parent layer, which enables you to hide multiple layers by changing the visibility of the parent layer.
Visible	Displays the layer and all its contents.
Hidden	Makes the layer and its content invisible.

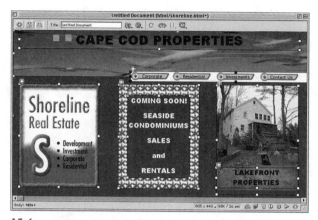

15.6   **You can specify background colors and background images for your layers.**

4. Specify a width and height for the default layer. These values are used when you select Insert→Layer to add layers. The default value is 200 pixels wide by 115 pixels high.

5. You can specify a background color for all layers. Click the color swatch to select a color or enter the color value in the Background Color field. Optionally, include a background image by entering the URL for the image in the Background Image field or by clicking the Choose button and locating an image **(15.6)**.

(T) I P

If the Nest When Created Within a Layer option is unchecked, you can nest layers by holding down the (Command) [Ctrl] key.

(N) O T E

Dreamweaver supports Netscape's <layer> and <ilayer> tags to create layers. The cool thing about using these tags is that you can import another HTML document into the layer, which makes changing the content of the layer from time to time easier. The <layer> tag is used for absolute position, whereas the <ilayer> tag is used for relative positioning. Because only Netscape browsers support these tags, you should use the <div> or <span> tags unless you're creating an intranet in which everyone is using Netscape browsers.

Setting the Position and Visibility of Layers

The layer properties are set from the Property inspector and, to some extent, the Layers panel. Many of the layer properties also can be manipulated by using JavaScript or VBScript, if you're game. Display the Property inspector and Layers panel to edit your layer **(15.7)**. Using the Property inspector, you can control the precise position of layers and make the layers visible or invisible.

1. Rename a layer with a name more meaningful than Layer 1, Layer 2, and so on, by entering a new name in the Layer ID box of the Property inspector. Stick with names that begin with a letter and do not contain any odd characters. Numbers can be used, except as the first character in the name.

2. Enter L and T values in the Property inspector to indicate the layer's position from the left and top of the parent layer when nested or from the Document window when the layer is not nested. Enter the W and H values for the width and height of the layer, respectively **(15.8)**.

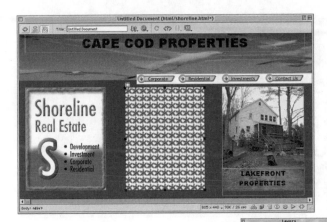

15.7

When a layer is selected, it is highlighted in the Layers panel and formatted with the Property inspector.

15.8

A) 291 pixels from the left (L)

B) 143 pixels from the top (T)

C) 218 pixels wide (W)

D) 276 pixels high (H)

E) 24 pixels from the left edge of parent layer (L)

F) 27 pixels from the top edge of parent layer (T)

15.9

When the eye is open the layer is visible, and when the eye is closed the layer is hidden. When the eye is not present next to a layer, it is visible because that is the default option in most browsers.

Click the eye at the top of the visibility column to set the visibility of all the layers at once.

15.10

3. Enter an integer value in the Z-Index field of the Property inspector. The z-index for a layer determines its place above or below other layers. Layers with higher numbers are placed above layers with lower numbers. You also can click the z-index value in the Layers panel to change the value, or simply drag the layers up and down in the Layers panel to reorganize them.

4. Set the visibility of the layer by selecting an option from the Vis pull-down menu in the Property inspector. Select Invisible to initially hide the layer or to hide the layer temporarily while you're working on the page in Dreamweaver (15.9). Choose Visible to always display the layer (15.10). Choose Inherit to inherit the visibility of the parent layer.

 I P

You can specify the measurements for L, T, W, and H in pixels, centimeters, millimeters, inches, points, percentage, or picas. The default measurement unit is pixels. Enter the values without spaces between the number and the measurement unit designation. Use px for pixels, cm for centimeters, mm for millimeters, in for inches, pt for points, % for percentage, and pc for picas.

Setting Background and Clipping Properties for Layers

Layers can contain a background color, background image, or both. When you specify a background image, the image tiles unless it is the same size as or larger than the layer. When the image is larger than the layer, it is displayed from the upper-left corner and clipped on the right and bottom. You can use the clip attributes to crop the contents of a layer, revealing the background color or background image.

1. Select a background image or background color for your layer in the Bg Image or Bg Color field of the Property inspector **(15.11)**.

2. Specify the HTML tags to use for the layer. `<div>` is the most dependable method, although you can mix the `<div>` and `<span>` tags if necessary.

3. Set the Overflow option controls to determine what happens when the content of a layer is wider or longer than its dimensions.

4. Enter values in the Clip field of the Property inspector to crop images in the layer. Specify how far from the left and top of the layer you want to crop the image by entering the L and T values, respectively. Indicate how far from the right and bottom you want to crop the layer in the R and B fields, respectively **(15.12)**.

Layer with a background color

15.11 **Nested layer with no background**

Table 15.2 Layer Overflow Options

Option	Description
Auto	Leaves it up to the browsers, which in most cases hides the overflow content.
Hidden	Crops the content at the size of the layer.
Scroll	Displays scrollbars in browsers that support this option.
Visible	Ignores the layer dimensions and resizes the layer to accommodate the content.

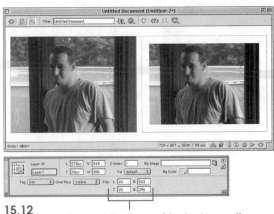

15.12 **To crop the layer 20 pixels on all sides, enter 20 as the Clip L and T values. Subtract 20 from the layer's W and H values to arrive at the Clip R and B values, respectively.**

Nesting Layers

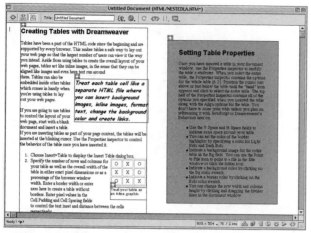

15.13

By nesting layers, you can enclose multiple layers in one parent layer and manipulate the layers as a group or individually. Nested layers also can be useful when you want to include a photograph with a caption that is wrapped into text or perhaps include a graph with a caption. Although you can't automatically wrap text around a layer, you can manually break lines to give the appearance of a runaround (15.13).

1. Create the parent layer by clicking and dragging in the Document window with the Layer object.

2. Click inside the layer to place the insertion point (blinking cursor) within the layer.

3. Create a second layer inside the first layer. The Layers inspector displays nested layers indented under the parent layer (15.14).

If you check the Prevent Overlaps check box in the Layers panel, nesting is disabled, as is overlapping of layers. If you nest or overlap layers before checking the Prevent Overlaps box, you must move the layers for this setting to take effect.

15.14

(T) I P

When drawing the nested layer, you might have to hold down the (Command) [Ctrl] key for the layers to be nested. Check the Nesting check box in the Layers Preferences to enable automatic nesting within layers.

Nesting Existing Layers

You can nest layers, even if they are already created and currently unnested. Use the Layers panel to nest and unnest layers.

1. In the Layers inspector, hold down the (Command) [Ctrl] key and drag the name of a layer on top of the name of the parent layer. The layer appears indented under the parent layer **(15.15)**.

2. To unnest layers, click and drag the layer's name in the Layers panel to the left so the name is no longer under the parent layer.

3. You can nest layers within nested layers. Hold down the (Command)[Ctrl] key and drag the name of a layer on top of the name of a nested layer. The parent layer now has two levels of nesting **(15.16)**.

 I P

Give your layers names that make sense to you, and simply click the layer name in the Layers inspector to select the layer.

 I P

Click and drag layers in the Layers panel to reorder them. You must set the z-index value for each layer to determine its position over other layers in the browser. Moving the layers around in the Layers panel automatically updates the z-index value.

Two unnested layers

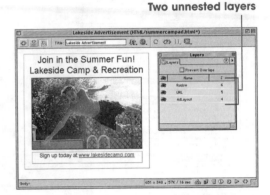

Two nested layers

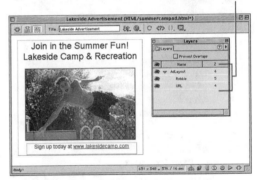

15.15

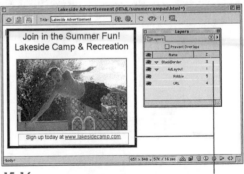

15.16

An empty layer with the background color set to black is the parent for the AdLayout layer, which has two children of its own.

Using Styles with Layers

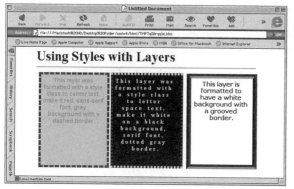

15.17

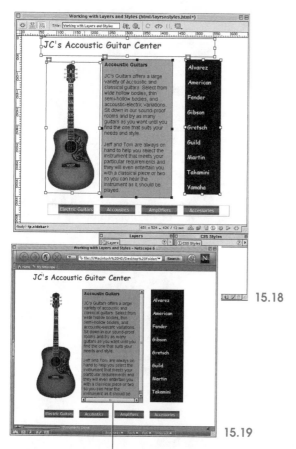

 15.18

15.19

Attributes such as the overflow scroll-bars do not appear in Dreamweaver.

Because layers use the `<span>`, `<div>`, `<layer>`, or `<ilayer>` tag to define the layer, you can use styles to redefine these tags—the same way you would redefine any other HTML tag. The positioning properties in styles are specifically for layers, but you also can define all the other style attributes, such as font, border, and background. Additionally, you can create a Style class that you can apply by selecting the layer and then clicking the class in the Styles inspector. See Chapter 14, "Working with Cascading Style Sheets," for information on how to create styles. In this example, the three layers have been formatted by creating Style classes (15.17).

(N) O T E

Cascading Style Sheets can come in handy when you want to specify formatting for layers in which the content dynamically changes based on some JavaScript function, such as Dreamweaver's Set Text of Layer behavior. You also can use styles with layers when you have multiple pages that follow a design that is generic but not consistent enough to merit using templates. You create Cascading Style Sheet classes with text formatting and positioning attributes, and then apply the styles directly to the layers (15.18). You must go back and forth between Dreamweaver and a Web browser because many of the style attributes do not appear in Dreamweaver at this time (15.19).

Aligning Layers with the Grid and Rulers

Dreamweaver's grid and rulers can be helpful in creating and aligning layers. The grid starts in the upper-left corner of the page and displays light blue grid lines spaced 50 pixels apart by default. The rulers display pixel values by default but can be changed to display inches or cen-timeters. The origin of the ruler also can be modified to aid in alignment and measuring spaces on your page.

Click and drag in the upper-left corner, where the two rulers intersect, to change the origin of the rulers.

You can turn the grid on and off here.

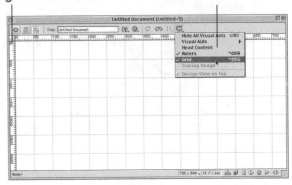

15.20

1. Choose View→Rulers→Show or press (Command-Option-R) [Ctrl+Alt+R] to display the rulers along the top and left of the document window.

2. Select View→Grid→Show to display the grid (15.20).

3. Select View→Grid→Snap To Grid to automatically snap objects to the grid lines when you get close to them.

4. Select View→Grid→Edit to dis-play the Grid Settings dialog box. Customize the grid spac-ing, color, display, and snap distance (15.21).

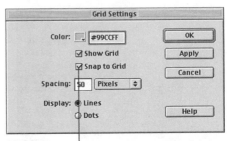

15.21

Snapping occurs even if the grid is not visible, but only if Snap to Grid is checked here.

T I **P**

Double-click the upper-left corner where the two rulers intersect to reset the ruler's ori-gin to the upper-left corner of the page.

15.22

5. Use layers to position elements on the grid **(15.22)**.

6. If you want to align layers, select the layers you want to align and select Modify→Align; then select an alignment option (Top, Left, Right, or Bottom) **(15.23)**.

15.23

Hold down the Shift key and click to select multiple layers. The last layer you select is the anchor layer for the alignment.

(N) O T E

Select more than one layer, and then select Modify→Align→Make Same Width to make all the selected layers the same width as the widest layer. Select Modify→Align→Make Same Height to make the selected layers the same height as the tallest layer.

(T) I P

If you used previous versions of Dreamweaver, you might have noticed that the grid always aligned with the margin of the page instead of the absolute upper-left corner. In Dreamweaver 4, however, the grid now aligns with the 0 point on the ruler in the upper-left corner.

Using a Tracing Image

The tracing image enables you to use a page mock-up as a basis for creating the Web page. For example, graphic artists can use a program such as Photoshop to create a bitmap image that depicts the desired design of a Web page, and the Web page developer can then use the image as a tracing image to position elements on the page using layers. You can display the tracing image at any level of transparency and can position the image anywhere on the page. The tracing image does not show up on your Web page and cannot be inadvertently selected by clicking. After you use layers to position the elements according to the tracing image, you can convert the layers to a table to support users with older browsers.

1. Select Modify→Page Properties to display the Page Properties dialog box **(15.24)**, and then click the Browse button to the right of the Tracing Image field to open a tracing image **(15.25)**. The tracing image should be in GIF, PNG, or JPEG format.

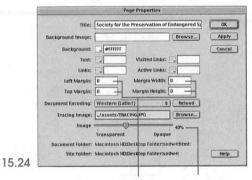

15.24

Set the Margin values to 0 if you want the tracing image to line up with the upper-left corner of the browser window.

An opacity of 40%–50% works best for most tracing images.

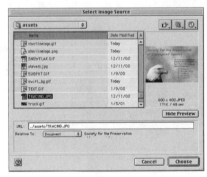

15.25

T I **P**

You also can load a tracing image by choosing View→Tracing Image→Load.

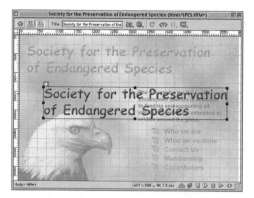

15.26

If you are using a background image, insert it after the page is designed with a tracing image.

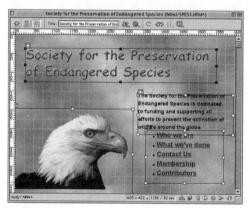

15.27

15.28

2. When you click OK, the tracing image appears in the Document window behind any objects already on the page **(15.26)**.

3. Draw layers to create the various elements necessary to re-create the tracing image **(15.27)**.

 O T E

Select View→Tracing Image→Adjust Position to change the x and y positions of the upper-left corner of the tracing image **(15.28)**. *You also can align the tracing image with an object that is selected by choosing View→Tracing Image→Align with Selection.*

 I P

Macromedia's Fireworks image editor enables you to save images in slices as GIF files, which you can then use as tracing images to re-create a designer's concept.

Converting Layers to Tables

To offer the widest support for the various browser versions currently in use, you can convert a page created using layers into a table layout. Because only version 4 and later browsers support layers, converting your layers to tables makes sense when you want to offer alternative Web pages.

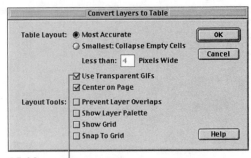

15.29

When you turn on Use Transparent GIFs, you are unable to reduce the size of a column by dragging the columns.

1. Save your page with the layers intact so you can edit the page at a later date.

2. Select Modify→Convert→Layers to Table to display the Convert Layers to Table dialog box (15.29).

3. Select the Table Layout options (Table 15.2) and click OK to convert the layers to a table (15.30).

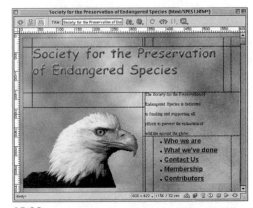

15.30

Table 15.3 Convert Layers to Table Options

Option	Description
Most Accurate	Creates a table cell for every layer as well as for any empty space between the layers.
Smallest: Collapse Empty Cells	Aligns the layer edges, if they fall within the specified number of pixels, and results in a table with fewer empty cells.
Use Transparent GIFs	Ensures that the table is displayed the same in all browsers by filling the last row of the table with transparent GIFs to prevent the columns from resizing.
Center on Page	Centers the resulting table from left to right in the browser window.
Layout Tools	The layout tools actually have no effect on your table and merely turn on the features used to edit layers.

Converting Tables to Layers

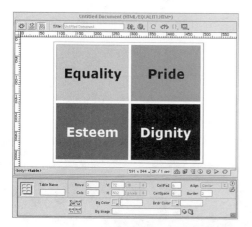

15.31

Converting the table to layers enables you to separate and move the boxes, or perhaps to use behaviors to make each box appear and disappear at given intervals.

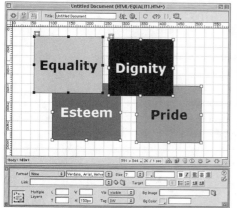

15.32

If you select more than one layer, you can move the selected layers as a group. You also can cut and paste layers, even nested layers.

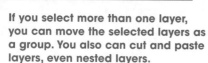

You might have some Web pages you created with tables that you now want to manipulate with layers, or you might simply have some table data that you want to move around freely. Because you can use behaviors and the timeline to animate and manipulate layers, converting a table to layers enables you to control and animate the table cell contents.

1. Save your tables file so you have a version to return to if you need to make changes within the tables.

2. Select Modify→Convert→ Tables to Layers to display the Convert Tables to Layers dialog box (**15.31**).

3. Check the boxes in the Convert Tables to Layers dialog box for the options you want turned on after the table is converted to layers.

4. Click OK to convert the table to layers. You can now freely move the layers in the Document window and arrange the layers in the Layers panel (**15.32**).

 I P

To show or hide the layer borders, select View→Visual Aids→Layer Borders. If you turn off the layer borders, the borders appear only when the layer is selected.

CHAPTER 16

In this chapter, you will learn how to...

Attach Behaviors and Use the Call JavaScript Behavior and the Change Property Behavior

Use Behaviors to Check Browser Type and Version

Check for Plugins Using Behaviors

Control Shockwave and Flash Playback with Behaviors

Control Sound and Display a Pop-Up Message with Behaviors

Create Links to URLs with Behaviors

Open Browser Windows and Preload Images

Show and Hide Layers

Swap Images and Validate Forms

Control Navigation Bars with Behaviors

Create Your Own Behaviors

*B*ehaviors are prewritten JavaScript code that performs particular tasks, such as playing a sound, preloading images, and checking browser versions. Behaviors are triggered by an event you specify with the Behaviors panel. A typical event is a mouse click, so in the Behaviors panel you specify both the event (in this case, onClick) and the actions that are to take place when the event occurs. Clicking the mouse, filling in a form

USING BEHAVIORS

field, loading and unloading a page, and many other actions can trigger events.

The behaviors that ship with Dreamweaver 4.0 are designed to work with all 4.0 and later browsers. Some behaviors do work with version 3 browsers, although none of the behaviors included with Dreamweaver work with Internet Explorer 3.x for the Mac, and some—such as the Set Text of Layer behavior—do not work on any of the version 3 browsers. In addition to the 20 behaviors that come preinstalled in Dreamweaver, a number of third-party developers offer behaviors for Dreamweaver. If you're adept at JavaScript programming, you can create your own behaviors and include them in Dreamweaver projects. See Chapter 22, "Customizing Dreamweaver," for more information on downloading and including third-party behaviors.

Attaching Behaviors

Behaviors in Dreamweaver work with all version 4.0 and later browsers. Behaviors can be attached to almost any object on your Web page, including links, images, form elements, and even the entire body of the page. You can even specify more than one action for an event. The actions will take place in the order listed in the Behaviors panel.

1. Select an object. This example uses an image object (smiley face button) (16.1).

2. Select Window→Behaviors to display the Behaviors panel if it isn't already onscreen (16.2).

3. Click the plus (+) button to select an action from the pop-up list (16.3).

4. Enter any parameters required for your action, and then click OK.

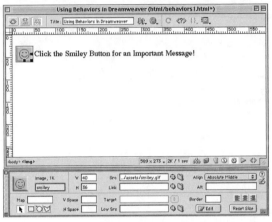

16.1

Name your images when you are going to use them in behaviors so they're easier to locate in the JavaScript code.

Behavior options ⌐
Change the
Remove behavior ⌐ order of
Add behavior ⌐ behaviors

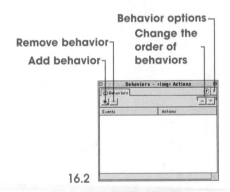

16.2

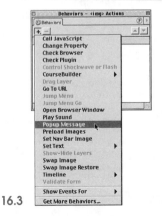

16.3

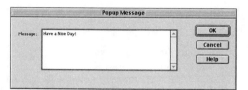

16.4

16.5

16.6

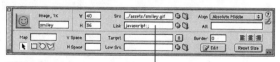

16.7

The null link makes an image behave like a button or text behave like hypertext.

5. The default event for the selected action appears in the Events column of the Behaviors panel. Click the arrow to the right of the event to select another event for this action, if necessary (16.5). I am using the onClick event to trigger the action of displaying a pop-up message box (16.6).

 O T E

Depending on the action you select, a dialog box appears in which you must enter the parameters for the action. In my example, the Popup Message dialog box appears with a field where I entered the message I want to display (16.4).

(N) **O T E**

The actions that appear in parentheses typically are used for links and will create a link for the selected object. Dreamweaver inserts the JavaScript null link (javascript:;) in the Link field of the Property inspector for the object with the attached behavior (16.7). You can use the # symbol as a null link, but it has the disadvantage of jumping to the top of the page when clicked, making the JavaScript null link preferable in most instances.

Using the Call JavaScript Behavior

Use the Call JavaScript behavior to perform a custom JavaScript that you either type directly into the field for the action or, if you created a function for the JavaScript, type the name of the function in the action field.

1. Select the text or objects on your Web page to which you want to apply the JavaScript action (16.8).

2. Select Window→Behaviors to display the Behaviors panel if it isn't already onscreen. Click the plus (+) button and select Call JavaScript to display the Call JavaScript dialog box. Enter the JavaScript for your action into the JavaScript field of the Call JavaScript dialog box (16.9). Click OK when you're finished.

3. The default event for Call JavaScript is onMouseDown, but you can change it to anything you like by clicking the arrow under the Events column of the Behaviors panel. Preview your page in a browser to test your JavaScript (16.10).

16.8

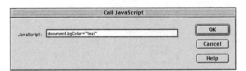

16.9 **This particular JavaScript code sets the background of the Web page to the indicated color.**

16.10 **Clicking the Background Teal button changes the background color to Teal.**

4. Enter a JavaScript function in the Call JavaScript behavior instead of the actual JavaScript code. To create a function, you must describe the JavaScript in the <head> section of your document and assign a function name. Select View→Head Content to display the head content at the top of the Document window. Icons represent the head content, and you already might have some icons in the head content area for the document title and meta information (16.11).

5. Click inside the head content area; then select Insert→Invisible Tags→Script to display the Insert Script dialog box and enter the JavaScript in the Content window (16.12).

6. Click OK when you've finished. You now can access the JavaScript code you just typed in the Call JavaScript behavior by simply typing the function name (16.13).

Title tag
Meta tag
JavaScript code

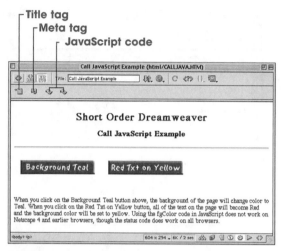

16.11

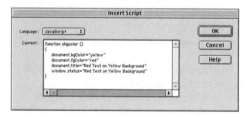

16.12

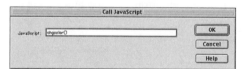

16.13

T I P

You can find a lot of JavaScript examples at http://www.javascript.com *and* http://javascript.internet.com. *For the most up-to-date information on JavaScript, visit* http://www.jsworld.com.

Using the Change Property Behavior

The Change Property action has more variables than any other action in the Behaviors panel. Use the Change Property action to change the properties of an object, such as an image, a layer, or a form. In the following example, the Change Property behavior is attached to a button that, when clicked, changes the background color of a layer and the text of an input text field (16.14).

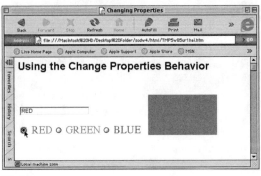

16.14

1. Click to select the object to which you want to assign the behavior, click the plus (+) sign in the Behaviors panel, and select Change Property (16.15).

2. In the Change Property dialog box, click the pop-up menu for Type of Object and select the type of object you want to change the property of.

3. Select a property from the pop-up menu or type a property into the Enter field. Select a browser version from the pop-up menu to display only the properties supported by that browser in the Property pop-up menu.

4. Type the new value for the specified property in the New Value field and click the OK button.

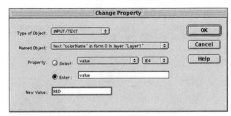

16.15

When you use the Change Property action, be sure to test your page on multiple browsers because the JavaScript used for this action can be very browser dependent. You have the option to select the browser type and version from a pop-up menu when you specify properties, but you must create multiple Change Property actions to accommodate multiple browsers in most cases.

16.16

Using Behaviors to Check Browser Type and Version

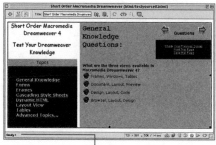

16.17 **Click to select the entire document and add behaviors to the <body> tag with the onLoad action.**

16.18 **You can include more than one Check Browser action in the Behaviors panel. If you need to broaden the criteria, select Stay on This Page from the pop-up menu and create another Check Browser action to check for other browser versions.**

16.19

Checking a site visitor's browser type and version is helpful if your Web page has elements that work only with certain browsers. You can use the Check Browser behavior to route the visitor to another page that is readable on all browser versions.

1. Create a new document and click the <body> tag in the lower-left corner of the Document window (16.17).

2. Click the plus (+) button in the Behaviors panel and select Check Browser to display the Check Browser dialog box (16.18).

3. Enter a version number for each browser type and select the action that is to take place when the specified criteria are met. Enter the URL and Alt (alternative) URL in their respective fields. When you click OK, the onLoad event is specified in the Behaviors panel, meaning that the behavior initiates when the page is being loaded (16.19).

You should attach the Check Browser/Version behavior to the <body> tag of a page that is compatible with all browsers and one that does not use any JavaScript in case the user has JavaScript turned off.

Checking for Plugins Using Behaviors

Use the Check Plugin action to direct visitors to pages, depending on whether a specific plugin is installed for their browsers. For example, you might want to check for the Shockwave plugin before taking users to a page that contains Shockwave. You can handle a missing plugin in two ways: Direct users without it to a page with a link to the plugin source, or simply take them to a page that does not use that plugin. Attach the Check Plugin action either to the <body> tag and use the onLoad event or to an empty link with the onClick event.

1. Click the <body> tag in the lower-left corner of the Document window.

2. Click the plus (+) button in the Behaviors panel and select Check for Plugin to display the Check Plugin dialog box (16.20).

3. Select a plugin from the pop-up menu or enter the plugin name in the Enter field. Enter the URL to display when the plugin is present and the Alt URL to display when the plugin is not present (16.21). Check the Always Go to First URL if Detection Is Not Possible check box if you want to display the page and let the user decide what to do about the plugin. Click OK.

16.20

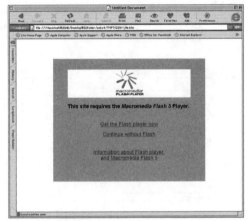

16.21

The Check Plugin behavior does not work with Explorer 3.0x for the Macintosh. Explorer 3.0x on the Macintosh will continue as if the behavior is not present. If you use this behavior for pages posted to the Internet, consider including a message indicating that a particular plugin is required on the pages that use the plugin.

Controlling Shockwave and Flash Playback with Behaviors

16.22

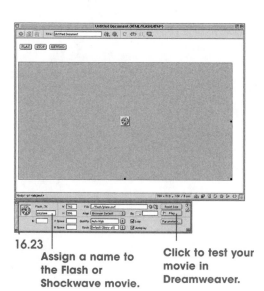

16.23 | Assign a name to the Flash or Shockwave movie.

Click to test your movie in Dreamweaver.

Use the Control Shockwave or Flash action to control the playback of a Shockwave or Flash movie. You can play, stop, or rewind a movie, and even go to a particular frame. This action is useful for stopping a looped animation from playing when the page is loaded or when a user clicks a button. If you're using layers, you can initially hide a layer containing a Flash or Shockwave file and then use the Behaviors panel to display the layer and begin playing the embedded movie. Although you can use almost any element on your Web page as a trigger for this action, this task's example is a form with three buttons to which behaviors for the example are attached (16.22).

1. Select Insert→Media→ Shockwave or Insert→Media→ Flash to insert a Shockwave or Flash movie into your document. Click OK.

2. Assign a name to your movie using the Property inspector. The Shockwave or Flash movie must be named to reference it in a behavior (16.23).

3. Display the Forms Objects in the Objects panel and click the Form button to create a form at the cursor position in the Document window.

Controlling Shockwave and Flash Playback with Behaviors continued

4. Click the Button object in the Objects panel to view the properties of that object. Click the None radio button and type **STOP** in the Label field in the Property inspector **(16.24)**.

16.24

5. Click the button in the Document window. Click the plus (+) button in the Behaviors panel and select Control Shockwave or Flash from the pop-up menu to display the corresponding dialog box **(16.25)**.

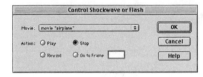

16.25

6. Select the movie from the Movie pop-up menu and click the radio button next to the action you want this button to perform. Click OK and preview your file in a browser. Repeat these steps to create buttons for Play and Rewind.

 I P

Shockwave and Flash files can contain embedded stops that make the movie stop playing at a specific frame. Use the Go to Frame option in the Control Shockwave or Flash dialog box to start playback at the frame succeeding the frame where the movie stopped. This method enables you to create a single movie that can be controlled using buttons to display various parts of the movie.

Controlling Sound with Behaviors

16.26

Change the event that triggers the action in the Behaviors panel. For example, if you are using a short sound burst and want the sound to play when your mouse is over an image, select onMouseOver **as the event.**

Controlling the playback of sound is pretty straightforward. Use the Play Sound action to play a sound. Depending on the sound format, some browsers might require the LiveAudio plugin or its equivalent to play sounds.

1. Select an object on your page to attach the behavior.

2. Click the plus (+) button in the Behaviors panel and select the Play Sound action to display the Play Sound dialog box (16.26).

3. To play a sound, enter the path of the sound file in the Play Sound field or click the Browse button to select it. Click OK.

Displaying a Pop-Up Message

16.27

16.28

The Popup Message action causes a JavaScript alert dialog box to appear with your message inside (16.27). Because the alert dialog box has only one button—OK—you should restrict the content to messages and not choices.

1. Click to select an object or some text with an empty link.

2. Select the Popup Message action in the Behaviors panel to display the corresponding dialog box and type your message in the Message field (16.28).

Creating Links to URLs with Behaviors

The Go To URL action enables you specify a URL to display in the current window or in a specified frame. The Go To URL is most useful if you want to change the contents of more than one frame with a single click.

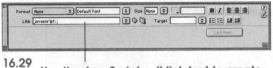

16.29 **Use the JavaScript null link text to create an empty link before attaching a behavior.**

1. Click an object on your Web page. If you want to use text, create an empty (null) link by typing javascript:; in the Link field of the Property inspector (16.29).

2. Click the plus (+) button in the Behaviors panel and select Go To URL to display the corresponding dialog box (16.30).

3. Select from where you want the URL to open within the Open In window and specify the URL in the URL field. Click OK.

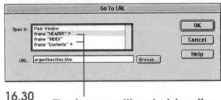

16.30 **The frames with asterisks after the name are frames that have URLs assigned to open in them. In this example, clicking a button makes two URLs open in two different frames.**

 I P

Use the Go To URL behavior to change a URL after performing some other behaviors. For example, make a sound begin, and then switch to a new URL with a single click.

 O T E

The Go To URL behavior is a useful tool for changing the content of all your frames with a single click.

Opening Browser Windows

16.31   **Browser windows can be any width you specify, but they must be at least 100 pixels high. The window seen here is 540 pixels wide and 197 pixels high.**

16.32   **Click the <body> tag to create a behavior that takes place when the page initially loads in the browser window.**

16.33   **The Window Name cannot contain any spaces or special characters.**

The Open Browser Window action is useful for presenting a floating window with some information or displaying a page on your site in its own window with its own navigation buttons. You can specify all the attributes about the window and even create a window with just a close box in the corner. You have, no doubt, encountered these little windows on Web sites, usually promoting some other site or telling you about new features.

1. Create an HTML page that is the width and height of your intended browser window and save the page (16.31).

2. In the main document, click the <body> tag in the lower-left corner of the Document window to create an onLoad event (16.32).

3. Select the Open Browser Window action from the pop-up menu in the Behaviors panel to display the Open Browser Window dialog box (16.33).

(T) I P

Use Dreamweaver to check the size of the file you want to place in a new browser window. Resize the document window until the placement of the file looks right and use those dimensions for your browser window.

Opening Browser Windows continued

4. Enter the URL in the URL to Display field and specify the width and height of the window (the width and height for which you designed the URL's page).

5. Click the check boxes of the attributes you want the window to have and type a name in the Window Name field if you want to refer to this window with JavaScript and other behaviors.

6. Click OK and preview the page in a browser. If you used the onLoad event for this action, the window appears as soon as the page starts loading (16.34).

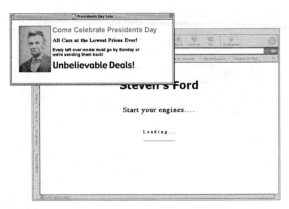

16.34

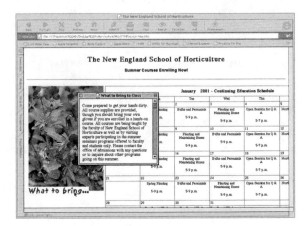

16.35

T I P

Use the Open Browser Window behavior to open windows with information that the user requests by clicking a button or text link. For example, if you have a link on your page for your company policy, make it a window that pops up so the user stays on the page after he has read your message **(16.35)**.

Preloading Images

16.36 Preloading images is important if you are creating rollovers using images. If you do not preload images to be used as rollovers, most likely a delay will occur when the user rolls over an image, which will defeat the desired effect. If you use the Rollover Image object in the Common Objects panel, you have the option of preloading the images in the Insert Rollover Image dialog box.

16.37 A Preload Images check box is included in the dialog boxes associated with behaviors that change the images on the Web page.

The Preload Images action preloads the images you specify to the browser's cache for later use by timelines, behaviors, or JavaScript. You can specify any number of images to preload, but keep in mind that the user's browser must have enough cache space to store the pre-loaded images. The Preload Images action usually works best when using the onLoad event.

1. To use the onLoad event, click the <body> tag in the lower-left corner of the Document window; then select the Preload Images action in the Behaviors panel to display the corresponding dialog box (16.36).

2. Enter the paths of the images and click the plus (+) button to add more images to the list. You must click the (+) button to add the images; otherwise, the next image you select will erase the current image. If you want to remove images from the list, click them and then click the minus (-) button. Click OK.

NOTE

The Preload Images behavior can be automatically inserted when you use other behaviors that affect images, such as Swap Image and Set Nav Bar Image **(16.37)**.

Showing and Hiding Layers

Use the Show-Hide Layers action to make layers visible, hide layers, or restore the default visibility for the layer. This action can be used to make things appear on your page when the mouse passes over an object or some text. See Chapter 15, "Creating Layers," for information on creating and manipulating layers.

1. Create a layer and add some content to the layer.

2. Click an image or some text with an empty link, and then select Show-Hide Layers in the Behaviors panel to display the Show-Hide Layers dialog box (16.38).

3. Click to select the layer you want to affect and click the Show, Hide, or Default button.

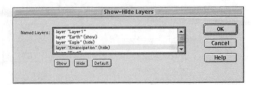

16.38

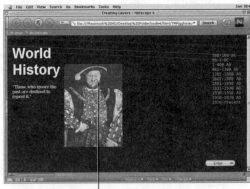

16.39 The onMouseOver event (shown here) and onMouseOut event can be attached to objects on your page to show and hide layers.

16.40 The onMouseOut event is triggered when the cursor is moved outside the object that contains the behavior.

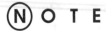 **O T E**

To create a rollover effect, create two Show-Hide Layers actions: one with the onMouseOver event (16.39) and one with the onMouseOut event (16.40).

 I P

To use a layer for a mouseOver and a mouseOut event, you must select Show Events For→4.0 and Later Browsers by clicking the plus (+) button in the Behaviors panel.

Swapping Images

In this example, hot spots were created for the navigation image using the map feature in the Property inspector, and the behavior is attached to the hot spot.

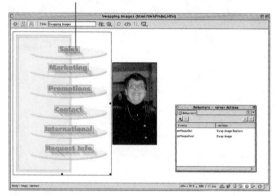

16.41

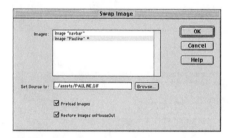

16.42

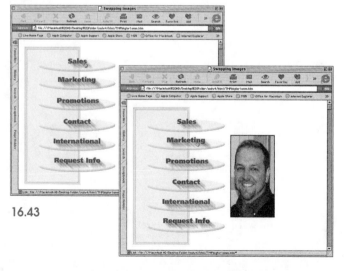

16.43

The Swap Image and Swap Image Restore actions substitute one image for another. The Swap Image action is useful for creating rollover effects or changing image content using buttons or rollovers on other images. To create a Swap Image behavior, you must have at least one image in your document to begin with. The Swap Image Restore action restores a previously swapped image to the original image.

1. Click an image or some text with an empty link to create the Swap Image behavior (16.41).

2. Select Swap Image from the pop-up menu in the Behaviors panel to display the Swap Image dialog box (16.42).

3. Select the image you want to swap in the Images list, and then enter the path for the image with which you want to replace the selected image. Check the Preload Images check box to avoid delays in swapping the image. Check the Restore Images onMouseOut check box if you want to restore the original image when the cursor is moved off the object that triggers the Swap Image action.

4. Click OK; then preview the page in a browser (16.43).

Validating Forms

The Validate Form action enables you to perform a limited amount of form validation before the form is posted to the Web server. This action checks the contents of text fields to ensure that the user has entered the correct type of data. You can attach this action to individual text fields with the `onBlur` event to validate the fields as the user enters the data. You also can attach this action to the entire form with the `onSubmit` event, which validates multiple fields at once when the Submit button is clicked. If you attach the action to the form, any invalid data prevents the form from being submitted until the fields are corrected.

1. Click any text field within a form to select it (16.44).

2. Select the Validate Form action in the Behaviors panel to display the Validate Form dialog box (16.45).

The First Name field is selected.

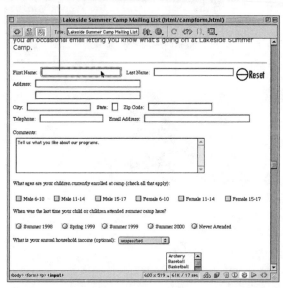

16.44

16.45

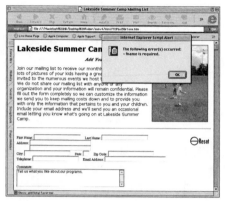

16.45

When you select the entire form, the
onSubmit event is used instead of the
onBlur event, which results when a
single field is selected.

16.47

**The criteria for the Validate Form
behavior are specified in parentheses
next to the form field in the Validate
Form dialog box.**

3. Select a field from the Named
Fields list. If you want to validate only the selected field,
click that field in the list. Click
the Required check box if the
user cannot leave this field
empty. Check a radio button to
specify the criteria for acceptance of the data. Click OK.

4. Preview the form in a browser.
In this example, when you
enter the wrong data in the
selected field, an error dialog
box appears in the browser
when you try to leave the field
(16.46).

(N) O T E

*To validate multiple fields when the form is
submitted, click the <form> tag in the lower-
left corner of the Document window before
creating the Validate Form action. When the
dialog box appears, specify all the validation
criteria for all the fields in the list* **(16.47)**.

Controlling Navigation Bars with Behaviors

You can control the way the buttons in a navigation bar behave using the Behaviors panel. See Chapter 9, "Inserting Interactive Images," for information on creating navigation bars.

16.48

Click any of the images in your navigation bar and view the Behaviors panel to see which behaviors were created for you when the navigation bar was created. Aside from the standard navigation bar settings, the Behaviors panel offers some advanced options for managing the buttons in the navigation bar. You also can use the Set Nav Bar Image behavior to add images to your navigation bar.

1. Click to select an image in your navigation bar and display the Behaviors panel if it isn't already onscreen (16.48).

2. Double-click the event you want to edit in the Behaviors panel to display the Set Nav Bar Image dialog box (16.49).

3. Click the Advanced tab in the Set Nav Bar Image dialog box to specify how other images on your page behave when you move over the image or click the image (16.50). Click OK when you're finished.

16.49

The Basic tab contains all the settings you specified when you created the navigation bar.

You can swap any image on your page using the Advanced tab options in the Set Nav Bar Image dialog box, not just images in the navigation bar.

16.50

Creating Your Own Behaviors

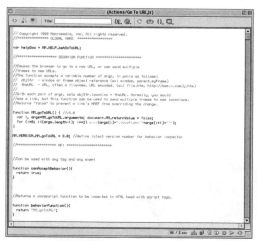

16.51

The Go To URL JavaScript file is located in the Actions folder and opened here in Dreamweaver.

You can link to external JavaScript files.

Create dialog boxes in tables.

16.52

If you're familiar with JavaScript and want to create your own actions, Dreamweaver provides a simple method to do so. You can use this procedure to add your own JavaScript to the Behaviors panel or to add third-party actions available on various Web sites, including Macromedia's.

1. Exit Dreamweaver if it is currently running.

2. Create your JavaScript in a text editor and save the file with the `.html` extension. This file should not contain any HTML code. Give the file a name that describes it; for example, the Dreamweaver action to control Shockwave or Flash is named `Control Shockwave or Flash.html`. It's okay to include spaces in the name of the file.

3. Put the new file in the Actions folder within the Dreamweaver folder:

- Windows users:
  `Dreamweaver\`
  `Configuration\Behaviors\`
  `Actions`

- Macintosh users:
  `Dreamweaver/`
  `Configuration/Behaviors/`
  `Actions`

4. Launch Dreamweaver and click the plus (+) button in the Behaviors panel to use your new action.

©HAPTER 17

In this chapter, you will learn how to...

Create Timelines

Add Keyframes to the Timeline

Use Behaviors with a Timeline

Create Animation by Recording a Layer's Path

Add Images to the Timeline

Make Animations Interactive with Behaviors

Create Multiple Timelines

Timelines enable you to add animation to a Web page using JavaScript without having to know how to write any code. Timelines do not use Java or ActiveX and do not require special plugins. Because timelines are created with JavaScript, the animation appears only in version 4 and later browsers.

In Dreamweaver, timelines work primarily with layers, creating animation by moving layers around on the Web page. You also can use

WORKING WITH TIMELINES

timelines to swap images on and off the page based on a span of time, rather than as a result of some event the Swap Image behavior handles. Animation is created by ordering a group of animation frames (layers in this case) and playing them in order at a specific frame rate, indicated as frames per second (fps). Because timelines use layers to create the animation effect, you can apply the behaviors in the Behaviors panel to your layers by including the behaviors in a special Behaviors channel of the timeline.

A single Dreamweaver timeline can contain up to 32 animation channels that can play simultaneously. Therefore, you can have 32 animated elements on your page at one time. Each animation channel can contain as many as 32,054 frames, which amounts to just about 36 minutes at 15fps—longer than you're likely to ever want an animation to play on a Web page. You also can create multiple timelines and control them by using the Timeline behaviors in the Behaviors panel.

Creating Timelines

The Timelines panel creates animation by placing layers in frames on various animation channels and represents the properties of layers and images over time.

1. Select Window→Timelines to display the Timelines panel (17.1).

2. Create a layer in the Document window and add some content to the layer.

3. Drag the layer onto the timeline and drop it in the first frame of the first row. The layer is added to the timeline with a keyframe (white circle) at the beginning and a keyframe at the end.

4. Click and drag the rightmost keyframe to set the length of the animation in frames (at 15fps) (17.2).

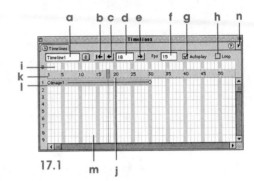

17.1

(a) Timeline name and pop-up menu

(b) Rewind button

(c) Back button

(d) Current frame

(e) Playback button (hold to play continuously)

(f) Frame rate

(g) Check Autoplay to use the onLoad JavaScript command

(h) Check Loop to play the animation continuously

(i) Behaviors channel

(j) Playback head

(k) Frame numbers

(l) Keyframes

(m) Animation Channels

(n) Click to display the Options menu

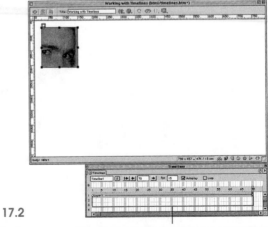

17.2

Keyframes are the control points of your animation.

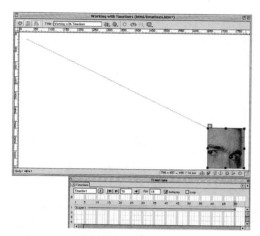

17.3   **Because this animation has only two keyframes, it plays in a straight line.**

5. Click the right-most keyframe to highlight it; then click and drag the layer to a new location in the Document window. When you release the layer in its new location, a line will appear between the first frame and the last frame, depicting the path of the animation (17.3). Because this animation has only two keyframes, the animation plays in a straight line.

6. Click the Rewind button to return the playback head to frame 1; then click and hold the Play button to preview your animation in Dreamweaver.

 I   P

(Ctrl-click)[Right-click] the timeline to display the context menu, where you can select menu options such as Add Frame, Add Keyframe, and Remove Frame. You also can click the triangle in the upper-right corner of the Timelines panel to display the context menu choices.

Adding Keyframes to the Timeline

Keyframes are placed on the timeline whenever you want to change the direction of the animation or when you want to add a behavior to the timeline. Insert keyframes on the timeline, and then drag the corresponding layer to modify the path of your animation.

1. Click the timeline, beneath the frame number where you want to make a change to the animation path **(17.4)**.

2. Select Modify→Timeline→Add Keyframe or press F6 to add a keyframe at the selected point on the timeline.

3. Drag the layer in the Document window to change the path of the animation at the point of the keyframe in the timeline **(17.5)**.

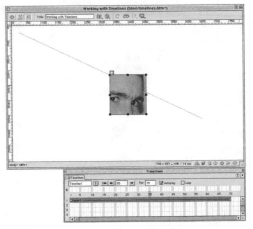

17.4

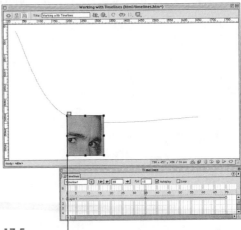

17.5 **You can use the Property inspector to specify the precise x and y position of the upper-left corner of the layer by setting the Left and Top values for the layer.**

 I P

Hold down the (Command)[Ctrl] key and click the timeline to add keyframes.

 I P

Click and drag the playback head to move to a specific frame within the animation.

Using Behaviors with a Timeline

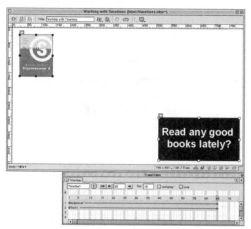

17.6

Here two layers are created, each containing some content. Each layer is animated to move to its opposite corner. When the timeline is played, the layer in the upper-left corner passes in front of the layer in the lower-right corner at about the center of the page.

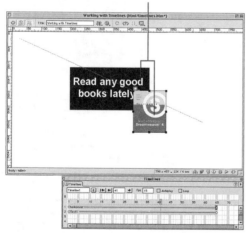

17.7

To add behaviors to your timeline, you first must add a keyframe in the frame where you want the behavior to take place. You can add any behavior to a timeline, and that behavior can contain any number of actions. When you add a behavior to the Timeline, the event for the behavior always is onFrameXX, where *xx* is the frame number in which the behavior takes place.

1. Create two layers positioned at opposite ends of the Document window; then add them to the timeline in channel 1 and channel 2. Drag the rightmost keyframes for each layer to set the overall length of the animation (17.6).

2. Click the ending keyframe of each layer, and then drag the layer in the Document window to a new position on the screen so the two layers intersect at some point along the animation (17.7).

 I P

If you change the frames per second (fps) to a value greater than 15, the animation will play more quickly locally on your computer, but will not play much more quickly than 15fps over the Internet.

Using Behaviors with a Timeline continued

3. Click and drag the playback head until the two layers are overlapping. Hold down the (Command)[Ctrl] key and click under the playback head and on the animation channel that contains the top layer (book-cover in my example) to insert a new keyframe **(17.8)**.

4. Double-click directly above the playback head in the Behaviors channel to display the Behaviors panel. Be sure the frame in the Behaviors channel of the timeline is highlighted. Click the plus (+) button in the Behaviors panel and select Show-Hide Layers **(17.9)** to display the Show-Hide Layers dialog box. Highlight the name of the bottom layer and click the Hide button; then click OK **(17.10)**.

17.8   **Keyframes are added to the timeline where you want to include a timeline behavior.**

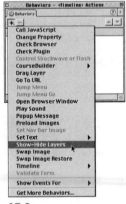

17.9

17.10

T I P

When you check the Loop option in the Timelines panel, a behavior is added in the frame after the last frame of your animation with the Go To Timeline Frame action.

You can add multiple actions to a single frame in the timeline.

Highlight a behavior and press (Delete)(Backspace) to delete it from the Behavior channel.

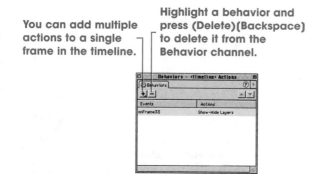

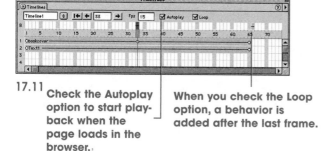

17.11 Check the Autoplay option to start playback when the page loads in the browser.

When you check the Loop option, a behavior is added after the last frame.

5. The event for the Show-Hide Layers action is onFrame33 (or whatever your frame number is) because the behavior was added to the timeline at frame 33 (17.11). View the animation in a browser. When you play the timeline, the bottom object should disappear when it reaches the specified frame.

6. Use this same procedure with the Change Property action in the Behaviors panel to change the Z-Index, Width, Height, Left, Top, and Visibility settings of the layer. See Chapter 16, "Using Behaviors," for information on using the Change Property action.

 I P

Instead of using the Change Property behavior to change the size of a layer, simply add a keyframe, and then click and drag the layer handles. For example, if you want a layer to gradually get smaller as the animation plays, click the last keyframe and make the layer smaller; Dreamweaver does the rest. Enter the Width and Height values in the Property inspector as an alternative way to change the size of the layer.

 I P

Remember to check the Autoplay button in the Timelines inspector before previewing in a browser.

Creating Animation by Recording a Layer's Path

Dreamweaver provides a method of creating timeline animation by dragging a layer. Keyframes are added automatically along the timeline where necessary, and the animation can be stretched to change the length (in time) of the animation after the initial animation is recorded.

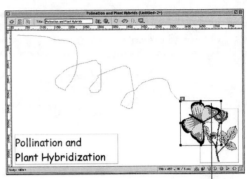

17.12 **In this example, the layer containing the butterfly was originally in the upper-left corner.**

1. Select a layer by clicking it in the Document window. Be sure to select the layer and not the contents of the layer.

2. Select Modify→Timeline→ Record Path of Layer.

3. Drag the layer to create the path for the animation **(17.12)**.

 I P

When you click the Autoplay button in the Timeline inspector, the Play Timeline behavior is added at the beginning of your document with the onLoad event. To see this behavior in the Behaviors panel, be sure a behavior in the Timeline inspector is not highlighted and click <body> in the lower-left corner of the Document window.

 O T E

The default playback rate is 15fps, which is most effective for playback on the Web. If you set the rate to a higher value, the animation might play back more quickly on your computer, but will still play at 15fps on a visitor's computer.

Adding Images to the Timeline

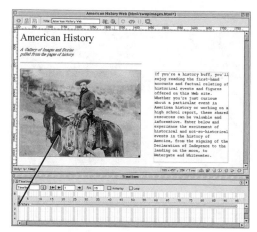

17.13

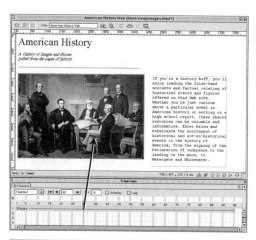

17.14

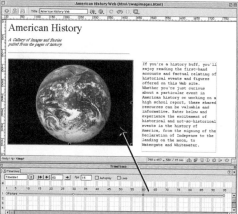

17.15

Add images to the timeline when you want to change the image source over time. This technique is a great way to transition multiple images on and off the page. You can add multiple images along a single channel by simply changing the image source at keyframe points.

1. Place an image on your page. Do not place the image in a layer.

2. Click and drag the image onto the timeline; then drag the last keyframe to the right to set the length of the animation (**17.13**).

3. Click to select a frame along the image channel and (Command-click) [Ctrl+click] to add a keyframe.

4. Select a new image source in the Property inspector (**17.14**).

5. Perform steps 3 and 4 to add more images to the timeline (**17.15**).

(T) I P

You should preload the images on your timeline by using the Preload Images action with the onLoad event in the Behaviors panel. Click the <body> tag in the lower-left corner of the Document window and specify the behavior to preload images using the Behaviors panel.

Making Animations Interactive with Behaviors

In addition to using behaviors within the timeline, you can control the start and stop of timelines, as well as jump to frame locations by using the timeline actions in the Behaviors panel. These behaviors are useful when you want to give the visitor interactive control over the timeline.

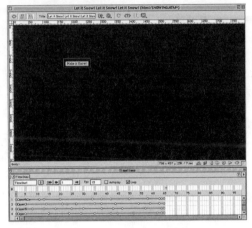

17.16

1. Create a timeline animation and a button using the Button object in the Forms Objects panel (17.16).

2. Click to select the button, and then select the Timeline→Play Timeline action in the Behaviors panel to display the Play Timeline dialog box (17.17). Select the Timeline you want to play and click OK.

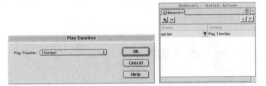

17.17

3. Be sure the Autoplay option is not checked before testing your page in a browser.

4. Create another button and select the Timeline→Go To Timeline Frame action in the Behaviors panel to display the corresponding dialog box (17.18).

17.18

 **O T E**

The default form button is the Submit button, so be sure to set the Action to None for the button in the Property inspector if you want to assign a behavior to the button.

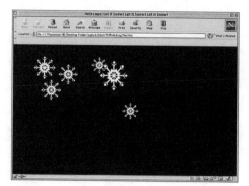

17.19

5. Enter the frame to which you want to jump. If you want the animation to loop back to the specified frame, enter a number in the Loop field to indicate how many times to loop. This is the same action that is inserted at the end of your timeline when the Loop check box is selected in the Timelines panel.

6. Preview the animation in a browser. When you click the button with the Go To Timeline Frame behavior, the animation jumps to the specified spot in the timeline and plays the timeline from that point **(17.19)**.

 I P

Click the behavior that appears after the last frame in the timeline and double-click the Play Timeline action in the Behaviors panel to set both the number of times the timeline loops and which frame it returns to when looping. This technique is useful if you want to put something in the first frame of your animation, such as a button, but don't want to include it in the loop.

Creating Multiple Timelines

You might want to create more than one timeline to have more than one animation on a page. Attach behaviors to various buttons or links to play and stop the multiple timelines, or check the Autoplay check box to play all timelines together when the page loads. Combine timelines that contain images with timelines using layers to animate your Web pages.

1. Select Modify→Timeline→Add Timeline to add a new time-line. The timeline name appears in the upper-left corner of the Timelines panel and is named by Dreamweaver automatically. Type a name for the new timeline if you do not want to use the default name (17.20).

2. Click the arrow to the right of the timeline name in the Timelines panel to switch among the available timelines (17.21).

The timeline name is entered here.

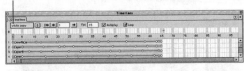

17.20

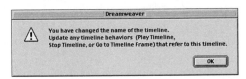

17.21

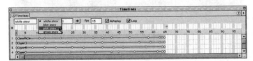

17.22

Select Modify→Timeline→Remove Timeline to delete a timeline.

If you rename a timeline that includes behaviors, you must go back and redefine the behaviors because the JavaScript code that is generated using the behavior refers to the specific timeline by its name (17.22).

CHAPTER 18

In this chapter, you will learn how to...

Use the Assets Panel

Add Assets to the Favorites List

Insert an Asset in a Document

Edit Assets

Copy Assets Between Sites

Create New Colors and URLs

Dreamweaver's Assets panel enables you to manage elements, such as images, templates, and movie files. The assets on your site are categorized in the Assets panel. The nine categories of assets found in the Assets panel are images, colors, URLs, Flash movies, Shockwave movies, MPEG and QuickTime movies, Scripts, Templates, and Library items. Only files that fit into these categories are presented in the Assets panel.

MANAGING AND INSERTING ASSETS WITH THE ASSETS PANEL

You can use the Assets panel in two ways. The Site list manages the categorized assets on your current site. The Favorites list, on the other hand, can contain the assets you use most frequently, such as logos, colors, and URLs. The contents of the Site list are automatically generated based on the assets used on your site. The Favorites list is empty until you add assets to it.

When you have more than one site defined in Dreamweaver, you can copy assets from one site to another using the Assets panel. Add frequently used colors and URLs to the Assets panel of one site, and copy those colors to the Favorites list of the Assets panel for another site. When copying assets from one site to another, Dreamweaver automatically duplicates the assets in the first site and places them in their respective places in the new site folder of the target site on your hard drive.

Using the Assets Panel

The Site list contains all the assets on your site that fit into the predefined categories and displays assets whether you use them on your Web pages or not. With the exception of the Library and Templates categories, the same categories are included in both the Site list of the Assets panel and the Favorites list.

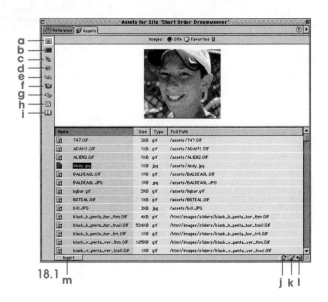

18.1

1. Select Window→Assets to display the Assets panel (18.1).

2. Click the Site radio button at the top of the Assets panel, and then click a category icon on the left side of the Assets panel to display the assets in that category (18.2).

3. If the Assets panel is open when you add or remove assets from your site, click the Refresh Site List button to update the list of assets.

4. Click an asset in the assets lists to preview the asset in the top section of the Assets panel.

(a) **Images**
(b) **Colors**
(c) **URLs**
(d) **Flash**
(e) **Shockwave**
(f) **Movies**
(g) **Scripts**
(h) **Templates**
(i) **Library items**
(j) **Refresh Site list**
(k) **Edit asset**
(l) **Add to Favorites list**
(m) **Insert selected asset in the current document**

 I P

To manually rebuild the site cache from scratch and refresh the Site list, (Command-click)[Ctrl+click] the Refresh Site List button at the bottom of the Assets panel.

N O T E

You must define a site and create a site cache before using the Assets panel.

The Site radio button does not appear when the Templates or Library assets are selected.

18.2

Adding Assets to the Favorites List

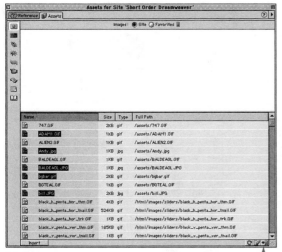

18.3

Add to Favorites button

18.4

18.5

Add assets you use frequently, such as colors, URLs, and images, to the Favorites list. You can add any asset to the Favorites list except Templates and Libraries.

1. Select one or more assets in the Site list of the Assets panel **(18.3)**.

2. Click the Add to Favorites button in the lower-right corner of the Assets panel. You also can add assets to the Favorites list in the following ways:

3. Click the Favorites radio button at the top of the Assets panel to view the assets in the Favorites list **(18.4)**.

4. Click the Remove From Favorites button in the lower-right corner of the Assets panel to remove assets from the Favorites list.

 O T E

When you add an asset to the Favorites list from the Document window's Design view, the context menu displays an option for the type of element selected. For example, if you (Ctrl-click)[right+click] a JPEG image, the context menu contains the Add to Image Favorites choice **(18.5)**.

 I P

When you remove an asset from the Favorites list, the asset still resides in the Site list of the Assets panel.

Inserting an Asset in a Document

Insert assets into your document by either dragging the asset from the Assets panel onto the Document window or selecting an asset in the Assets panel and clicking the Insert button. To use URL and Color assets, select some text and drag the asset onto the text in the Document window. URLs also can be applied to images in the Document window. See Chapter 19, "Creating Templates and Libraries," for information on inserting Template and Library assets.

1. Place the insertion point in the Document window's Design view where you want to insert an asset.

2. Select Window→Assets to display the Assets panel if it's not already onscreen (18.6).

3. Click to select a category on the left side of the Assets panel.

4. Select either Site or Favorites at the top of the Assets panel.

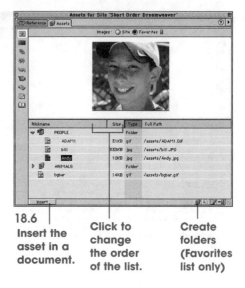

18.6
Insert the asset in a document.

Click to change the order of the list.

Create folders (Favorites list only)

NOTE

When inserting a template or library item, you must use the Site list in the Assets panel. Templates and library items do not appear in the Favorites list.

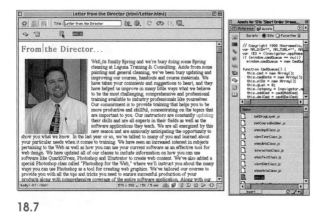

18.7

5. Drag the asset from the Assets panel onto the document in the Design view.

6. To insert a script from the Assets panel, select View→Head Content and drag the script from the Assets panel into the head section (18.7).

To change the color of text in the document using the Assets panel, select the text, and then drag a color from the Assets panel onto the selected text. Use the same method to add a URL to text, or click an image and drag a URL from the Assets panel onto the image.

Editing Assets

Some assets, such as images, launch an external editor application when you edit the asset. You can edit colors and URLs in the Favorites list, but not in the Site list.

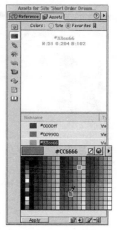

1. Double-click an asset in the Assets panel or select an asset and click the Edit button in the lower-right corner of the Assets panel.

2. If an editing application is launched to edit the asset, make any necessary changes and save the file.

18.8

3. To edit colors, create Favorites for the colors you want to edit; then click the radio button for Favorites at the top of the Assets panel. Double-click a color in the Favorites list of the Assets panel. When the color palette appears, select a new color (18.8).

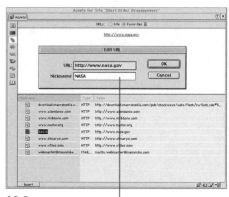

4. To edit URLs, create Favorites for the URLs you want to edit; then click the radio button for Favorites at the top of the Assets panel. Double-click a URL and change the URL in the Edit URL dialog box (18.9).

18.9

Assign a nickname to display in the Assets panel instead of the URL address.

 **O T E**

If an external editor does not launch when you double-click an asset, specify the editor in the Preferences dialog box. Select Edit→Preferences, and then select the File Types/Editors category.

Copying Assets Between Sites

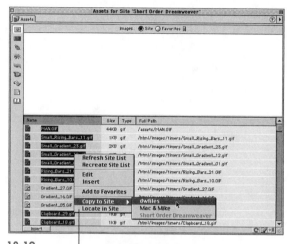

18.10

**Select Locate in Site to find the
selected file(s) in the Site window.**

You can copy assets from the Assets
panel of one site to another site
defined in Dreamweaver. If you
copy a color or URL to another site,
the color or URL is added to the
Favorites list only. You can select
multiple assets and copy them to
another site or select folders in the
Favorites list of the Assets panel to
copy to another site.

1. Select the assets in the Assets
   panel you want to copy to
   another site.

2. (Ctrl-click)[Right+click] to display the context menu; then
   select Copy to Site to select a
   site defined in Dreamweaver
   (18.10).

When you copy assets to another site, the
assets are added to both the Site list and
Favorites list, except in the case of colors
and URLs, which are added only to the
Favorites list.

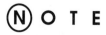

The assets that appear in the Assets panel
relate to the current site and not just the
current document.

Creating New Colors and URLs

You= can use the Assets panel to
create colors, URLs, templates, and
library items. Colors and URLs must
be added to the Favorites list
because they don't relate to any
files. For information on creating
new templates and library items, see
Chapter 19, "Creating Templates
and Libraries."

1. Click the radio button for
   Favorites in the Assets panel.

2. Click the Color or URL category list on the left side of the
   Assets panel.

3. To add a new color, click the
   New Color button at the bottom of the Assets panel; then
   select a color from the color
   palette (18.11).

4. To add a new URL, click the
   New URL button at the bottom
   of the Assets panel; then type a
   new URL and optional nickname (18.12).

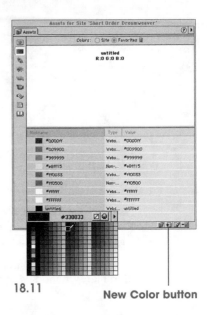

18.11

New Color button

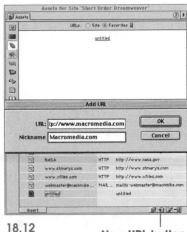

18.12

New URL button

O T E

*You can change the name of any color in the
color list to a unique name of your choice.
Click the color name in the Nickname column, and then type a new color name.
Double-click a color in the color list to
change the hexadecimal color value shown in
the Value column.*

CHAPTER 19

In this chapter, you will learn how to...

Create a Template

Specify Editable Regions of a Template

Create a New File from a Template

Export XML Content

Import XML Content

Use Libraries to Organize Content

Use Server-Side Includes

Templates are a great tool to ensure uniformity on your Web sites. In Dreamweaver, you start off by creating a document, making use of the tools available in Dreamweaver. The file is then saved as a template with a .dwt extension. After the document is saved, you specify which parts of the Web page are editable. When you subsequently use the template to create a new Web page, everything on the page—aside from the areas you marked as

CREATING TEMPLATES AND LIBRARIES

editable—are protected from change. Templates are a useful tool if your site contains a constant theme or if you have common items, such as navigation bars, e-mail links, or copyright information.

Libraries are useful for storing Web content you use repeatedly. You can store either single elements or groups of items—include text, images, and even plugin files, such as Shockwave and Flash—in libraries. After you've stored library items, you can open them in Dreamweaver and edit them as separate entities. When you change a library item, you are prompted to update all pages on your Web site that contain that particular library item. With a little planning, you can streamline the updating of your Web site by using templates and libraries and Dreamweaver's capability to update an entire site when you make changes to the templates and libraries.

Creating a Template

When you create a new template, it is available in the Templates category of the Assets panel and stored in a Templates folder in your site Root folder.

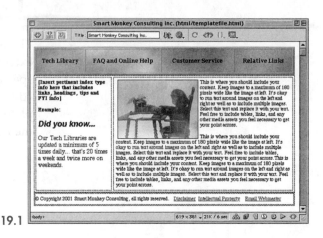

19.1

1. Create an HTML document in Dreamweaver the way you ordinarily would for any other Web page. As you design your page, keep in mind that you will be selecting items to be edited while locking others (19.1).

2. Select File→Save as Template to display the Save As Template dialog box (19.2) and specify the site for the template as well as a name. When you click Save, the new template appears in the Templates category of the Assets panel (Window→Templates).

You cannot save a frameset as a template, but you can save the individual HTML source pages used in the frameset as templates.

19.2

Template category

3. Click the template name in the Templates category of the Assets panel to display a preview of the template (19.3). You can open and delete templates directly from the Templates category of the Assets panel.

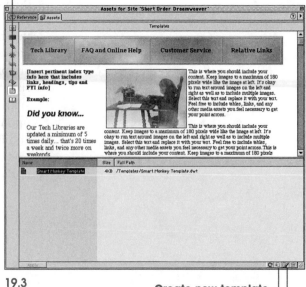

N O T E

When you open and make changes to a template, you can choose to also update all other pages created from that template.

19.3

Create new template ┐
Edit selected template ┘

Specifying Editable Regions of a Template

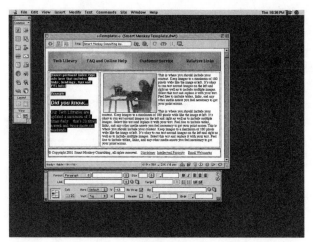

19.4

Specify the individual regions of the page separately because you are prompted to name the regions for easy access later.

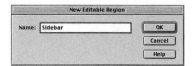

19.5

When you first create your template, everything on the page is protected, which prevents another user from making changes to the template items. You must specify which regions of the page are editable to enable the user to make changes to specific parts of the document created with the template file. The user always has the option to detach from the template, in which case all content can be edited. An editable region called `doctitle` is automatically specified for a template so the user can change the title of the page but not the rest of the page properties, such as background color and text color.

1. Select the content on the page that you want to mark as editable (19.4).

2. Select Modify→Templates→ New Editable Region. When the New Editable Region dialog box appears, type a name that identifies the editable region (19.5).

 **O T E**

The following characters are not valid for region names: apostrophes ('), quotation marks ("), angle brackets (< >), and ampersands (&).

Specifying Editable Regions of a Template continued

3. Select Modify→Templates→
New Editable Region and enter
a name for the editable region
in the Name field of the New
Editable Region dialog box. An
editable region is defined in
the Document window with
curly braces, such as {Optional
By Line} (19.6).

4. Select Edit→Preferences→
Highlighting to customize the
highlight colors for the
editable and locked regions of
a template (19.7). Boxes surround the editable regions
with tabs in the upper-left corner containing the region
names. The locked region color
appears in documents that use
the template. To view the highlighted regions in the
Document window, select
View→Visual Aids→Invisible
Elements. The highlighted
regions appear in the
Document window when
Invisible Elements are turned
on (19.8).

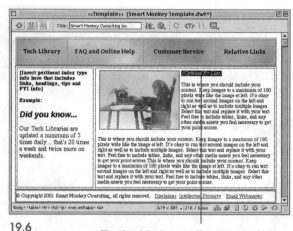

19.6

**The text between the braces is the
Region name.**

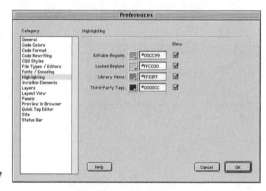

19.7

I P

*You can mark an entire table or an individ-
ual table cell as editable. You cannot, however, mark multiple cells as editable at one
time. Layers and layer content are separate
elements, and both can be marked as
editable.*

19.8

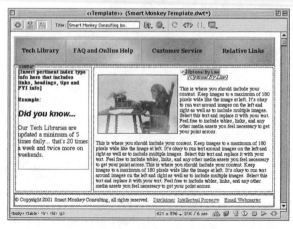

Creating a New File from a Template

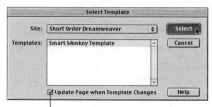

19.9 **Changes made to the template will automatically update pages created with the template.**

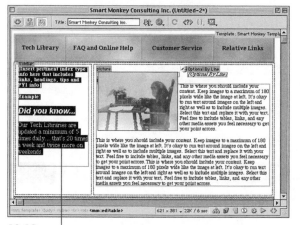

19.10 **Styles, timelines, and behaviors can be applied only to editable regions of a document that uses templates.**

After a template is created, you simply create a new document from that template. If you edit the template at some point after it has been applied to Web pages, upon saving the modified template, you are prompted to update all files that use that template. Conversely, you can detach the template from the file to prevent changes to the template from affecting a particular document.

1. Select File→New from Template and select the template from the dialog box that appears onscreen (19.9).

2. Select Modify→Templates to select the editable regions by their names, which appear at the bottom of the menu. The selected editable region is highlighted in the Document window (19.10).

3. Select Modify→Templates→ Update Current Page to update pages manually, one at a time.

N O T E

Custom styles, timelines, and behaviors are fully supported for editable regions of templates, although any document that uses a template cannot have its own style sheet, timelines, or behaviors; it must use the style sheet, timelines, and behaviors defined for the template.

Exporting XML Content

You can use the Extensible Markup Language (XML) export features to export the editable regions of a template as an XML document. Using this function, you can export your content to a format that can be modified outside Dreamweaver using a text editor.

1. Open a document that uses a template with editable regions.

2. Select File→Export→Export Editable Regions as XML.

3. When the Export Editable Regions as XML dialog box appears, select a tag notation and click OK (19.11).

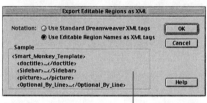

19.11

 A sample is created from your data when you click the radio buttons in this dialog box.

Importing XML Content

XML content can be imported into a document that is using a template.

1. Select File→Import XML into Template.

2. Locate an XML file and click Open. When the XML file is imported, Dreamweaver merges the XML content with the template specified in the XML file and displays the result in a new Document window. If the specified template is not found, Dreamweaver prompts you to select a template to use.

 O T E

XML is a language for defining tags and their relationships, similar to HTML tags and their attributes, except you can define your own tags with XML. The beauty of XML is that it can be anything you want it to be. It's simply a mechanism for coding data with tags that are understood by some other program.

T I P

For the latest information about XML, go to http://www.xml.com. *For a simplified explanation of XML, go to* http://www.w3.org/ XML/1999/XML-in-10-points.

Using Libraries to Organize Content

Options menu for library items

Refresh Site List

Click the New Library Item button to create a library item from scratch.

Click the Edit button to edit the selected Library item.

Delete selected library item(s).

19.12

A Library folder is created in the site Root folder, so each site can have its own library.

Use Dreamweaver's libraries to store content you use frequently and content that's likely to change on a regular basis. Library items should include content that appears on many pages in your site and content that must be updated frequently. When you place a library item in a document, a copy of the HTML is inserted into the file, creating a reference to the original, external item. This behavior enables you to update the content on an entire site all at once by changing the library item.

1. Select Window→Library to display the Library category of the Assets panel. The library items are listed in the bottom part of the Assets panel. When you click the name of library item, a preview of the content appears in the upper half of the Assets panel (19.12).

 O T E

When you place layers in the library, the x and y position of the layer is retained. When you drag a layer library item onto the Document window, the item is placed in the same position it was in when it was saved to the library.

 O T E

Select Edit→Preferences and select Highlighting from the Category list to change the highlighting color of library items.

Using Libraries to Organize Content continued

2. Click and drag items from your Document window into the bottom section of the Library category of the Assets panel to add items (19.13).

3. Click and drag items from the library into the Document window to place library items on your page.

4. Click the Detach from Original button in the Property inspector to break the link between a library item and its source file (19.14). The instance of the library item is no longer updated by the library update functions.

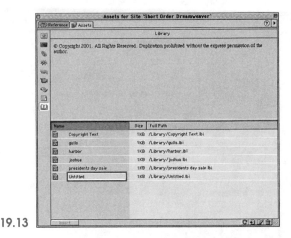

19.13

Type a descriptive name for the library item in the Library panel.

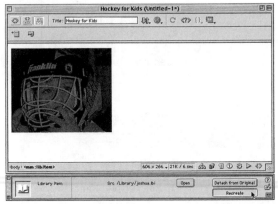

19.14

Restore a library item that is placed on a page to the library if the item has been deleted from the library or does not exist in the current library.

Editable items on a page using a template cannot be added to the Library inspector, although you can replace editable items with library items. If you need to add items from a document created from a template, detach the template from the file first by selecting Modify→Templates→ Detach from Template.

19.15

Select Update Site from the
Asset panel options menu.

19.16

19.17

5. Double-click an item in the
Library category of the Assets
panel to edit the item. When
you save the file, you are
prompted to update any existing library items on pages
(19.15). If you do not update
the pages at this point, you can
update them later by selecting
Modify→Library→Update
Pages (19.16). When the
Update Pages dialog box
appears, click the Start button
to update pages on your site
that contain the changed
library item (19.17).

(N) O T E

*Library items can include any <body> ele-
ment, including text, tables, forms, images,
Java applets, plugins, and ActiveX elements.
Because Dreamweaver stores only a reference to linked items, such as images, the
original file must remain at the original
location for the library item to work correctly. Library items can contain behaviors,
but you can edit behaviors only when they
are not library items. Behaviors store the
code in the <head> section, and the <head>
content is not editable in libraries.
Unfortunately, you cannot store timelines or
style sheets in libraries because this code is
also stored in the <head> section.*

 I P

*If you want to add a detached library item, (Option)[Ctrl] drag the
item from the Library inspector into the Document window. Be sure
the working file is saved to your site before performing this step;
otherwise, the relative link for the library item does not work.*

Using Server-Side Includes

Server-side includes are instructions to a Web server to include a specified file in the current document. Typically, the content is in HTML format and is saved with the `.shtml` or `.shtm` extension.

1. Select Insert→Server-Side Include or click the Insert Server-Side Include button on the Common Objects panel (19.18).

2. When the dialog box appears, enter the path to the file you want to include; alternatively, click the Folder icon to browse and select the file, and then click OK (19.19).

3. In the Property inspector, the Virtual radio button is highlighted when the server-side include file is relative to the document or the Site root. Click the Edit button to edit the server-side include file; then save the edited file (19.20).

O T E

Because the HTML file used as the server-side include becomes part of the current HTML file, the server-side include file should be saved without the <html>, <head>, <title>, or <body> tags and without any tags pertaining to <frameset>. Just the content for the body of the document is necessary. You can use Dreamweaver to create the server-side include, but delete these elements from the source code before saving.

Because Includes are processed only on the Web server, the included content does not typically appear when you open the document locally in a browser. However, if you select File→Preview in Browser from within Dreamweaver, the content is available because Dreamweaver processes the include instructions locally.

19.18

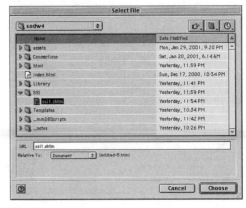

19.19

If you want to enter the precise path of the file when it's on the remote server, enter the remote path of the server-side include file, and then click the File radio button.

19.20

CHAPTER 20

In this chapter, you will learn how to...

Add Sound to Your Site

Link Audio Files to Images or Text

Embed Sound Files

Set Sound File Parameters

Insert Shockwave and Flash Files

Embed Java Applets

Add ActiveX Controls

Dreamweaver's plugin support provides a method for incorporating virtually any file that requires a plugin on your Web pages. Support is directly available for Java applets, ActiveX, Flash, and Shockwave in the Objects panel. The Plug-in object enables you to incorporate other plugins, such as QuickTime, Acrobat, RealAudio, and a variety of others. As with all plugin technology, the end user usually must download a plugin for

ADDING MULTIMEDIA TO YOUR WEB PAGES

his browser to view Web content that uses a particular plugin.

Plugins offer a variety of options for adding dynamic content to your Web pages. QuickTime movies enable you to incorporate video and audio content in a digitized format, whereas plugins such as RealAudio enable you to incorporate streaming audio. QuickTime VR is also a popular format today because it enables the user to get a virtual reality view of a panoramic image in 360°. With Shockwave you can incorporate movies created with Macromedia's Director and incorporate interactive content on your Web pages, including audio, video, and multimedia effects. Macromedia Flash creates vector-based animations of relatively small size that can be scaled right on the Web page. If a plugin isn't available for your needs, you always can create a Java applet or ActiveX control and incorporate customized features on your Web pages.

Adding Sound to Your Site

You can incorporate sound on your Web pages in a number of ways. Sounds can be played in the background, as the result of some trigger using behaviors, or as links using a browser's built-in Audio Playback tool. Unfortunately, sound files are handled differently on the various browsers, and support for sound formats seems to come and go with various versions of the browsers as well. Sounds typically are handled by specific plugins defined in the browser preferences, where the sound file's extension is associated with a helper application or plugin (20.1). (Table 20.1) describes the most common digital audio file formats in use on Web pages today.

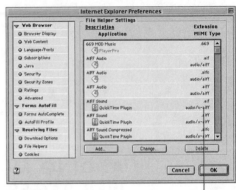

20.1 **The AIFF Sound format is associated with the Apple QuickTime plugin in this example.**

Table 20.1 Audio File Formats

File Extension	Description
.au	The AU format was used early on to add sound because Unix was the only system enabling sound on Web pages. This format is used by NeXT and Sun Unix Systems.
.aiff	The Audio Interchange File Format originally was developed by Apple Computer and is sometimes used by Silicon Graphics (SGI) computers.
.midi or .mid	The MIDI format is actually a set of instructions that control built-in sounds and musical instruments on the computer. MIDI files tend to be the smallest of the sound files because they don't actually contain any digitized audio, just text commands.
.mp3	The MPEG2 Audio Layer 3 format takes advantage of the MPEG compression engine to produce high-quality sound with optimum compression. This format often is used for lengthy audio samples, such as tracks from an audio CD.
.ra, .rpm, or .ram	The RealAudio format was developed by Progressive Networks and was the first live streaming-audio plugin. This format is still the standard for streaming audio.
.rmf	The Rich Music Format was developed by a company called Headspace and is supported by the Beatnik plugin. Beatnik also supports .mod, .aiff, .au, .mid, and .wav formats.
.swa or .dcr	The Shockwave audio format was developed by Macromedia and uses the MPEG compression of MP3. With the appropriate plugin, the Shockwave audio format can be streamed or downloaded.
.wav	Microsoft and IBM developed the Waveform audio format, and it is the format still used predominantly on Windows computers.

Linking Audio Files to Images or Text

20.2

20.3

20.4

The simplest way to incorporate sound on your Web page is to create a link to the sound file. Because support for sound formats varies from browser to browser, it's not unusual to see links to a sound in multiple formats. Another good idea is to let users know the size and format of the files they are downloading by typing this information in as part of the link (20.2).

1. Select some text or an image to use as a link to your sound file.

2. Enter the link in the Link field of the Property inspector or click the folder to the right of the link field to locate and link a sound file (20.3).

(T) I P

Be sure to test your sound files on multiple browsers and platforms because sound files are notorious for causing problems in browsers.

(N) O T E

When a browser has an application or plugin associated with a linked sound, the plugin or application will play the sound (20.4). When the sound file is not handled in some way by the browser, the user is prompted to save the file to disk.

Embedding Sound Files

When you embed a sound or music file, the floating controller used by the browser is embedded on the page as though it were an image. With embedded sound, you can control the volume, visible controls, and the starting and ending points of the sound. The player for a particular sound file depends on which plugin is designated for that sound file in the browser, so the Plug-In object and ActiveX object can be used to embed the sound.

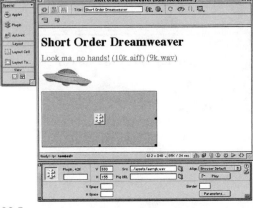

20.5

1. Position your cursor in a document where you want the sound controller to appear.

2. Click the Plug-In object in the Special Objects panel and locate the sound file you want to embed. The plugin icon appears in place of the controller in Dreamweaver because the controller used to play the sound depends on the browser in which it is viewed **(20.5)**.

 **O T E**

Embedded sound files display the sound controller just like an image, and you can treat it like an image as well. Set the horizontal alignment to enable text wrapping and indicate the V Space and H Space values. You also can put a border around the controller by specifying a Border value in the Property inspector.

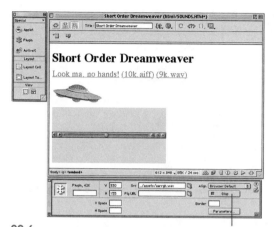

20.6

**The Play button changes to the Stop button
when the sound is playing in Dreamweaver.**

3. You must specify a size for the
plugin in the Property inspector. Use a width of 144 pixels
and a height of 60 pixels for
the generic audio plugins.
These dimensions are the size
of Navigator's audio player,
and they accommodate most
other audio players, including
Internet Explorer's audio controls.

4. Click the Play button in the
Property inspector to preview
the sound file in Dreamweaver
(20.6).

 I P

*You might have to edit the preferences for
your browser to identify the sound file
extension with the proper plugin. For example, Netscape's preferences might be set to
play AIF files with the QuickTime controller,
but not AIFF files. It's a good idea to stick to
the three-character extensions for sound files
even if you're working on a platform that
doesn't limit you to three.*

Setting Sound File Parameters

You can specify the parameters for a sound file in the Property inspector. In the HTML source code, parameters are specified as attributes to the <embed> tag (20.7). See (Table 20.2) for the parameters you can specify for sound files and their controllers.

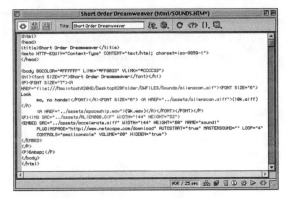

20.7

Table 20.2   Sound File Parameters

Parameter	Values	Description
name	A unique name you assign	Along with the mastersound parameter, name controls a sound with more than one controller.
mastersound	Enabled when no value is specified; disabled when None is specified	When you assign more than one controller the same name parameter, the mastersound parameter enables the same sound to be played by each.
autostart	true or false	Determines whether the sound begins playing automatically when it is loaded.
controls	console, smallconsole, playbutton, pausebutton, stopbutton, or volumelever	Specifies which sound controls appear. The default is console.
endtime	minutes:seconds	Specifies the point at which the sound stops playing.
hidden	true	Hides the controller and plays sounds in the background.
loop	true, false, or a number	Specifies whether the sound file loops or how many times it loops.
starttime	minutes:seconds	Specifies where in the sound file the sound begins playing.
volume	1–100	A percentage value that sets the audio volume.

20.8

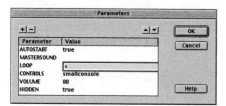

20.9

1. Select the Plugin icon in the Design view of the Document window and expand the Property inspector to show all properties (20.8).

2. Click the Parameters button in the Property inspector to display the Parameters dialog box and enter the parameters for the sound file (20.9).

T I **P**

The order in which you enter the parameters in the Parameters dialog box doesn't matter because the browser reads all parameters before executing the sound.

Inserting Shockwave and Flash Files

Both Flash and Director are made by Macromedia, as is Dreamweaver. So it stands to reason that Flash and Director Shockwave files are fully integrated with Dreamweaver, enabling you to preview them right in the Dreamweaver Document window.

1. Click in the Document window at the point where you want to insert the Director Shockwave or Flash file.

2. Click the Insert Shockwave or Insert Flash object in the Common Objects panel and locate the Shockwave or Flash file.

3. The Design view of the Document window displays the Flash or Shockwave icon in a gray box representing the size of the file (20.10).

4. Specify the parameters for the file in the Property inspector. Include an ID number in the ID field for ActiveX controls. See the section "Adding ActiveX Controls," later in this chapter (20.11).

5. Click the green Play button in the Property inspector to preview the Flash or Shockwave file in Dreamweaver (20.12).

20.10

20.11

20.12 **Dreamweaver automatically inserts both the `<object>` and `<embed>` tags in the HTML source code to enable Netscape and Explorer to play the Flash or Shockwave file.**

Embedding Java Applets

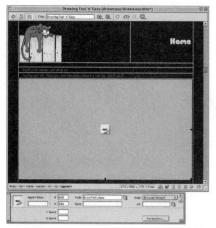

20.13

20.14

Java applets run on Netscape 2 or later and Internet Explorer 3 or later.

Java *applets* are little programs that can be run inline on your Web page. Java is a programming language, based on C++, that was developed by Sun Microsystems to enable true cross-platform application programming.

1. Click in the Document window at the point where you want to embed the Java applet.

2. Click the Insert Applet icon in the Special Objects panel, and then locate the Java applet to embed. Java applets typically have the .class file extension.

3. The Java placeholder appears in the Document window at a default size of 32×32 pixels. If you know the size of the Java applet, enter the width and height values in the Property inspector. Some Java applets adjust to fit the width and height you specify **(20.13)**.

4. Preview the Web page in your browser to ensure that the applet plays and has the correct dimensions **(20.14)**.

(T) I P

One of the most comprehensive sites for all things Java is www.javashareware.com, where you will find shareware Java applets. Be sure to read any usage requirements before implementing these applets on your site.

Adding ActiveX Controls

ActiveX is a programming language written by Microsoft for use in Internet Explorer 3 and later. An ActiveX control acts like a plugin in many instances, although it also can act like Java and JavaScript—playing miniprograms in the browser window. At this writing, support for ActiveX is not built into Netscape, but you can download an ActiveX plugin for Netscape 4 and later that handles some of the ActiveX controls. Macintosh browsers do not support ActiveX. Dreamweaver enables you to specify an ActiveX control along with the Netscape plugin equivalent, including both sets of code in the HTML source code.

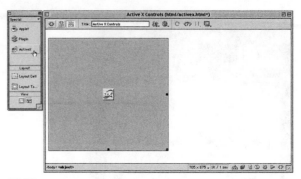

20.15

1. Click in the Document window where you want to insert the ActiveX control.

2. Click the Insert ActiveX object in the Objects panel to insert the ActiveX icon in the Document window (20.15).

 I P

If you click the minus button to the right of the ClassID field in the Property inspector, the selected ClassID is removed from the pull-down menu list.

20.16

20.17

3. Specify the parameters for the ActiveX control in the Property inspector (20.16). Select a ClassID from the pull-down menu or enter it in the ClassID field. If the class is not in the list, type the URL of the ActiveX control in the Base field.

4. To include the Netscape `<embed>` codes, click the Embed check box to the left of the Src field and indicate a source file in the Src field.

(N) O T E

Some ActiveX controls access a data file. Specify the data file URL in the Data field. The ID number is used to pass information from one ActiveX control to another.

(N) O T E

A full explanation of ActiveX controls is beyond the scope of this book, but a number of books have been written about ActiveX. If you want to try out some free ActiveX controls, visit www.coolstf.com or www.download.com. To see examples of ActiveX, visit http://night-fall.com/activex.html **(20.17)**.

CHAPTER 21

With Dreamweaver's powerful site management tools you can perform all of the maintenance and management tasks associated with site design. When you're ready to upload your Web site to a server, use Dreamweaver commands to clean up the HTML code, eliminating unwanted and redundant source code. You can even clean up Word HTML files to remove the special codes Microsoft Word inserts to make Web pages appear correctly in Word.

MANAGING, SYNCHRONIZING, AND CLEANING UP YOUR SITE

Synchronize your local site files with the remote files to be sure you have the most up-to-date content on your remote Web site and local hard drive. Find and fix broken and orphaned links using Dreamweaver's site window. Dreamweaver keeps track of everything on your Web site and lets you know when links are not working or whether you're trying to link to a file that no longer exists. If you use Check In/Check Out and Design Notes on your site, take advantage of Dreamweaver's new reporting features to generate a report detailing the status of your site and any potential problems.

Synchronizing Remote and Local Files

Use the Synchronize command to synchronize the files between your remote site and your local site. Dreamweaver generates a list of files that need to be put on the remote site and optionally removes any files on the remote site that do not currently exist on the local site. Be sure to have both a remote site and a local site defined before proceeding **(21.1)**.

1. Select Site→Synchronize to display the Synchronize Files dialog box **(21.2)**.

2. To synchronize only selected files, choose Selected Local Files Only from the Synchronize pop-up menu. Select the Entire Web Site option to synchronize the entire site.

3. From the Direction pop-up menu, select the direction in which you want to synchronize the files **(Table 21.1)**.

4. Check the Delete Remote Files Not on Local Drive check box if you want to remove any files that exist on the remote site but do not exist on the local site.

5. Click the Preview button. Dreamweaver evaluates and compares the files on your local and remote sites **(21.3)**.

Remote site   Local site

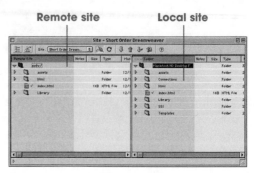

21.1

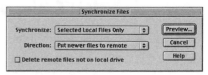

21.2

Table 21.1   Direction Options for Synchronizing Files

Option	Description
Put Newer Files to Remote	Uploads all the local files that have more recent modification dates than their counterparts on the remote server
Get Newer Files from Remote	Downloads all remote files that have more recent modification dates than the local files
Get and Put Newer Files	Places the most recent versions of the files on both the local and remote sites

21.3   **Synchronize preview in progress**

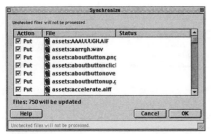

21.4

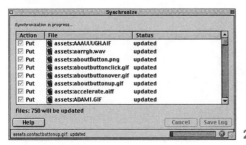

21.5

21.6

6. In the Synchronize dialog box that appears when Dreamweaver has finished checking your site, put a check mark in the Action column for all the files you want to update. Uncheck any files you don't want to update (21.4). Click OK.

7. Dreamweaver reports the status of the synchronization in the Status column of the Synchronize dialog box (21.5). Click the Save Log button to save the status log to a text file (21.6).

To see which files are newer on the local site or which files are newer on the remote site, without synchronizing, select (Site→Site Files View→Select Newer Local) [Edit→Select Newer Local] or (Site→Site Files View→Select Newer Remote) [Edit→Select Newer Remote].

If you select Get Newer Files from Remote in the Synchronize Files dialog box, and you also check the Delete Remote Files check box, Dreamweaver deletes any files in your local site for which no corresponding remote files exist.

Cleaning Up HTML Source Code

Use the Clean Up HTML command to remove empty tags, combine nested <font> tags, and improve the overall format of the HTML code. You can end up with redundant tags and nested font tags when creating pages using the Design view of the Document window. For example, if you select a word and make it red, the HTML code <font color="red">word</font> is created. Click somewhere else; then select the same word again and make the size 5. The resulting HTML code is <font size="5"><font color="red">word</font></font>. The Clean Up HTML command would combine the two nested font tags into one font tag, resulting in cleaner and more correct HTML code. The combined HTML code is <font size="5" color="red">word</font>.

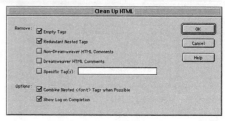

21.7

1. Open an existing document and select Commands→Clean Up HTML to display the Clean Up HTML dialog box (21.7).

2. Select the appropriate Remove and Options check boxes (Table 21.2). Click OK.

Table 21.2   Clean Up HTML Options

Option	Description
Remove Empty Tags	Removes any tags that have no content between them.
Remove Redundant Nested Tags	Removes all redundant instances of a tag.
Remove Non-Dreamweaver HTML Comments	Removes all comments not inserted by Dreamweaver, including any comments you manually insert in the code. For example, Dreamweaver inserts the comment `<!--#BeginEditable "doctitle" -->` to mark the beginning of an editable region.
Remove Dreamweaver HTML Commentss	Removes all comments that were inserted by Dreamweaver. Removing Dreamweaver comments turns template-based documents into ordinary HTML documents and library items into normal HTML code.
Remove Specific Tag(s)	Removes any tags you list in the adjacent text field. Separates multiple tags with commas.
Combine Nested `<font>` Tags when Possible	Consolidates two or more font tags when they control the same range of text. For example, `<font size="5"><font color="red">word</font></font>` is changed to `<font size="5" color="red">word</font>`.
Show Log on Completion	Displays an alert box with details about the changes made to the document as soon as the cleanup is finished **(21.8)**.

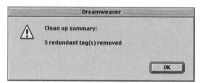

21.8

N O T E

The source formatting options you specify in the HTML Format preferences and the `SourceFormat.txt` file apply only to subsequent new documents created with Dreamweaver. If you want to apply these formatting options to existing HTML documents, select Commands→Apply Source Formatting.

Cleaning Up Microsoft Word HTML

Microsoft Word inserts a lot of extraneous code in the HTML documents it creates. These codes help Microsoft Word display the content correctly in Word, but they have no effect on the way the code is displayed in browsers, or Dreamweaver, for that matter. You should retain a copy of your Word document if you plan on using Word to make changes in the future. The Clean Up Word HTML command is available for documents saved as HTML by Word 97 and later.

1. In Microsoft Word, save your document as an HTML file.

2. Open the HTML document in Dreamweaver (21.9).

3. Select Commands→Clean Up Word HTML to display the Clean Up Word HTML dialog box (21.10).

4. Click the check boxes for the options you want to use. The Basic tab of the Clean Up Word HTML dialog box displays the options (Table 21.3). Click OK.

Document created in Microsoft Word

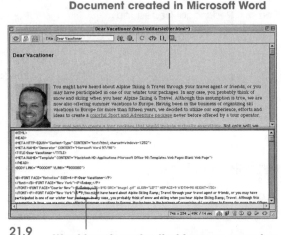

21.9

Word inserts codes that have no meaning in Dreamweaver and are ignored.

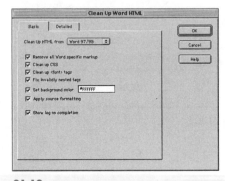

21.10

(N) O T E

After you've applied the Clean Up Microsoft Word HTML command, the HTML file no longer displays correctly in Microsoft Word. Save a copy of the original Word document if you want to use Word to make changes.

Table 21.3 Basic Tab Options for the Clean Up Word HTML Command

Option	Description
Remove All Word Specific Markup	Removes all Word-specific HTML, custom meta data and link tags in the \<head\> section, Word XML markup, conditional tags and their contents, and empty paragraphs and margins from Word styles. You can select each of these options individually using the Detailed tab **(21.11)**.
Clean Up CSS	Removes all Word-specific CSS (Cascading Style Sheets), including inline CSS styles when possible (if a parent style has the same properties), style attributes beginning with mso, non-CSS style declarations, CSS style attributes from tables, and unused style definitions from the \<head\> section. You can further customize this option in the Detailed tab, shown in Figure 21.11.
Clean Up \<font\> Tags	Removes HTML font tags, converting body text to size 2 HTML text.
Fix Invalidly Nested Tags	Removes the font tags inserted by Word outside the paragraph and heading tags.
Set Background Color	Enables you to enter a color value for the background of the document. Dreamweaver inserts the hexadecimal value for white by default.
Apply Source Formatting	Applies the source formatting options you specify in the HTML Format preferences and SourceFormat.txt file.
Show Log on Completion	Displays an alert box detailing the changes made to the document when cleanup is completed **(21.12)**.

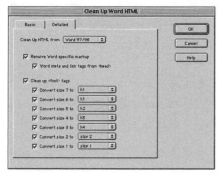

21.11

21.12

N O T E

It can take several seconds to complete the cleanup command, depending on the complexity of the document. The options you select in the Clean Up Word HTML dialog box become the default settings for that dialog box.

Finding and Fixing Broken Links

Broken links are links that no longer follow a valid path or point to a nonexistent file. Large sites can contain hundreds of links to both internal documents within your site and external documents outside your site. Managing and fixing these links can be a daunting task if you try to perform it one file at a time. Orphaned files (files that exist on the site but are no longer linked to any file) can also be a problem. Dreamweaver's Check Links feature can find and fix broken links and orphaned files with a single command.

The Check Links feature searches for broken links and unreferenced files in an open file, a portion of a local site, or an entire local site. Dreamweaver verifies only links to documents within the local site. External links are reported, but Dreamweaver does not verify them.

1. Select Site→Check Links Sitewide to display the Link Checker dialog box (21.13).

2. Select a link report from the Show pop-up menu: Broken Links, External Links, or Orphaned Files.

3. To fix a broken link, select a broken link in the Broken Links column of the Link Checker dialog box; then click the folder button that appears to locate the missing file (21.14).

Select a specific link report.

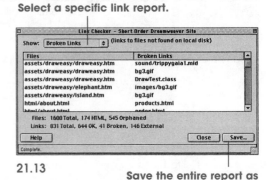

21.13

Save the entire report as a tab-delimited text file.

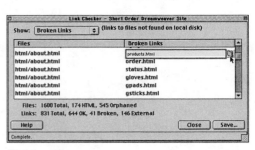

21.14

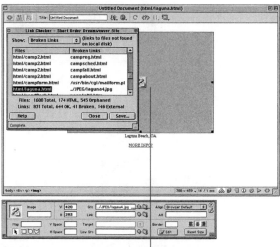

21.15

The linked object is selected in the document so you can fix the link using the Src field of the Property inspector.

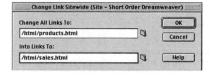

21.16

21.17   **The Orphaned Files report is only available when you check the entire site.**

4. Double-click a filename in the Files column of the Link Checker to open the file in Dreamweaver with the related link highlighted. Use the Property inspector to fix the link (21.15).

5. Click Save if you want to save a tab-delimited report (21.16), or click Close to close the Link Checker dialog box without saving the report.

(N) O T E

If you selected Orphaned Files from the report pop-up menu in the Link Checker dialog box, you can delete orphaned files by selecting files in the list and pressing the Delete key.

(N) O T E

To change a link sitewide, select Site→Change Link Sitewide and enter the link you want to change in the Change All Links To field of the Change Link Sitewide dialog box (21.17). Enter the new link in the Into Links To field, and then click OK.

Generating and Using Reports

Dreamweaver can generate a number of reports to help you get a picture of the possible problems with HTML files and the overall workflow on your site when Check In/Check Out and Design Notes are in use.

1. Select Site→Reports to display the Reports dialog box (21.18).

2. Select an option from the Report On pop-up menu (21.19).

3. Select a report type by clicking the appropriate check box (Table 21.4).

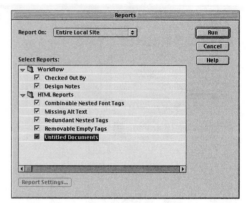

21.18

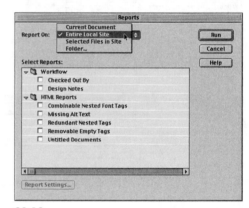

21.19

Table 21.4   Reporting Options

Report Type	Description
Checked Out By	Produces a list of files that are checked out for each person in the work-group.
Design Notes	Reports on files that contain Design Notes along with the status information from the Design Note.
Combinable Nested Font Tags	Creates a report that lists all nested font tags that can be combined to clean up the code.
Missing Alt Text	Creates a report listing all the `<img>` tags that do not have alternative text in the `alt` attribute of the `<img>` tag.
Redundant Nested Tags	Creates a report of nested tags that should be cleaned up.
Removable Empty Tags	Creates a report of all empty tags that can be removed.
Untitled Documents	Creates a report of all documents that contain the default untitled title in the `<title>` tag of the `head` section. Duplicate titles and missing `<title>` tags also are reported.

Double-click a file
to open it in the
Dreamweaver
Document window.

Click the column headers
to change the sort order
of the list.

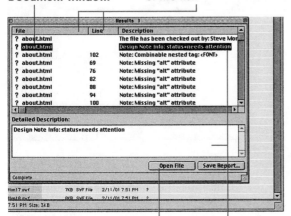

4. Click Run to create the report.
A list of results is displayed in
the Results window (21.20).

5. Click Save Report to save the
report as an XML file.

21.20

Open a selected file
in the Dreamweaver
Document window.

Select a list item to see
the details in the lower
half of the Results window.

 O T E

*You can import the XML file of the report
into a Dreamweaver template file or import
the file into a database or spreadsheet program.*

 **I P**

*Use the Clean Up HTML command to
correct any HTML errors reported.*

Adding, Editing, and Removing File View Columns

You can customize the columns displayed in the Site window's Local Folder and Remote Site lists. You can reorder columns, add new columns, delete columns, hide columns, associate Design Notes to column data, and indicate which columns are shared with other users connected to a site.

1. Select Site→Define Sites, select a site, and click the Edit button to display the Site Definition dialog box (21.21).

2. Click the plus (+) button to add a new column and assign a column name in the Column Name field (21.22).

3. In the Associate with Design Note field, select a Design Note field from the pop-up menu.

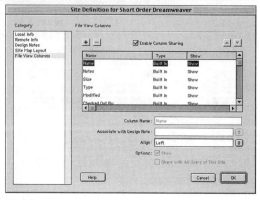

21.21

This box must be checked if you want to share columns with others on the site.

Add columns   Remove columns   Rearrange the order of the columns

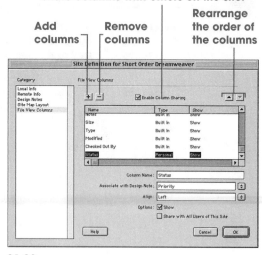

21.22

N O T E

You must assign a new column with a Design Note, so data exists to display in the column. For more information on Design Notes, see Chapter 2, "Setting Up Your Site in Dreamweaver."

The new Status column gets its information from the Design Notes attached to the file.

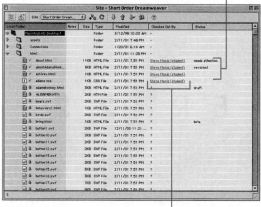

21.23

Click to send an e-mail to the person with the file checked out.

4. Select an alignment for the column and click the Show check box to display the column in the Site window.

5. Click OK. The new column is added to the Site window (21.23).

 **N O T E**

You cannot delete, rename, or associate a Design Note with a built-in column, such as Name, Notes, Size, Type, Modified, and Checked Out By. You can, however, change the order and alignment of these columns. You can hide all the columns except the Name column.

CHAPTER 22

In this chapter, you will learn how to...

Change the Default File Type

Modify the Objects Panel

Create an Object

Edit the HTML Source Formatting Profile

Create and Edit Browser Profiles

Create a Browser Profile

Dreamweaver offers a true open architecture environment, enabling you to modify and edit virtually every aspect of the application's interface. Aside from affecting the way things look in Dreamweaver, you also can specify precisely how the HTML code is generated and edit the browser profiles to accommodate newer versions of the browsers or tweak the existing browser profiles.

CUSTOMIZING DREAMWEAVER

You can rearrange the objects in the Objects panel to better reflect the way you like to work, create additional objects, move existing objects to new panel groups, and remove the objects you never use. True, it helps to know some JavaScript and even some C++. However, with a little work, you can use the existing code to build your own objects, which insert HTML and JavaScript code into your document.

Dreamweaver's extensibility enables you to seamlessly connect to e-commerce tools and create connections to virtually any external source, such as databases, scripts, and proprietary applications.

Changing the Default File Type

When you select FilefiOpen in Dreamweaver, the Open dialog box has a pop-up menu that displays all the file types Dreamweaver can open. By default, the All Documents choice is selected, displaying all the document types Dreamweaver can open in the file list. If most of your work requires a specific file type, such as JavaScript documents, you can modify the Dreamweaver Extensions.txt file to set the default file type to list only JavaScript documents. In the Extensions.txt file, the file type listed on the first line is the default file type.

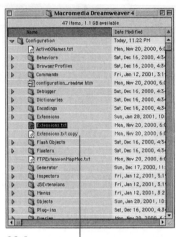

22.1

Be sure to make a backup copy of the Extensions.txt file before editing it.

1. Make a backup copy of the file named Extensions.txt in the Configuration folder. The Configuration folder is located inside the Dreamweaver application folder (22.1).

2. Open Extensions.txt in Dreamweaver or in a text editor (22.2).

3. Cut the line of text corresponding to the file type you want to make the new default; then paste it at the top of the list.

4. Save the file, quit Dreamweaver, and then start Dreamweaver again. Select File→Open to see the change to the default file type (22.3).

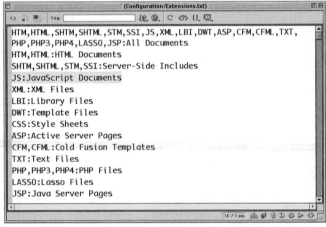

22.2

New default file type —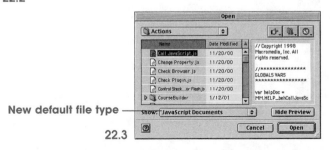

22.3

Modifying the Objects Panel

The Objects folder

Folders appear as menu choices in the Objects panel.

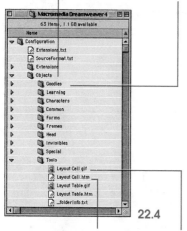

22.4

Code inserted when the Object is selected in the Objects panel

Icon that appears in the Objects panel

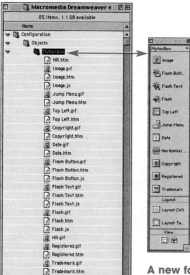

22.5

A new folder in the Objects folder creates a new menu choice in the Objects panel. Rename the folders in the Configuration/Objects folder to rename the Object panel menus.

The Objects panel is divided into six panels: Characters, Common, Forms, Frames, Head, and Invisibles. These panels correspond to folders inside the Configuration/Objects folder within the Dreamweaver application folder. An additional folder named Tools contains the Layout Cell and Layout Table objects. Each folder contains an HTML file and corresponding GIF file for each object in the panel. The GIF file is the icon that is displayed in the Objects panel, whereas the HTML file is the code inserted when the object is clicked (**22.4**).

1. Navigate into the Dreamweaver application folder on your hard drive and open the Configuration folder; then open the Objects folder.

2. Move the HTML and GIF files corresponding to an object in the Objects panel from one folder to another.

3. Delete any files corresponding to an object in the Objects panel that you never use, or move them somewhere else on your hard drive.

 I P

*Create a new folder in the Configuration/Objects folder and move the HTML and GIF files into the new folder to add a panel to the Objects panel (**22.5**).*

Creating an Object

You can create either relatively simple objects using only HTML or more complex objects using a combination of HTML and JavaScript. Create objects for HTML code that you use over and over again or to insert JavaScript functions with the click of a button.

1. Create a new blank document in a text editor.

2. Type or paste in the tags you want this object to insert into your document (22.6). For example, type what is shown in Figure 22.6.

3. Save the file in one of the existing Objects folders, if you want the new object to appear on one of the existing panels (22.7). To create a new panel, create a new folder within the Objects folder and save your file there.

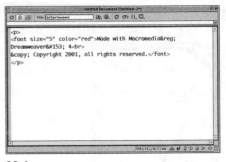

22.6

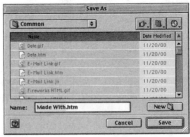

22.7

 **O T E**

If you create additional folders inside any of the Objects folders, the folder and its contents will be ignored.

 **O T E**

You can use Dreamweaver's Code inspector as your text editor, but you first must delete all the HTML tags.

22.8

If you don't supply a GIF image for the object, Dreamweaver inserts a generic icon.

4. Use a graphics program, such as Photoshop or Fireworks, to create an 18-pixel×18-pixel GIF image to act as the icon in the Objects panel.

5. Name the GIF file the same as the HTML file you created and save it in the same folder as the HTML file. For example, if you saved the HTML file as Made With.htm, name the GIF file Made With.gif.

6. Launch or restart Dreamweaver to try your new objects.

(N) O T E

*If you create an image larger than 18-pixels square, Dreamweaver automatically scales it to 18 pixels×18 pixels. Dreamweaver inserts a missing image icon in the Objects panel if you fail to include a GIF file (**22.8**). Use one of the existing icon files if you need an idea of how to proceed.*

Editing the HTML Source Formatting Profile

Edit the HTML Source Formatting profile to specify how Dreamweaver formats the HTML source code for your documents. Inside the `SourceFormat.txt` file, you will find formatting preferences for individual tags and groups of tags, as well as the HTML Format preferences (usually set with Dreamweaver's Preferences command). Quit Dreamweaver before you edit the `SourceFormat.txt` file and use a text editor, such as BBEdit or Simple Text on the Macintosh, or Notepad, Wordpad, or HomeSite on Windows.

You must follow a specific format when editing the HTML Source Formatting profile, which is indicated in the file (22.9). Each section of the profile begins with a keyword, which looks just like an HTML tag with a question mark preceding the keyword—for example, `<?options>`, `<?elements>`, `<?attributes>`, and so on. The parameters for each section appear directly above the section and are enclosed within HTML comment tags (`<!-- -->`).

The parameters for each keyword are described above, between the comment tags.

The keyword is always in angle brackets and preceded by a question mark.

22.9 **All parameters are enclosed in angle brackets.**

IGROUP 1

22.10

IGROUP 2

Individual tags can be marked as belonging to indention groups (IGROUPs) in the `<?elements>` section. IGROUP 1 contains table rows and columns, and IGROUP 2 contains framesets and frames (22.10). These groups directly correspond to the Indent Table Rows and Columns and Indent Framesets and Frames options in the HTML Format Preferences dialog box (22.11).

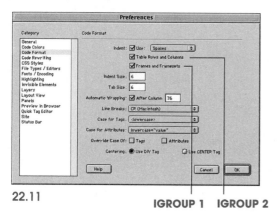

22.11

IGROUP 1   IGROUP 2

Editing the HTML Source Formatting File continued

The break attribute in the <?ele-ments> section determines how the HTML tags break. The break attribute has four values separated by commas (break="1,0,0,1"). The first value sets the number of line breaks before the tag, whereas the second value determines how many breaks after the opening tag. The third value is how many breaks before the closing tag, and the last value represents how many breaks after the closing tag (22.12).

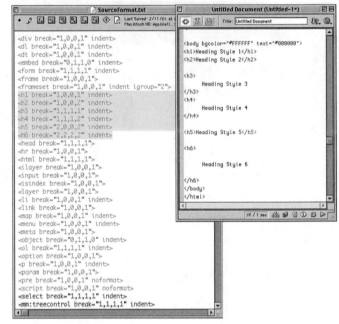

22.12

You can turn off indention for the entire group by removing its number from the active *attribute in the* <?options> *section.*

You can add other tags to IGROUP 1 or 2 and control them with the options in the HTML Format preferences within Dreamweaver.

Editing Browser Profiles

22.13

The unique name of the browser profile must be on the first line.

Anything preceded by two hyphens (–) is ignored.

The profile type must be indicated on the second line.

22.14

When you preview your pages in a browser, Dreamweaver compares your documents to the browser profile for the particular browser. The browser profiles contain information about the HTML tags and attributes that are supported by the browser. This file also contains warning and error messages, as well as suggestions for which tags to substitute for the tags that are not supported.

Browser profiles are stored on your hard drive in the Configuration/BrowserProfiles folder within the Dreamweaver application folder. You can edit existing profiles or create new ones with a text editor (for example, BBEdit, HomeSite, Notepad, or SimpleText).

1. Navigate into the Configuration/BrowserProfiles folder within the Dreamweaver application folder on your hard drive (22.13).

2. Use any text editor to open one of the browser profiles, or create a new profile that is named the same way as the browser application with a .txt extension.

3. Edit the browser profile (22.14) and save it with the same name. See (Table 22.1) for an explanation of the variables used in browser profiles.

Editing Browser Profiles continued

- The first line is reserved for the name of the profile. The profile name must be unique and followed by a single carriage return. The Target Browser Check dialog box and the target check report use this name.

- The second line is reserved for the designator `PROFILE_TYPE=BROWSER_PROFILE`. Dreamweaver uses this line to determine which documents are browser profiles. It must not be changed or moved.

```
<!ELEMENT htmlTag    NAME="tagName" >
<!ATTLIST htmlTag
unsupportedAttribute1 !Error !msg="The unsupportedAttribute1
    of the htmlTag is not supported."
supportedAttribute1
supportedAttribute2 ( validValue1 | validValue2 |
    validValue3 )
unsupportedAttribute2 !Error !htmlmsg="<b>Warning:  Use of
    unsupportedAttribute2 of the htmlTag can result in the
    browser crashing!!</b>">
```

Listing 22.1

The syntax for a tag entry is seen in Listing 22.1

Table 22.1   Variables for Browser Profiles

Variable	Description
HtmlTag	Enters the tag as it appears in an HTML document but without the brackets (< >).
tagName	What the tag is called or commonly known as, such as "horizontal rule" for the <HR> tag. The tagName is used in error messages when you don't specify an error message. If a tagName is not specified, the value of htmlTag is used in error messages.
UnsupportedAttribute	Attributes not supported by the browser you are profiling. Any tags or attributes not specifically included in the browser profile are assumed to be unsupported. You must specify unsupported tags or attributes only when you want to create a custom error message.
SupportedAttribute	Any attribute supported by htmlTag. Basically, if you don't include the !Error designation, the attribute is deemed supported by the browser.
validValue	Some HTML tags and attributes have specific values, such as the FrameBorder attribute of the Frame tag, which accepts a yes or no value. Use the validValue variable to specify the values supported by the attribute (22.15).

Use the underscore character (_) instead of spaces when naming the browser profiles.

Valid values are separated by the piping symbol (|).

22.15

Table 22.2   Rules for Editing Browser Profiles

Item	Rule
Spaces	A space must appear before the closing angle bracket (>) on the !ELEMENT line, as well as after the opening parentheses, before the closing parentheses, and before and after each pipe (|) in the value list.
!	An exclamation point without a space must appear before the words ELEMENT, ATTLIST, Error, msg, and htmlmsg (!ELEMENT, !ATTLIST, !Error, !msg, !htmlmsg).
!Error, !Warning	You can include !Errors and !Warnings within the !ELEMENT or the !ATTLIST area.
!msg, !htmlmsg	The !msg messages must contain only plain text. The !htmlmsg messages can contain any valid HTML codes, including hyperlinks.
Comment tags	The HTML comment (<!-- -->) tags are supported by all browsers. Do not specifically include them in the browser profile because they will cause havoc when Dreamweaver parses the HTML file.

You must follow specific rules about the format of the browser profile to avoid parsing errors when performing browser checks (see **(Table 22.2)** *for a detailed list).*

You don't have to quit Dreamweaver before editing or creating browser profiles, so you can use Dreamweaver as your text editor if you want.

Creating a Browser Profile

You can create a browser profile by simply modifying any existing profile. For example, to create a profile for Netscape Navigator 6.0, open and edit the profile for Navigator 4. Add any new tags or attributes introduced in version 6.0, and save the profile as Navigator_6.0.txt.

1. Using any text editor, open the profile closest to the profile you want to create or open the profile to which you want to make changes (22.16).

2. Change the name of the profile that appears on the first line of the browser profile.

3. Add any new tags or attributes supported by the new version of the browser.

22.16

N **O** **T** **E**

You must remember to change the browser name at the top of the file, even if you save the file with a new name.

T **I** **P**

If you want to avoid error messages for unsupported tags, include the tags in the list of supported tags.

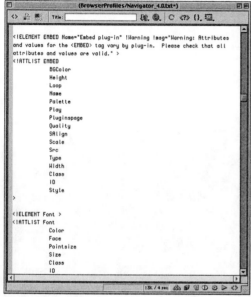

22.17

4. If any tags exist that are not supported by the browser, delete them. New versions of browsers typically support all previous tags, even if newer ones are introduced to replace them. You might want to add an !Error message informing the user that she is using a deprecated tag or attribute and telling her what to use instead.

5. Use the !msg or !htmlmsg to indicate any custom error messages (22.17).

The profiles included with Dreamweaver include all supported tags. Some lines in these profiles might include commented-out lines for some commonly used but unsupported tags. To include a custom error message, remove the two hyphens (--) and add the !msg or !htmlmsg after the !Error.

For further information on extending Dreamweaver, visit www.macromedia.com/ support/dreamweaver/extend.html.

APPENDIX A

In this appendix, you will learn...

About Web Applications and Dynamic Pages

INTRO TO DREAMWEAVER ULTRADEV

Macromedia Dreamweaver UltraDev is a professional environment for building Web applications. A *Web application* is a collection of pages that interact with each other and with other Web resources, such as databases, on a Web server. UltraDev is also a professional editor for creating and managing Web sites and pages and uses the same design interface as Dreamweaver. Because UltraDev uses the same page-design and site-management tools as Dreamweaver, experienced Dreamweaver users can concentrate on incorporating the unique features of UltraDev, such as database connectivity. UltraDev supports Microsoft Active Server Pages (ASPs), Sun JavaServer Pages (JSPs), and Allaire ColdFusion. Using UltraDev, you begin by designing a Web page, and then define a data source, such as a recordset from a database. Using the data imported from a database, you then incorporate server behaviors to make the page functional. If you want to connect your site to a database—or build ASP, JSP, or ColdFusion applications—Dreamweaver UltraDev is the application for you.

 **O T E**

To learn more about Active Server Pages (ASPs), visit http://msdn.microsoft.com/workshop/server/toc.htm. *To learn more about JavaServer Pages ges (ASPs)(JSPs), go to* http://java.sun.com/products/jsp/. *Information on ColdFusion can be found at* http://www.allaire.com/Products/ColdFusion/ productinformation/.

About Web Applications and Dynamic Pages

A Web application is just a collection of static and dynamic Web pages. A standard HTML page is an example of a *static* page. Even an HTML page that contains JavaScript, VBScript, or Flash buttons is still considered a static page. *Dynamic* pages are Web pages that contain server-side scripts used to access and control data on the server. To build Web applications in UltraDev, you need the following: a Web server; an application server that runs on your Web server or a Web server that is also an application server, such as Microsoft Personal Web Server (PWS) or Internet Information Server (IIS); a database or database system; and a database driver that supports your database system. The requirements depend on whether you use UltraDev to create ASP applications, ColdFusion applications, or JSP applications.

You might, for example, create a company directory for your Web site in which users can search for employees.

1. Start by creating a static HTML page using the Forms Objects panel to make search fields and a search button **(A.1)**.

A.1

2. Create a results page to display the results of the search, and insert field placeholders using a database linked into Dreamweaver UltraDev **(A.2)**.

Fields are inserted as placeholders using the Data Bindings panel.

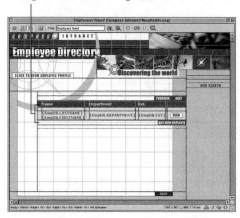

The Data Bindings panel contains the fields of the linked database.

A.2

3. Preview the live data in the Live Data View of UltraDev (A.3).

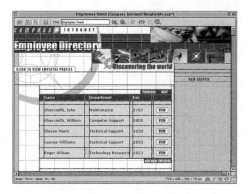

The Live Data View displays actual record data from the linked database.

A.3

4. Create a details page that displays the details of individual records in the database **(A.4)**.

A.4

5. Use the Server Behaviors panel to add server-side scripts to your pages **(A.5)**.

A.5

 **O T E**

You will need a good understanding of databases and database connectivity to initially set up the database links for UltraDev. Ask your database administrator for help in setting up connections to databases.

$\widehat{A}$ P P E N D I X B

USING COURSEBUILDER FOR DREAMWEAVER

CourseBuilder is a Dreamweaver extension that enables you to create online training and testing Web pages. Using CourseBuilder's built-in interactions, you can create an online learning environment that includes tutorials and testing interactions, such as multiple choice, drag-and-drop, mapped images, and text entry fields. You also can create scoring scenarios that enable the user to track his progress and keep track of a user's progress over multiple visits to your Web site. CourseBuilder is a free extension you can download from Macromedia Exchange, and it works with both Dreamweaver and Dreamweaver UltraDev. See Appendix C, "Enhancing Dreamweaver with Extensions," for instructions on downloading extensions from Macromedia Exchange (`http://www.macromedia.com/exchange/`).

Setting Up CourseBuilder Interactions

The CourseBuilder extension enables you to add interactive learning components to your page by using *interactions*. Interactions are the layout graphics necessary—such as check boxes for multiple choice questions—along with attached scripts that check for a correct answer and respond in some way. All the interactions that come with CourseBuilder use a select group of images and scripts that are located in the CourseBuilder folder. Before creating Web pages that contain CourseBuilder interactions, you must have a site defined and a document open in Dreamweaver that already has been saved in the site. In the following tasks, a multiple-choice question is created. Dialog box options will differ depending on the type of interaction you create.

1. Begin by copying the support files, which include the images and scripts used by the interactions, to your site folder. An Images folder and a Scripts folder are added to your site. Choose Modify→CourseBuilder→Copy Support Files.

2. Create and save a new document in your site folder or open an existing page to add interactions.

3. Click in the document to position the cursor where you want to add the interaction; then click the Insert CourseBuilder Interaction button located in the Learning Objects panel **(B.1)**.

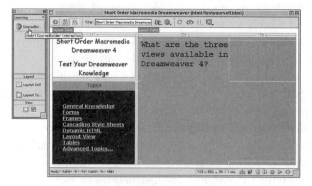

B.1

4. In the CourseBuilder Interaction dialog box, select the type of interaction and click a graphic in the gallery tab to indicate how it looks **(B.2)**.

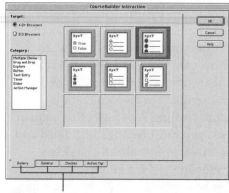

After you select a graphic from the gallery tab, other tabs appear at the bottom of the dialog box.

B.2

5. Click the General tab at the bottom of the dialog box and fill out the fields to specify how the interaction is handled (B.3).

Determine when the interaction is to be judged.   **Type a name for your interaction.**   **Type the text for the question.**

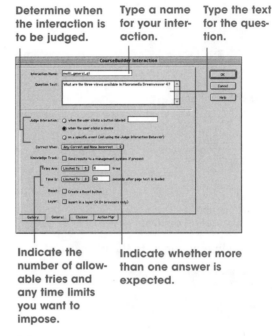

Indicate the number of allowable tries and any time limits you want to impose.   **Indicate whether more than one answer is expected.**

B.3

6. Click the Choices tab and enter the options for each of the choices, including which one is the correct choice (B.4).

You can use text or images for choices.
Click to add and remove answers.

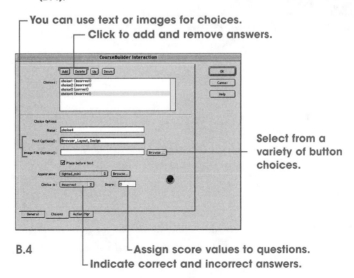

Select from a variety of button choices.

B.4   **Assign score values to questions.**
Indicate correct and incorrect answers.

7. Click the Action Mgr tab and edit the scripts used to handle the results of the interaction **(B.5)**.

Highlight an action and click the Edit button.

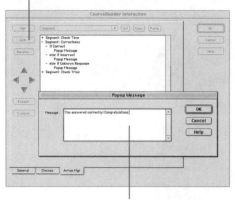

B.5 **Type the messages that will appear when a particular action occurs.**

8. Click OK to insert the interaction onto the page **(B.6)**.

B.6

After you create an interaction, you can edit the images and text used in the interaction using standard Dreamweaver tools.

Use templates and libraries to create a uniform interface for your learning pages. Provide navigation aids and links to user statistics if you are keeping track of them.

Editing Interactions

Use the Property inspector to edit interactions on your pages. Each interaction includes invisible buttons for the JavaScript and interaction settings. If you are proficient in JavaScript, you can edit the client-side JavaScript code. To change the text of a question, simply change the text on the Web page. To change the answer values, click the invisible CourseBuilder button and edit the interaction through the Property inspector.

1. Choose View→Visual Aids→Invisible Elements to display the invisible CourseBuilder and JavaScript buttons that appear below the interaction.

2. Click the CourseBuilder button beneath the interaction to display the options in the Property inspector; then click the Edit button in the Property inspector (B.7).

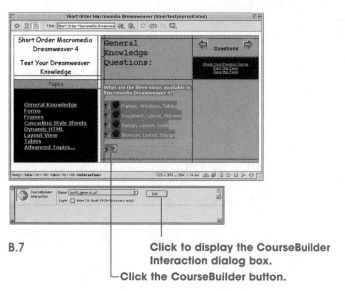

B.7   **Click to display the CourseBuilder**
                                        Interaction dialog box.
                                  └─**Click the CourseBuilder button.**

3. If you want to edit the JavaScript for the interaction, click the JavaScript button beneath the interaction, and then click Edit in the Property inspector (B.8).

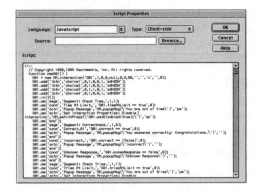

B.8

Using Knowledge Track

The Knowledge Track option on the General tab of the CourseBuilder Interaction dialog box enables you to send result data to a server running computer-managed instruction (CMI) software. Lotus Pathware is a popular CMI that complies with standards set for computer-based training (CBT). Pathware, among others, can be used with a variety of databases. When you check the box for Knowledge Track in the CourseBuilder Interaction General tab, additional tabs are added to the bottom of the dialog box to set the tracking functions. Knowledge Track has two components:

- **The Tracking tab in the CourseBuilder Interaction dialog box**—This contains settings you use to specify interaction properties that are recorded by a CMI or database server application (B.9).

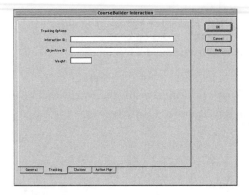

B.9

- **The Modify→CourseBuilder→Create Pathware Frameset and Modify→CourseBuilder→Create Tracking Frameset commands**—These create a parent HTML document with two frames. The top frame displays the HTML page that contains the CourseBuilder Interaction. A hidden bottom frame is used by the CMI system to communicate with the CourseBuilder Interaction.

When you select Knowledge Track, the following information is sent to the CMI server every time the CourseBuilder Interaction is judged:

- The current date (DD/MM/YYYY)

- The current time (HH:MM:SS)

- The string entered in the Interaction ID field of the Tracking tab

- The string entered in the Objective ID field of the Tracking tab

- The type of the interaction

- The correct answers for the CourseBuilder Interaction

- The answer given by the student

- Whether the student's response was correct or incorrect

- The weight given to the question for scoring

- The time it took for the student to answer the question (HH:MM:SS)

Connecting with Databases

CourseBuilder for Dreamweaver sends data to a computer-managed instruction (CMI) system when Knowledge Track is enabled. You can modify Knowledge Track features to collect data without using a CMI system, such as Pathware, by using server applications, such as Microsoft Active Server Pages (ASPs) and Allaire ColdFusion. If you are using Dreamweaver UltraDev, you can incorporate the database interactivity of UltraDev with CourseBuilder. Explicit instructions for sending data to a database are included in the CourseBuilder documentation available on the Macromedia Web site.

Ⓐ P P E N D I X   C

In this appendix, you will learn...

Download Extensions

Install Dreamweaver Extensions

ENHANCING DREAMWEAVER WITH EXTENSIONS

Macromedia has a special area on its Web site called Macromedia Exchange where you can download extensions to enhance the performance of Dreamweaver and add tools, commands, and objects to your Dreamweaver software. Many extensions on the site are tested by the folks at Macromedia and given a seal of approval that means they install correctly and do what they're supposed to do. If you're a developer interested in creating your own extensions, you will find all the information you need on the Macromedia general Web site and also on the Macromedia Exchange site.

Downloading Extensions

A number of places within the Dreamweaver application link you, via your Web browser, to the Dreamweaver Exchange page. In the Commands menu you will find a Get More Commands option. In the Behaviors panel, the last Behavior in the list is Get More Behaviors. You can add more Flash buttons to Dreamweaver by clicking the Get More Styles button in the Insert Flash Button dialog box. All these options and others link you to the Dreamweaver Exchange site. You can enter the Internet address for Dreamweaver Exchange (http://www.macromedia.com/exchange) or use any of the links provided in the Dreamweaver application.

N **O** **T** **E**

If you used the previous version of Dreamweaver with extensions, you were required to first download the Extension Manager. The Extension Manager is built into Dreamweaver 4.

1. Choose Help→Dreamweaver Exchange to launch your
default Web browser and connect to Dreamweaver
Exchange (C.1).

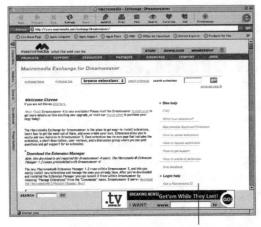

C.1 **You will need a Macromedia ID to download
extensions. It's free; just click this link to set it up.**

2. Scroll down in the browser window to see a list of
Featured Extensions, or click the pop-up menu to view
extensions by category (C.2).

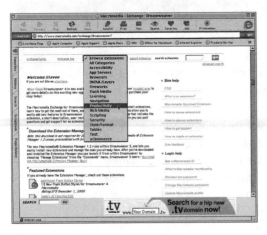

C.2

3. When the table of extensions appears in the browser,
click the name of the extension you want to download.

4. The Web page that appears next contains specific information about the extension you select, including reviews and user comments. Click the link for your computer platform to download the extension (**C.3**).

Link to the developer's Web site
Description and key features

Click to download

Reviews
User comments and impressions

C.3

Installing Dreamweaver Extensions

After you have downloaded the extensions you want to add to Dreamweaver, use the built-in Extension Manager to install them. The Extension Manager enables you to turn extensions on and off, install extensions, remove extensions, and even submit your own extensions.

 I P

Dreamweaver extensions appear on your hard drive with the .mxp file extension. You must use Dreamweaver to install the extension with the Extension Manager.

1. Choose Commands→Manage Extensions to launch the Macromedia Extension Manager **(C.4)**.

C.4 **(a) The Extension Manager has its own File menu and Help menu.**

(b) Installed extensions.

2. Choose File→Install Extension and select an extension you downloaded (with the `.mxp` file extension). Click the (Choose)[Install] button to install the extension.

3. Click the extension in the Macromedia Extension Manager window to display information about the extension **(C.5)**.

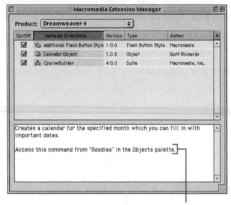

C.5 **The information about the extension usually tells you where you will find the features of the extension in Dreamweaver's interface.**

4. Close the Extension Manager and try your new extension.

APPENDIX D

In this appendix, you will learn how to...

Run the Debugger

Find and Fix Syntax Errors

Set Breakpoints and Find Logical Errors

Watch and Edit Variable Values

DEBUGGING JAVASCRIPT WITH DREAMWEAVER

Dreamweaver's built-in JavaScript Debugger can significantly reduce the time it takes to find and isolate errors in client-side JavaScript code. You can write the code with the Dreamweaver Code view or Code inspector, and then run the debugger to check for syntax and logical errors. Syntax errors cause the browser to report an error message, whereas logical errors make the page function improperly but do not result in a browser error. The Dreamweaver Debugger works with Microsoft Internet Explorer and Netscape Navigator on the Windows platform and with only Netscape Navigator on the Macintosh platform.

The JavaScript Debugger checks JavaScript code for syntax errors first, and then runs with the browser to check for logical errors. If logical errors are encountered, the JavaScript Debugger window isolates the errors in the code, enabling you to examine variables and document properties while the JavaScript routine is running. You can optionally set breakpoints in your code to stop the program execution in specific places, displaying the values of JavaScript objects and properties in a variable list. You also can step through the JavaScript code one statement at a time and monitor variable changes.

Running the Debugger

After you have written some JavaScript code, start the JavaScript Debugger to check for errors. The debugger scans the code for syntax errors first, and then opens the page in the browser to check for logical errors.

1. Select File→Debug in Browser; then select the browser from the list **(D.1)**.

D.1

2. The JavaScript Debugger window appears and is stopped at the first line of code **(D.2)**. Click the Run button to start debugging.

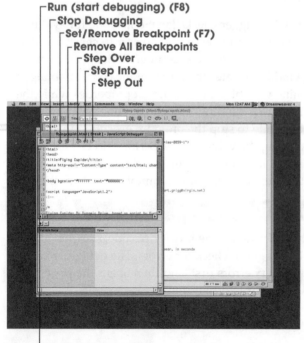

D.2 └─ Current line of code

3. Click the Stop Debugging button in the JavaScript Debugger window to close the debugger and stop debugging.

D.3

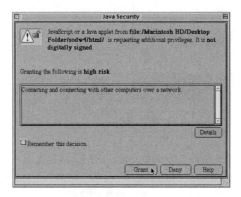

D.4

 **O T E**

*If you are using Netscape Navigator, click OK when the debugger warning box appears **(D.3)**; then click Grant in the Java Security dialog box **(D.4)**. Windows users running Internet Explorer must click Yes in the Java Security dialog box and then OK in the debugger warning box. If you have already accepted a Macromedia Security Certificate, the Java Security dialog box might not appear.*

Finding and Fixing Syntax Errors

If the JavaScript Debugger finds syntax errors, it stops and lists the errors in the JavaScript Syntax Errors window.

1. When the debugger finds a syntax error, select the error in the JavaScript Syntax Errors window **(D.5)**.

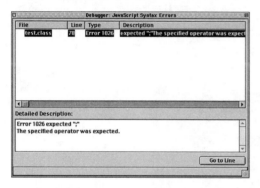

D.5 Click to go to the line in the Code view or Code inspector of Dreamweaver.

2. Double-click the syntax error or select the error and click the Go to Line button to view the line of code in the Dreamweaver Code view or Code inspector **(D.6)**.

The syntax error is highlighted in the source code so you can make the necessary changes.

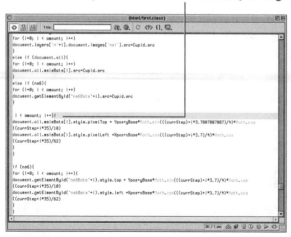

D.6

Setting Breakpoints and Finding Logical Errors

When the debugger finds logical errors, the JavaScript Debugger window opens. A breakpoint is automatically set in the first line of your code, but you can insert your own breakpoints throughout the code. The debugger stops execution at each breakpoint in the source code, where you can view the values of JavaScript objects and properties in the variable list window at the bottom of the debugger window.

1. To insert breakpoints in your JavaScript code using the Dreamweaver Code view or Code inspector, click the Code Navigation button in the toolbar at the top of the Document window and select Set Breakpoint **(D.7)**.

Jump to variables in the
JavaScript code

Breakpoints

Code Navigation button

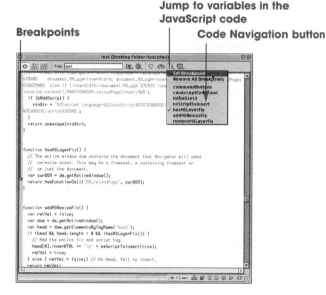

D.7

2. Select File→Debug in Browser to start debugging the JavaScript code. The debugger will stop at each breakpoint inserted.

3. Click the Step Over button at the top of the JavaScript Debugger window to step over a statement, stopping at the next statement **(D.8)**.

D.8

4. Step into a valid JavaScript function by clicking the Step Into button at the top of the JavaScript Debugger window. Click the Step Out button to step out of a function and continue debugging.

Watching and Editing Variable Values

You can watch the variable values in the bottom section of the JavaScript Debugger window. You enter the variable names in the Variable Name column. The current values of the listed variables are shown in the Value column when the debugger stops at breakpoints or when you step into the code.

1. Select the name of a variable in the code portion of the JavaScript Debugger window (D.9).

D.9   Variable

2. Click the plus (+) button and press Enter. You can, alternatively, click the plus (+) button, type the variable name, and then press Enter.

3. When you run the debugger, the variable values are displayed in the lower section of the JavaScript Debugger window **(D.10)**.

D.10

4. To edit a variable value, click the variable name in the bottom section of the JavaScript Debugger window; then click in the Value field. Type a new value and press Enter to continue debugging (D.11).

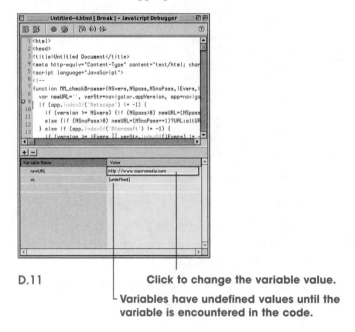

D.11

Click to change the variable value.

Variables have undefined values until the variable is encountered in the code.

 **O T E**

If the variable is an object with properties, you can expand the variable to show its properties and values by clicking the (Triangle button)[Plus button (+)] next to it in the list. The expanded variable is automatically collapsed each time you step through the code.

 **O T E**

To remove a variable, click the variable in the list, and then click the minus (-) button.

INDEX

Q-R

W-Z